GREAT ISSUES IN POLITICS

GREAT ISSUES
IN
POLITICS

Compiled & Edited
by
Dr. R.K. Pruthi

DISCOVERY PUBLISHING HOUSE
NEW DELHI-110002

First Published-2005

ISBN 81-8356-010-5

Published by

DISCOVERY PUBLISHING HOUSE
4831/24, Ansari Road, Prahlad Street,
Darya Ganj, New Delhi-110002 (India)
Phone: 23279245 • Fax: 91-11-23253475
E-mail:dphtemp@indiatimes.com

Printed at:

Amit Enterprises, Delhi

Preface

Political phenomena is studied through different approaches to enable us to understand political reality and the art of government.

What are the dynamics of political change? How is the state related to society. Why is the freedom of governed essential?

We have selected, for our readers, some of the interesting and innovative material on the subject. Essays on government and citizen, role of a modern state and national states vs. international order have been included which are some of the great issues of politics of our times.

We take this opportunity to gratefully acknowledge the authorities on the subject.

We record our thanks to the librarians and their staff members for co-operation and kindness.

My publisher and his staff members have worked hard and rendered every possible assistance. Our readers satisfaction with the work will constitute our highest reward.

R.K. Pruthi

Contents

1

Introduction

A clear understanding of the scientific method in reaching theories is necessary for you, if you are to form judgements for ourselves, and not merely learn and repeat the theories of other people. This is peculiarly important in studying Political Science, for we shall find, as we proceed in our study, that many conclusions are vitiated by the entire exclusion of relevant facts recorded in Indian history. In Professor Seeley's text-book, in Professor Bluntschli's careful study, and in the fine work of Dr. Woodrow Wilson, for instance, save for a few preliminary allusions, the Political Science, nominally based on the history of the world, beings with Greece. We shall have, therefore, to add to our historical data those contained in Indian history, rendered available by historical research and discoveries. Doubtless rich stores of knowledge still remain hidden from us, and these will be available for future students. The facts on which Political Science is based are to be found in history, supplemented by present observations, and to omit the history of Asia as a storehouse of relevant facts is a most unwarrantable narrowing of the foundation of facts on which our Science must be built.

Do not suppose that this criticism is due to my love for, to my admiration for, India; the ignorance is patent, and Sir Henry Maine has preceded me in my judgement. In your study of western books, you must remember this omission of relevant facts, and decide for yourselves how far it affects the theories that are submitted.

Remembering that theories are built up by inductions from collections of facts, you will not fail to observe the seriousness of the non-inclusion, in the collection of facts on which Political Science is based, of the mass of facts existing in the East. The omission will certainly result in many errors, and the supply of the omitted facts may seriously modify the theory.

We shall see that History is our storehouse of facts, and History may be roughly separated for our purpose into the History of the East and the History of the West. In Political Science, as studied in the West, then, the History of the East is ignored. Even in Germany, where it has been studied far more fully than elsewhere, we find such a man as J.K. Bluntschli, Professor of Political Science in the University of Heidelberg, saying:

Political Science does not properly begin till we come to the Greeks. As it was in Greece that the self-consciousness of man first unfolded itself in art and philosophy, so it was in politics. (*The Theory of the State*. J.K. Bluntschli. Authorised translation. Third Edition. Chap. iii, p. 34. Clarendon Press, Oxford).

Dr. Woodrow Wilson, after a very incomplete Section on "Early Forms of Government," occupying 24 pages in a book of 639, plunges into "The Governments of Greece". Professor Seeley blunders in the same way; starting with the Greeks, he naturally says:

It flashes on us after a time that by a State the ancients mean a city, and that we mean a country. When I say the ancients, I mean, of course, the Greeks and Romans. Outside the classical world we see traces of a similar arrangement in antiquity, for Carthage seems to be a sovereign city like Rome or Athens. But antiquity too has large Country States, the, Macedonian Monarchy, the Persian Empire, the primeval Egyptian State. Substantially we have to deal with the fact that in two countries, Greece and Italy, the political vital principle seized small groups of populations and turned them into highly developed organisms, whereas in modern Europe (and now also in America) and in Asia, the political organism is very large and tends also to become larger, (*Introduction to Political Science*. Sir J.R. Seeley. Lecture iv. p. 80. Macmillan, London.)

Hence the City-State is the beginning of Political Science for the West, and this leads Professor Seeley into the further mistake of regarding representative Government as a modern discovery. He says:

One of the most fundamental facts that I have to put before you is, that whereas both personal Government and Government by majority are found in antiquity as well as in modern States, on the other hand the representative system was scarcely known to the ancient world. This grand difference between the ancient and modern world is closely connected with that other broad difference which strikes our attention so instantaneously. Etc. (Lecture vii, p. 158.)

But this fundamental fact in non-existent, for Indian villages from time immemorial have had their village councils, Panchayats, elected by the villagers, lists of voters and of persons eligible for election being kept, and the qualifications of voters laid down. Sir Henry Maine states that "the families within the village or township seem to be bound together through their representative heads" (*Village Communities.* Sir Henry S. Maine. Seventh Edition. Lecture iv, p. 117. John Murray, London) by an intricate system of law, and he regards the fact that they invented rules to meet new cases, as described best by the word legislation (p. 116). Moreover he says that the Village Council "is always viewed as a representative body, and not as a body possessing inherent authority," and speaks of the "essentially representative character of the Village Council" (p. 122). It shows the persistence of custom in India, that even now, uneducated people elect by the method shown by old inscriptions to have prevailed in the election of Village Councils.

I am speaking of this omission of Indian fact as a matter of fact, not as a matter of blame. The material for the History of the East is mostly buried in ancient languages, and very partially translated. The Indian material is large in amount, to be found in extant treatises, and also in inscriptions only lately studied; it is still most imperfect, but Indian scholars are constantly increasing it by their researches. Moreover, as Sir Henry Maine recognised in his *Village Communities in the East and West,* there is the immense advantage in India that much still survives which renders the literature of the past more vividly intelligible than it would otherwise be. For the City-States of Greece are dead, and can only be studied in a few books. The Past is Past. But in India it is not so. As Sir Henry Maine says:

We take a number of contemporary facts, ideas and customs, and we infer the past form of those facts, ideas, and customs not only from historical records of that past form, but from examples of it which have not yet died out of the world, and are still to be found in it. When in truth we have to some extent succeeded in freesing ourselves from that limited conception of the world and mankind, beyond which the most civilised societies and (I will add) some of the greatest thinkers do not always rise; when we gain something like an adequate idea of the vastness and variety of the phenomena of human society; when in particular we have learned not to exclude from our view of the earth and man, those great and unexplored regions which we vaguely term the East; we find it to be not wholly a conceit or a paradox to say that the distinction between the Present and the Past disappears. Sometimes the Past *is* the Present; much more often it is removed from it by varying distances, which, however, cannot be estimated or expressed chronologically. Direct observation comes thus to the aid of historical enquiry, and historical enquiry to the help of direct observation. (Lecture i, pp. 6. 7.)

Again, he writes:

If an ancient society be conceived as a society in which are found existing phenomena of usage and legal thought which, if not identical with, wear a strong resemblance to certain other phenomena of the same kind which the Western World may be shown to have exhibited at periods here belonging chronologically to the Past, the East is certainly full of fragments of ancient society. Of these, the most instructive, because the most open to sustained observation, are to be founding India. The country is an assemblage of such fragments rather than an ancient society complete in itself. The apparent uniformity and even monotony which to the new comer are its most impressive characteristics, prove, on larger experience, to have been merely the cloudy outline produced by mental distance; and the observation of each succeeding year discloses a greater variety in usages and ideas which at first seemed everywhere identical. (Lecture i, p. 13.)

Under these circumstances, we shall begin our study of the State in India, since it rests on works older than, and contemporaneous with, Plato and Aristotle. We must not, however, forget that Chinese antiquity is still practically unknown and that research in that ancient non-Aryan land may, nay, is sure to, yield us many treasures.

There is one small but not unimportant matter, as to the method of utilizing the information gained through listening to lectures. I strongly advise you to take very few notes while the lecture is being delivered. Attention divided between listening and writing can never be concentrated on the matter of the discourse. At the most a few heads of the lecture may be put down, and the attention concentrated on the speaker as he deals with them. As soon after the lecture as possible, the student should write under each head the gist of what was said thereon.

To conclude these preliminaries, let me mention the spirit in which you should study. I spoke just now of the need of study, so that you might be equipped to meet such fully trained rivals as the German commercial men. You have to overcome the further difficulty that, at present, you have not a Government of your own, devoted to your interests, and pushing your Commerce. What that means you can see by comparing the commercial progress of Japan with that of India. Inadequately and over a small area, we shall try to do here, so far as education is concerned, what every wise National Government, such as those of Germany and Japan, do for their own Nations, and our hope is that such Colleges as this, justified by your further success, will multiply.

I pray you to remember that you form part of a great Educational Movement intended to serve the Motherland by preparing for her high-minded and useful citizens. If in all your studies, theoretical and practical, in your work and in your play, you are inspired by the Ideal of Service, and do all for the sake of the Mother, then, and then only, will this College deserve the name of National.

THE PLACE OF POLITICAL SCIENCE

The specialisation of knowledge has been one of the most remarkable mental phenomena of the Age, and more and more, as accurate knowledge of the facts of the world around us increases in amount, it has been found necessary to divide large areas of study into smaller ones, and to classify the smaller according to common resemblnaces, assigning to each class a name of its own.

Thus Biology, the Science of living things, has been divided into Zoology and Botany; and Zoology into Invertebrates and Vertebrates, and these again we study not only in smaller classes, but from another view-point, in their inner composition and their mental equipment, under Anatomy, Physiology and Psychology, our field becoming less in extent and but more intensively cultivated.

Similarly Political Science is a subdivision of History, and also of Psychology, founded on a certain class of facts contained in the first, and on observation of the workings and evolution of the human mind. These facts relate to the organisation of men into groups, their inter-relations and external relations, their methods of government, their laws, their evolution as a group, the aggregation of groups into a larger group for a common purpose, and the like.

The Science itself results from this innate tendency in men to live together. Man is called by Aristotle "a political animal," from his point of view "a city animal"; in Biology he is called " a social animal". The temperament of the beast of prey leads him to live apart, or with his mate, though smaller beasts of prey, being weak, combine into hunting packs; the "social animal" not living on flesh-though man has departed from this wholesome rule-prefers company, feeding together, to solitude. The beast of prey growls and snarls over his food, if another comes near him; the social animal grazes in friendly contact with his fellows.

Man's need for society is shown in the fact that human nature does not grow, expand, become beautiful, in isolation. Language itself is the result of the social instinct, the desire to communicate with others. Emotion cannot give any happiness except where it flows outward to another or to others. Without this, it causes only pain of the most acute kind, and is a continual source of misery. Love, friendship, the joy of comradeship, of fellow-feeling—all that renders fertile the desert of life, making it blossom into beauty—all these depend on contact with another. The family, originally beginning in passion, is sublimated by mind into lasting emotion, and this one universal and stable institution, springing from the deepest wells in human nature, is the foundation of society. Moreover the capacity and the need for love is most developed in the finest types of human nature and is least in the lowest; it is the former who pour it out most richly, and they who suffer most from its absence. Solitary confinement maddens, and is the heaviest punishment known to human law. At all times and in all places man seeks companionship; he cannot live, nor develop to his highest, alone. Says Aristotle:

As we see that every city is a society, and every society is established for some good purpose—for an apparent good is the spring of all human actions—it is evident that this is the principle upon which they are every one founded, and this is more especially true of that which has for its object the best possible, and is itself the most excellent, and comprehends all the rest. Now this is called a City, and the society thereof a political society. (*A Treatise on Government.* Trans. From the Greek of Aristotle by Willian Ellis in 1776. Edition of 1888. Book I, Chap. I, p. 9. G. Rontledge. The book is more often named *Politics*).

INDUCTIVE AND DEDUCTIVE SCIENCES

Political Science in the West is a very modern product, so modern that Sir J. R. Seeley complaints that no satisfactory text-book existed on the subject. For a modern science, as we know it, begins with the observation and collection of facts; then follows the classification of the facts, their arrangement into groups; to these the mind applies itself studying their juxtapositions and arrives at certain underlying general connections, sequences, similarities amid diversities; finally, disregarding the irrelevant and accidental and clinging to the relevant and suggestive, by a process of induction a hypothesis or theory is reached, which illumines the hidden interrelations and shows them as coherent and intelligible. Working with that theory as guide, experiments to test it are devised, which gradually eliminate the irrelevant and link together the relevant, and a great generalisation emerges, or some hitherto unknown law, thereafter recognised as a truth. Through these processes the modern man builds up his science. In ancient times another process was followed: certain truths were recognised by the intellect as congruous with its own nature—"whose nature is truth" says an Upanishat—and therefore as self-evident, needing no exeternal proof. The intellect recognises these as true when they are presented to it, by a direct intellectual vision, far more reliable than the vision of the physical eye. Sciences, such as mathematics, were developed by deductions from such truths, by sheer intellectual effort, long sustained.

Modern nomenclature has classified as Science the concrete study which leads up to general, or abstract, truths; the abstract truth is reached by stripping away from the concrete truths all the differences by which we distinguish them, and uniting that which they have in common. Where this is the method, we call it scientific. Where an abstract truth is first seen by the intellect, and its results are thought out speculatively, we speak of Philosophy, and the method as philosophical. The end sought alike by Science and Philosophy is one—Truth. The methods vary. One ascends, the other descends, but they meet and coalesce on a common ground; the synthetic Truth. Both methods are useful, even necessary; the use of the first evolves mental faculties—observation, analysis, judgement, and the like; the use of the second develops the Intellect. They are not really enemies, as they used to be in Germany; they are complements.

Plato, in his *Republic,* Aristotle, in his *Treatise on Government,* create by their intellectual imagination an ideal State, perfect, beautiful. They then lay down its laws, its methods, its customs, such as would train the citizens to the ideal as conceived, and carry out its purpose. (Professor Seelley, we shall find, objects to the view that we are to seek for a purpose in Society; he would examine, only the facts, and not trouble about any purpose, any object aimed at.) Similarly wrought Sir Thomas More in his *Utopia.* Then we have another class of thinkers, using imagination to construct that which they think must have existed. Hooker, in his *Ecclesiastical Polity,* Locke, in his *Civil Government;* Hobbes in his *Leviathan;* Jean Jacques Rousseau, in his *Contrat Social*—these all imagine unobserved primitive conditions, out of which the State emerges by contract—a theory which is in the air, not formed out of facts by induction, nor deduced from truths self-evident to the intellect, and thus without a scientific basis, however scientifically it may be worked out from the supposed contract.

POLITICAL SCIENCE AND HISTORY

If we are to build up a Political Science, whence can we collect our facts save from History? History gives the material for the Science; the Science illuminates History, and renders it intelligible. Professor Seeley puts this very well:

> This Science is not a thing distinct from History, but inseparable from it. To call it a part of History might do some violence to the usage of language, but I may venture to say that History without Political Science is a study incomplete, truncated, as on the other hand Political Science without History is hollow and baseless—or in one word:
>
> History without Political Science has no fruit:
> Political Science without History has no root.
>
> (Lecture i, pp. 3, 4.)

Professor Sidgwick says in his Preface to this book:

> As regards the general view that these lectures enforce and illustrate—the two-sided doctrine (1) that the right method of studying Political Science is an essentially historical method, and (2) that the right method of studying Political History is to study it as material for Political Science—I think it may be said that this was one of his deepest and most permanent convictions (pp. X. XI.)

That Professor Sidgwick is right in this view is shown not only in the passage above quoted, but also in another passage in which Professor Seeley pleads that the first modern attempts at a Political Science are based on a wrong method, and "that States *can* be treated in the same way as plants or as animals". He proceeds:

> Let us now enquire what aspect our science would wear if it pursued this method. Inductively pursued, Political Science would live and move among historical facts. It would begin by collecting these facts with great industry, and verifying them with most scrupulous care, for it would be keenly alive to the danger of confounding mere rumour, or legend, or party-statement with such facts as science can recongnise. Next it would not attempt to bolster up with the facts so obtained some preconceived theory; all such theories it would put on one side, and honestly wait to see what theories arose naturally out of the facts. For this purpose it would begin by grouping and classifying the facts, placing together, for example, such facts as bear on the internal growth of States, and in another group such as relate to their external action, or the interaction of States on each other.... Everything here depends upon a large supply of—what shall I say? I was going to say historical facts—facts carefully observed and exactly registered. (Lecture i, pp. 21, 22.)

Further, it must be remembered that Political Science is meant to be applied in practice, as well as studied in theory, that it is an Art as well as a Science. Professor Sidgwick truly says in his Preface that "in order to know what England ought to be and do now, they must study what she has been and done in the past". Similarly President Wilson writes:

> Each people, each Nation, must live upon the lines of its own experience. Nations are no more capable of borrowing experience than individuals are. The histories of other peoples may furnish us with light, but they cannot furnish us with conditions of action. Every Nation must constantly keep in touch with its past. (*The State.* Woodrow Wilson, Ph.D. Revised Edition. Chap. XVI, § 1535. Heath & Co., London.)

A Nation is a growth, with its roots deeply buried in its Past, and that Past is to be found in its history. National self-respect, pride of country, patriotism, all grow out of the knowledge of ancestral virtue, ancestral achievement, ancestral greatness. *Noblesse oblige*—"Nobility compels"—is as true of Nations as of men. The intense patriotism of the Scotch grows out of and is nourished by their intimate knowledge of their history, interwoven with the places, towns, mountains, rivers, fields of their native land. Here a battle was fought; there some martyrs died for freedom; yonder a Highland charge swept all before it; in that glen a massacre took place; in this spot Bruce was hidden; in that fort Mary was imprisoned; so will a Scot talk to you, if you travel with him through his country. If countries have not a long past of their own, their people look for it in the Past of the land whence they came. The British Colonies look back to their Mother Country for historical inspiration. The United States with pride nurse the memories of the land whence the "Mayflower" brought their fathers. This is why every boy and girl should grow up in the atmosphere of their own country's history, and be fed with the stories of the heroes and heroines, of the sages and saints of their race. The history of foreign Nations should be read for instruction, but the history of one's own country should be the daily food, until it is assimilated into the life of the boy and girl, grows with their growth and strengthens with their strength. Thus can Patriotism become an overpowering emotion.

Only when they grow up thus, can Indians know what India "ought to be and do now," what institutions will best suit her, what lines of progress can best be chosen by her, what are the directions in which she can best advance.

The fundamental reason why a foreign Government can never be either successful or stable is that it has no common Past with the Nation over which it rules.

It is, therefore, continually blundering, however well-intentioned it may be. It has no "feel" for the suitable, the acceptable, and wonders at its own failures, regarding the Nation it rules as being to blame, and ungrateful. If it invades and conquers, it must settle down, it must become National, part of the Nation, assimilated to the Nation, one with the Nation, or it must pass away, and leave the Nation to come to its own.

INDIVIDUALS OF GRADE COMPLEXITY

One other principle of Evolution we must grasp, still as a generalisation, before we enter on the details of our special subject. It is the well recognised scientific idea of graded Bodies, or organisms, becoming more and more complex as they ascend the ladder of evolution, but retaining their own individuality, even when entering into a higher organism as forming part of it. Every organism is a Life embodied in a Form. The conception is a familiar one in the East, each Life being recognised as a fragment of the Life Universal, that shapes for itself through innumerable stages, the forms suited to its unfolding powers. Each such life is technically called by the Hindu a Jive, or a Jivatma, a Living Being, or a Living Self, and is seen as the cause of evolution, by slow and gradual changes creating from the surrounding matter the organs necessary for the more and more complete working of his latent powers, or functions. In the familiar presentation by the *Chhāndogyopanishaṭ* (VIII, xii, 4) it was the will of the Self to see, to smell, to hear, to think, that brought about the appropriate organs of enjoyment. That luminous generalisation was reached by Modern Science towards the latter part of the nineteenth century, when we find it laid down that in the simplest organism, the plastid, the functions of the Life—taking in food, digestion, respiration, circulation—are all performed by any part of the plastid; there are no organs. As the Life-functions go on, the part of the body which is most convenient for the carrying on of a particular function becomes appropriated by that function, and is shaped into its organ by the exercise of the function through it. Thus the taking in of food fabricates in the course of ages a mouth and esophagus; the function of digestion slowly builds a stomach and intestines; the function of respiration gradually forms lungs; and the function of circulation a heart. It may be noted that while the plastid is floating freely in all directions, no mouth forms, since food particles may touch it anywhere. When it becomes fixed, the part of the body opposite the fixed point is that which touches food constantly, and there gradually the mouth is formed, and there sense-organs develop. Very curious and interesting are the many transformations through which these organs pass, ere they reach their, at present, highest forms—a most fascinating study. Out of it all, Science definitely says that the exercise of the Life-function creates the organ; the exact opposite of the position taken by Science in the middle of the century, that the organ produced the function. It is the Life, with its Will to live, that creates a form for its own use and more efficient exercise.

Even before Biological Science had rêcognised Life as being, as Sir William Crookes said, the shaper and organiser of From, it has seen graded organisms on an ascending ladder, and had regarded each as an Individual, that is, as a Life embodied in a Form, the form being composed of less developed lives also embodied in forms, that is of less evolved Individuals, the place of the Individual being higher or lower according to the greater or less complexity of the Form, and the more or less numerousness of the aspects of the Life. (Organs are not biological individuals, because they are differentiation's within a body, and neither have, nor have had, any separated existence.) The Life which inhabits the Form is the controlling, directing, harmonising, and co-ordinating power, holding the organism together, whether it be simple or complex, and using the form to express its Will, its Intelligence and its Activity. Thus we have as Biological Individuals:

A simple Cell.
A group of Cells forming an Organism.
A simple or complex Organism up to a Human Being.
A group of Human Being, forming a Family.
A group of Families, forming a Tribe.
A group of Tribes, forming a Nation.
A group of Nation, forming an Empire or Commonwealth.
A group of Commonwealths or Empires, forming organised Humanity.

The first six of these are patent and can be studied. The seventh in its imperfect form as Empire has existed, and in its higher form of Commonwealth is in the process of making at the present time. The eighth is, as yet, in the future, in the scientific imagination as in the religious vision. The point for us to realize in our study is that there *is* a life, a Jiva, a Jivatma, a fragment of the Divine Life, with more and more of its latent powers unfolded in each successive Form, each such Form being a true Individual. In this individualised Life, or Jivatma, inhere the characteristics, or unfolded powers, brought out by the special evolution of the successive forms in which it dwells, family characteristics, tribal characteristics, national characteristics. This family, tribal, national, Life, or Jivatma, is not a mere word, a metaphor; it is a fact in Nature. It is the controlling, directing, harmonising and co-ordinating power as much in the family, the tribe, and the Nation, as in the single human being, for they are all alike Individuals, a Life embodied in a form.

This idea is very familiar in the West from the use made of it by S. Paul, who speaks of it as a "mystery" to the Ephesians, and who points out to the Corinthian Church:

As the body is one, and hath many members, and all the members of that one body, being many, are one body, so also Christ... That there should be no schism in the body, but that the members should have the same care one for another. And whether one member suffer, all the members suffer with it; or one member be honoured, all the members rejoice with it. Now ye are the body of Christ, and members in particular (*1 Cor.,* xii, 12-27.)

The German writer, Professor J. K. Bluntschli, has put this idea very strongly and well. "The State," he says, "has a moral nature" (Book I, chap. iii, p. 2.). He writes:

The State is in no way a lifeless instrument, a dead machine; it is a living and therefore organised being. This organic nature of the State has not always been understood... It is the especial merit of the German school of historical jurists to have recognised the organic nature of the Nation and the State. This conception refutes both mathematical and mechanical view of the State, and the atomistic way of treating it, which forgets the whole in the individuals.....In the State sprit and body, will and active organs, are necessarily bound together in one life. The one National Spirit, which is something different from the average sum of the contemporary spirit of all citizens, is the Spirit of the State; the one National Will, which is different from the average will of the multitude, is the Will of the State. The constitution.....is the body of the State, it is the form in which the Nation manifests its common Life. Individual States differ like individual men in spirit, character and form. The progress of mankind depends essentially on the emulation of its component Peoples and States....While history explains the organic nature of the State, we learn from it at the same time that the State does not stand on the same grade with the lower organisms of plants and animals but is of a higher kind: we learn that it is a moral and spiritual organism, a great body which is capable of taking up into itself the feelings and thoughts of the Nation, of uttering them in laws, and realizing them in acts; we are informed of moral qualities and of the character of each State. History ascribes to the State a personality which, having spirit and body, possesses and manifests a will of its own.

The glory and honour of the State have always elevated the heart of its sons, and animated them to sacrifices. For freedom and independence, for the Rights of the State, the noblest and best have in all times and in all Nations, expended their goods and their lives. To extend the reputation and the power of the State, to further its welfare and its happiness, has universally been regarded as one of the most honourable duties of gifted men. The joys and sorrows of the State have always been shared by all its citizens. The whole great idea of Fatherland and love of country would be inconceivable, if the State did not possess this high moral and personal character....The State is, par excellence, a Person, in the sense of public law. The purpose of the whole constitution is to enable the Person of the State to express and realize its will, which is different from the individual wills of all individuals, and different from the sum of them. (Book I, chap. I, pp. 18,19,20,22.)

This conception of the State, fundamentally true, has been wrought into the mind of the German people, and has given them the marvellous coherence, endurance under suffering, and power to sacrifice all that makes life dear, which they are manifesting in the present War. So powerfully do Ideas work out in the conduct of a Nation, so important are literary teachings to the State. The German error lies, as we shall see, in making the State supreme, and in sacrificing everything to it, as Machiavelli taught, even morality, truth, justice, righteousness. We need to add to this the Indian idea, that above the State is the Supreme Law, Dharma, the expression of the Divine Nature. The most absolute Indian monarch was regarded as the administrator, not as the creator, of Law, and if he disregarded it, so the Shastras taught, the Law he disregarded would sweep him away, he and his House with him.

But for the moment, we are concerned only with the State as an organism—natural, because inherent, as said, in universal human nature, but also, in a sense, artificial, because shaped and modified by human intelligence. Some writers, in recognising the immense work of the latter have overlooked the former, as though a race-borse ceased altogether to be a natural product, because carefully bred by human intelligence selecting certain parents, so as to develop certain characteristics.

Professor Seeley presses this same idea, asking: "Are not States living organisms?" He points out that "it is a characteristic of life, which has been made every prominent in recent science, that substances informed by it [I would substitute 'informed by life at a certain stage of its unfoldment'] receive what is called organisation, that is, the different parts acquire different capacities and adapt themselves to perform different functions. Each part becomes more or less a living tool or organ." Then he proceeds:

But this is precisely what characterises a State. A State is a number of human beings not merely crowded or massed together, but organised. This is so strikingly true that all the technical terms applied to physical and political organisation are interchangeable, and the word organisation itself is applied in both departments alike without metaphor. We say a man is a member of a State. What does the word member mean? It means "limb". We say the eye or the ear performs a function. What does function mean? It is a political term, meaning the discharge of a public office. These examples show how early and how instinctively the analogy between that differentiation which in the physical body creates organs, and that selection which in the State assigns special functions to special men, or to special classes, was perceived. The same thing is illustrated by the ancient fable of the Belly and the Members, which you may read either in Livy or in Shakspeare, and by passages well known to all of you in Plato's *Republic* and in S. Paul's Epistles. There should be no schism in the body, says S. Paul, and Plato says: as we do not say "a finger has pain" but "a man has a pain in his finger," so in the State we ought not to say, "Some one suffers," but "the State suffers in some one". (Lecture ii, pp. 43, 44.)

When we speak of a man being public spirited, we mean that he feels a wrong inflicted on another as keenly as though it had been inflicted on himself; that he resents a general injustice as though it were done to himself personally; that he protects the weak, though the person protected be neither a friend nor a relative; that he regards a public duty as more imperative than a private one. In such a man the State-consciousness is active; he has realised himself as one with the State, his life as identical with the life embodied in the State. It is the parallel of the Realisation of the Self, the "I am Brahman" of the Yogi.

The love of country, the pride in country, the composite emotion that we call Patriotism, already spoken of, is, then, not an emotion directed to a Nothingness, but to a Reality—to that fragment of the Life Universal, the Divine Life, which is the Self, the Jivatma, of the State to which we belong.

Professor Seeley, in his favourite Socratic way, has put this very well:

When I say, "I am an Englishman," what do I mean? Does it refer to my parentage or family? Well, I cannot absolutely say that it does not. I regard myself as being of some sort of kin to other Engishmen, as though we were all alike descended from some primitive Anglus. I feel this very strongly in the presence of foreigners, for I find that they speed a different language and seem both mentally and bodily of a somewhat different type. But whether it really is so, is after all of no practical importance. I am an

Englishmen, and should be so just as much if my ancestors were Frenchmen. And yet that I am an Englishman and not a Frenchman is all-important to me. (Lecture i, p. 15.)

I have been using the word "State" as though we all knew exactly what is its content; yet probably the ideas of most of us are very hazy on the subject. We shall have to discover a definition for the word State, which will apply to it in the Family, the Tribe, the Nation, the Empire or Commonwealth, and finally in organised Humanity, or the World-State. We shall try to find such a definition in the next lecture. We shall also, probably next week, trace the origin of the State and try to understand its essential nature.

CONCLUSION

In concluding this Introductory Lecture, I would earnestly ask you to make an effort to understand clearly any principle or generalisation which may be new or unfamiliar to you, because these will govern all I say, and if they be not thoroughly comprehended the whole subject is likely to remain dim and vague, lacking in clearness and accuracy of thought. You need to grasp the long and laborious method of establishing a scientific truth—the "sublime patience of the investigator", as W.K. Clifford rightly called it. You need also to remember the weakness of the method—the likelihood that all relevant facts may not have been collected. You need to think over very carefully the meaning of the Biological Individual, to realise its two factors, Life and Form, and to understand the building up of higher Individuals out of lower ones, and the functions of the Life in the higher Individual, controlling, directing, harmonising and co-ordianting the lower individuals who form his Body.

You will then come to our Science will prepared to study it.

One difference between East and West should be noted, though it does not affect our actual study of the facts. In the East, the State is regarded not only as inherent in human nature, but also, as the creation of men who were superhuman in their knowledge, and the existence of its Life, with its controlling, directing, harmonising and organising powers rests on their authority, and this on their knowledge of Ishvara, of God. In Greece, Nature is the authority, and that which is nearest to the Order of Nature is best. In modern days, these powers are sometimes regarded as the inherent life-forces, belonging to what Professor Seeley called the "political vital principle," and there can hardly be said to be any authoritative basis for the views taken, since they are still in the region of an imperfect theory, not having yet been based on sufficient research into facts, nor subjected to experiment for final verification. Still, as I said, the origin of the organising force in the State need not affect our study of the facts which result from it.

—Annie Besant

2

Approaches to Politics

Political phenomena is studied through different approaches in order to understand the true nature of political reality. Philosophers, historians, scientific observers and analysts have contributed to enlighten us on the distinction between appearance and reality by following various methods to examine political issues.

The name and identity of each approach conveys a specific thrust. Thus the historical approach is inspired by perspectives of development, decay and evolution in history. The normative approach is concerned with issues of values, preferences, ideals and what ought to be' in Political Science. The behavioural approach lays emphasis on how people behave in political life. The post-behavioural approach is a reaction to, and a consequence of the behavioural approach. It seeks to learn from experiences of the beahvioural enquiry. It is an extension of and in continuity with the behavioural approach. It lays emphasis on 'relevance' and 'action'.

Each approach is a particular way of studying and understanding politics. Generally approaches to the study of politics are identified as 'traditional' and 'modern'. For instance, the historical and the normative approaches would be counted under the traditional perspective since these have been followed from the ancient times. The behavioural and post-behavioural approaches fall under the category of the modern perspective. Approaches which are identified as modern, are considered more scientific.

THE HISTORICAL APPROACH

It uses the knowledge of history and applies it to understand political life. History signifies and manifests an ever-changing process, affecting social life in its entirety. To study politics as a significant human activity, we enquire into the past. When facts about the past are sought, we are really concerned with the origin, nature, development and evolution of ideas, institutions and processes. This is the basic purpose of the historical approach. Knowledge regarding organised existence in the past provides the background to our understanding of politics as it has evolved. Since we are removed from actual happenings and events in the past, we need to take special care to identify the nature of facts of political life. History supplies the accumulated wisdom of the past successes and failures of political scientists.

It cannot be denied that political life today has historical moorings. Freeman is of the view that History is past Politics and Politics is present History. History leads the wise and drags the foolish. History provides relevant information, and we have to distinguish between what is of no significance today and what is likely to offer useful lessons in our search for a meaningful understanding of political life. This approach should help us to identify meaningful patterns of political life.

The historical approach is chronological and descriptive and seeks to explain linkages of political life with the changing social situation.

Political scientists who subscribe to the historical approach are Sabine, Dunning, McIlwain, Burgess and Seeley. In the past, Herodotus and Thucydides followed this method. Aristotle and Machiavelli relied substantially on history though they were not true followers of the historical method. The historical approach indicates broad trends, patterns and linkages. A total perspective, therefore, is necessary.

LIMITATIONS OF HISTORICAL APPROACH

To draw inferences, formulate generalisations and make laws based on the historical experience of political life, should be by caution. Historical understanding is essential, it does not mean that such attempts always succeed in formulation of laws of universal relevance.

Laws formulated on experiences of the past are not necessarily applicable to situations at present or in future which are different and are likely to change. It is partially correct that history repeats itself. Indentical situations might not recur and yet some similarities could be discerned by a careful study of the past political life. Political life in our own times has special characteristics, identity, features, problems and issues.

The past serves as a window to the long process of evolution. Not all the information about antecedents of political life is necessarily relevant today. Political life in our own times might not, in all the cases, be understood by what had happened in the past.

The danger is that in our effort to understand the historical content of political life, and learn from it, we might be carried away by our own preferences and biases. We might only see what we like to and miss what is relevant. This is likely to distort our knowledge. Facts and fiction are likely to be mixed up. Hence reliability of the historical approach is weakened.

If laws of universal relevance could be formulated on the basis of historical experience, it would mean that political life is bound by determinate.

THE NORMATIVE APPROACH

This approach is identified with preferences and values. That is, individual and social priorities, choices, goals, biases and interests comprise the norms. The emphasis is on moral and rational premises. The motivating concern is for what ought to be or what should be.

For instance, if we come across the statement that only men of wisdom should become rulers, or, that every citizen ought to assess the capabilities of candidates before casting his or her vote, the normative concern is predominant. The normative approach is value laden, that is, values determine perceptions, analysis and prescription. In ancient Indian thought and Greek philosophy, the concern for the good life and quality of life is indicative of value laden, normative objectives. It is based on the view that values are inevitable and essential for understanding and evaluating political phenomena and facts.

Since political life concerns human beings, it is not possible, nor desirable, to study facts, phenomena and processes without taking into account the reality that human beings have choices, preferences and values. The moral aspect alone helps us to test whether facts about political life are right or wrong. What is to be studied, how is it to be studied, and, why we study, what we do, are issues viewed from moral perspectives.

The normative approach stresses the belief that relevance of political life lies in the values that motivate and inspire it. Political analysts and author philosophers have been making value judgements all the time. The normative approach states that it is not possible to make political studies value neutral. In order to make the right choices, act in the right manner, make right decisions and ensure betterment of political life, value preferences cannot be ignored.

It does not ignore or minimize the significance of facts. The assertion is that the study of facts and values is necessary for a viable and clear understanding of political life.

It was believed that if Political Science attained the level of reliability of science, it would be possible to build an empirical theory of political life. There is, however is word of caution. By neglecting values, Political Science would become a dry and rudderless discipline. It will miss its destination and fall to inspire the individual and the community to perform duties.

Critics point out that normative approach shuts its eyes to political reality and seeks to build castles in the air. Hence this approach is unrealistic. Politics deals with capture and retention of power. There is hardly any place for scruples in this game of power. Unarmed prophets who preached norms in public life met with a sad end e.g. Socrates, Christ and Gandhi. Men are not Gods. They are made of flesh and blood prone to all weaknesses and mistakes.

Thus Political Science must take into consideration these hard facts in order to build up a dependable body of knowledge.

THE BEHAVIOURAL APPROACH

The historical and the normative approaches fit into the category of traditional perspectives. The emphasis was on descriptive chronological, value-based and moral priorities.

The behavioural approach is identified as a contemporary and scientific alternative, it stresses the study of political behaviour as against the role of institutions alone. It claims to induct scientific methodology and tools of analysis, and empirical, propositions for the study of political life. The approach evolved owing to several factors and causes, the most important being growing dissatisfaction with the traditional approaches.

The behavioural approach is identifiable with behaviouralism in Political Science. This was largely projected by exertions of political scientists in the USA.

Kirkpatrick called behaviouralism a 'revolution'.

David Easton stated that behaviouralism signifies a plea for 'methodological rigour' and concern for 'empirical theory'.

Robert Dahl believes that behaviouralism manifests a 'mood' which calls for greater unity between empirical political studies and concern for general theory.

Easton has given an elaborate explanation about the behavioural approach. He distinguished between behaviouralism and behaviourism. Behaviourism is a psychological concept, associated with the contribution of J.B. Watson.

Eston is one of the pioneers of the behavioural approach. The stance of Easton deeply affected the evolution of the behavioural approach. He however modified his original views and sought to combine both theory and practice. He had provided eight major tenets of the behavioural approach.

1. *Regularities:* Political behaviour has discoverable uniformities. These can be expressed as generalisations or theories with explanatory and predictive values.

2. *Verification:* Such generalisations must be testable for their validity with reference to political behaviour.

3. *Techniques:* For observing, recording, and analysing political behaviour, rigours means have to be found. These need to be refined and validated.

4. *Quantification:* Precision in the recording of data and exactitude of findings require that measurement and quantification be done in a systematic way.

5. *Values:* For the sake of clarity, ethical evaluation and empirical explanation need to be kept analytically distinct.

6. *Systematisation:* Research and theory are intimately inter-twined as parts of a coherent and orderly body of knowledge. This elaborates the concern for making political analysis scientific.

7. *Pure Science:* The knowledge of applied human behaviour and theoretical understanding comprise scientific enterprise. Understanding and explanation of political behaviour form the core of this knowledge, which should be really effective to resolution of practical problems in a society.

8. *Integration:* Social sciences deal with the totality of the human situation. Political research has to take into account the findings of other disciplines. This inter-relationship will help Political Science to once again regain its former glory and status. Moreover Political Science should be drawn into a basic unit of social sciences.

Thus the behavioural approach brought about a distinct changes in perspectives and method of studying political life. This also signified a departure from traditional perspective and approaches.

Limitations of the Behavioural Approach

Behaviouralism has generally been criticised for its over reliance on methods and techniques borrowed from the natural sciences. Critics of this approach have argued that the behaviour of people is not as predictable as the behaviouralists claim. Therefore the behaviouralists have been accused of 'scientism' i.e. a method which only appears to be scientific without actually being so. Further, critics have focused their attack on the behaviouralists for ignoring ethical and moral considerations of politics, i.e. for ignoring 'values'.

David Easton, himself a behaviouralist, pointed out that this approach by ignoring important political values like the commitment to democratic institutions and processes had revealed a conservative bias. In fact, the main emphasis in the behaviouralist approach was on 'system maintenance', that is, on how the political system could maintain its own existence. There was little acceptance of the need for reform of the political system, much less on possibilities of systemic change or a total change in the system itself.

Major criticism of the behaviouralists related to a basic feature of the discipline of Political Science itself, that is, to their ignoring the nature and role of the state.

In the behaviouralist approach the character and functioning of the state did not come into their analysis at all, reducing their analysis into one of 'hyperfactualism', that is an exhaustivc collection of facts which had little relation to the most crucial fact of all; the organisation and social basis of the state which actually shaped the political system.

The behavioural approach, contributed to the incorporation of scientific methodologies and techniques into Political Science, but failed to examine some of the most basic and relevant issues that had traditionally the basis of the discipline.

THE POST BEHAVIOURAL APPROACH

It is a search for perspective going beyond the behavioural approach. The post-behavioural approach is a recent development, is indicative of process of revaluation as well as a restatement of new priorities and obligations. It is an extension of the behavioural approach. There is conscious effort to spell out perceived change.

David Easton, in the presidential address to the American Political Science Association in New York in 1969 stated that increasing social and political crises of our times overlook the behavioural 'revolution'. His call for post-behavioural perspectives was also identified as a 'revolution'. Let us remember that just as the behavioural approach emerged as an alternative to overcome inadequacies of the traditional approach, post-behaviouralism was an attempt to reassess the validity as well as the limits of the behavioural approach.

He identified relevance and action as the major bases of the post-behavioural approach.

Easton expressed deep dissatisfaction with behavioural research and teaching in Political Science. The objective of converting the study of politics into a more rigorous scientific endeavour modelled on the methodology of natural, physical science, was not fully achieved post-behavioural approach was intended as more than a reaction to behaviouralism. Easton claimed that post-behaviouralism was future-oriented, seeking to propel Political Science towards new directions. He equated the new perspectives with a movement and an intellectual tendency.

Tenets of the Post-Behavioural Approach

1. The behavioural insistence upon techniques of study and research has to be revised. Substance must precede technique. Contemporary urgent problems need to be examined intensively. The obligation, therefore, is to be relevant and meaningful, to ensure the quality and reliability of issues and subject-matter of concern. What we perceive, identify and investigate has to be specifically identified. Mere abstractions are of no use. Emphasis on sophistication of tools and technique of investigation would be ineffective if the substance of manifold problems and challenges of politics is ignored or minimised.

2. Easton cautioned that in the contemporary situation, it is better to be value-laden than non-relevantly precise. That is, if political analysts do not comprehend the situational

relevance of issues and problems, they would fail to assess the social reality. The objective of precision would become meaningless. On the other hand, if substantial identification of relevant issues is achieved, even vagueness of some sort would not adversely affect the study of issues. Vagueness could be corrected at some stage but failure to be relevant would only add to the complexity and meaninglessness of issues and bases of the substance of political life.

3. The behavioural approach was restricted and limited in several ways. Over-emphasis and exclusive concern for description and analysis of facts at the empirical level resulted in a limited and narrow perspective. This was empirical conservatism. The behavioural perspective was overly devoted to abstraction and 'analytic' formulation (at the intellectual level). Crude realities of political life were not taken into consideration. The post-behavioural approach seeks to recognise the real needs of mankind in times of crisis.

4. Departing from the stance of the behavioural perspective, the post-behavioural approach conceded that study of politics is inseparably connected with values. Even science could not be totally value-neutral. There are limits to our knowledge. Value premises help us understand the contexts of issues and problems.

5. Dissatisfied with the abstract and soulless perspectives, methodology and inferences of the behavioural approach, the post-behavioural alternative calls upon intellectuals of Political Science to fulfil vital tasks and social obligations. The intellectuals role could not ignore protection of human values of civilisation.

6. The post-behavioural approach seeks to transform the study and analysis of political life into an Action Science. The nineteenth century perspective of political Science was largely contemplative. The argument was that Action Science reflects contemporary conflicts in society over ideals. Study and research could not ignore this vital aspect. Therefore, the intellectuals must accept the logic that to know is to bear

responsibility for acting. To act is to engage in reshaping society. Knowledge must be put to work in the larger social context.

7. Once the intellectuals understand, accept and implement their transformed role and obligations, it is the task of institutions of learning including universities to get involved in the struggles of the day. This is inescapable as well as desirable.

P.H. Merkl explains that the post-behavioural approach does not mean a new wave of methodological innovations. It signifies stock-taking and re-appraisal. There is a noticeable trend back to the vital aspect concerning value-preferences, identified with the normative approach. This should explain that from the traditional approaches to the post-behavioural approach, there is not only change but also continuity.

Thus the historical approach is meant to study political life as an integral part of the total historical context. Political life is seen in meaningful relationship with forces operating at a given time and place. The historical approach places political life in the moving stream of development, decline and evolution. It provides the basis for identifying options to move in the desired direction.

The normative approach seeks to study political life with emphasis on inevitability and desirability of values. Preferences, priorities, goals, biases and interests need to be assessed from a normative point of view. The political reality should not be ignored.

The behavioural approach relies on the study of political behaviour. This approach is a clear and conscious departure from the traditional approaches. It aims at methodological precision, scientific rigour, theory-building, interdisciplinary integration leading to unity of the social sciences, and, above all, it opens up new possibilities for evolution and development of Political Science as a discipline. The behavioural approach represents an important stage in making political knowledge scientific and precise.

The shift from historical and normative approaches to the behavioural was a departure. The move from the behavioural approach to the post-behavioural did not amount to a radical departure. It signifies a process of reassessment. There is apparent concern for making political studies more relevant by resolution of social crises. The call for action is innovative.

Arguing for the priority of substance as against technique, Easton recongnizes the fact that political dynamics could not be understood in isolation. The imperative determinants are the individual and his preferences and values. Post-behaviouralism accepts the relevance of the social purpose of Political Science absolute and final laws. It would mean that human beings are not free to progress from one phase of civilisation to the other. Since political life is not static, society has also to adjust to the changing situation. Absolute laws of political life, therefore, are neither possible nor desirable.

Scope of history is much more comprehensive than Political Science. History records a variety of aspects and phenomena. But Political Science is to necessarily dependent upon that knowledge to explain evolution of organised and ordered political life.

Plato's theory of the Philosopher King, or Communism of family and property are historically irrelevant. These theories are relevant to Political Science. Similarly, Hobbes, Locke and Rousseau stated that the state originated in a Social Contact. The theory is historically unfounded, but it is significant for understanding several aspects of Political Science.

History of past political events cannot be recreated fully and objectively. Historians have made their own selective studies. A few facts were considered and others ignored. What we know as history may neither be comprehensive nor impartial. History, therefore, can provide only broad patterns and trends of political life in the past.

References

Appadorai, A. 1985: *The substance of Politics,* Oxford University Press, Madras.

Easton, David. 1971. *The Political System,* Scientific Book Agency: Calcutta.

Varma, S.P. 1988. *Modern Political Theory,* Vikas Publication: New Delhi.

Davies, Morton R. and V.A. Lewis. 1971. *Models of Political Systems,* Vikas Publications: New Delhi.

Verma, S.L. 1988. *Modern Political Theory.* Meenakshi Prakashan: New Delhi.

3

The Dynamics of Political Change

Politics is the process in which a community confronts a series of great issues and chooses between opposing values. Almost universally the institution through which this is done is the state, though on occasion the same role has been performed by religious, economic, or kinship groupings. Government consists of the machinery, personnel, and methods used by the state to carry out its functions. In every political situation, in every type of state, and under all forms of government, the same basic issues are always present and they must all receive a solution. Since each issue admits of more than one choice, states and their governments differ in the choices they embody and in the manner of combining them.

This way of understanding politics offers insights into some of its characteristics whose significance would otherwise be missed. Too many political analyses reduce the subject to terms and categories that are primarily static. That is an unfortunate by-product of an attempt that is laudable in itself—the effort at logical exposition. Logic aims at concepts and propositions which are, as far as possible, unambiguous and mutually exclusive. But the actualities of politics—as distinct from theories about them—are fluid and mobile. Hence it is difficult, and can be inaccurate, to impose a rigid framework on shifting materials. A political philosophy, which satisfies the conceptual tests of a logical system, often fails at the no less rigorous task of explaining political phenomena as they have been, as they now are, and as they may be. To be successful, a political analysis must meet two criteria. It should designate the underlying problems that are the invariable constrants and indicate the variable modes of resolving them.

The reasons for these requirements, and for the necessity of both, are implicit in the treatment attempted in this book. To argue that the political process is composed of constant factors is to recognize the similarity between situations separated in time and place if one speaks of politics, state, and government in Greece of the fifth century B.C. Rome of the first century A.D., the age of Thomas Aquinas, the revolutionary century from 1688 to 1789, or the world of Roosevelt, Churchill Stalin, and Hitler, there must be some unifying threads which, despite the manifold differences, persist unbroken. Presumably the problems confronting Pericles or Augustus, Louis IX or Louis XIV, Lincoln or Nehru, were similar, and may appropriately be grouped as incidents in our constant striving to control the present and shape the future. To conceive of the Connecticut Yankee at King Arthur's Court was a stroke of fancy. But a Pericles in the While House would have found himself as much in his element as a Roosevelt in the Athenian Assembly. The issues that both statesmen faced and the skills they practiced were sufficiently alike for their abilities to be transferable. Likewise a Clodius with his gang fights in the streets of Rome could have changed places readily with a Capone in Chicago. As a stream of history flows uninterruptedly from prehistoric times to the present without regard for our divisions into periods, so does a stream of politics rise at a source concealed in our primeval past and follow its single course down to the rapids and whirlpools of our century.

PERMANENT PROBLEMS, CHANGING SOLUTIONS

But, though its flow be continuous, a stream will change direction. Its main channel can shift. Its current may be fast for a while or sluggish. Similar is the action of politics. For its continuity represents the unity of energy, not of mass. It is a unity of flux and movement. It extends over time, not over space. Throughout its process runs a rhythm that is ever changing because it is patterned from issues whose solutions change. In the opportunity for choice conferred by each issue lie the springs of political dynamics.

How are such changes manifested? Many examples have been noted in this work of the human tendency to tack and turn like sailors taking advantage of the wind. The history of politics reveals an expanse of creative activity which allows wide room for inventiveness and resource. After making what progress they can in one direction, people veer around and strain toward another point. Thus the monistic city-state of Greece and Rome was replaced by the Christian experiment in church-state dualism. This in turn gave way to the monism of nation-state sovereignty, which was later followed by the attempt to separate the economic order from politics. The unit of government has likewise passed through a succession of forms. City-state, empire-state, and nation-state have all been tried and tested. Each yielded what benefits it could and then succumbed to conditions for which it ceased to be appropriate. So too with the other great issues. Humanity perennially explores new ways of meeting old problems, as the United States in 1987 pioneered with the structure of federalism; or we revive under different circumstances a system used centuries before, just as the American Republic designed its institutions with a separation of powers similar to what the Roman Republic once employed.

INTERACTION BETWEEN THE GREAT ISSUES

There is, however, another aspect of the process of political change whose operation is more intrucate than what has so far been described. If politics forms a single compound which can then be analysed into five basic elements, it would follow that when one component undergoes a major alteration, the remainder are likely to be affected. The probability raises a fundamental question: When people turn to a different solution of any issue, are there consequent changes which that decision tends to produce among the rest? Does the evidence of history suggest that specific solutions of the respective issues ordinarily accompany each other in pairs or groups? If so, one could indicate which alternatives are mutually compatible and which are not—and that would constitute a valuable guide for interpreting the past and predicting the future. On the other hand, one may find that no relation—positive or negative—can be traced between some pairs of issues, in which case a choice among one set of alternatives would be unconnected with, and thus irrelevant to, a choice among another set. There is only one way to discover whether this is the case. Every issue must be discussed in relation to every other, in order to detect any possible pattern in which their solutions tend to combine.

The Relations of Privilege or Equality to Other Choices

Take the first choice between regimes of privilege and equality. What correlation is there between either of these and the manner in which other issues are solved? Does a swing from privilege to equality, or vice versa, lead to corresponding reversals in the treatment of other issues? Wherever a few privileged persons are in a position of superiority over a much larger number, the dominant oligarchy will use all means to enable them to stay on the top of the heap. Necessarily, the favoured few must possess political power and therewith must control the state—or they will eventually be ousted from influence by those who do. Does this mean, however, that when an elite monopolizes the government, the entire society is subordinated to the state in monistic fashion? Or is it possible for privilege to be associated with pluralism, in which case, though politics would be reserved for the few, the functions of the state vis-à-vis other associations would somewhere be limited?

The historical answer is that the principle of oligarchy, as such, does not necessitate either a pluralist or monistic policy by the state toward society. Oligarchies have in fact been associated with one or the other. Thus in the medieval period, when the state was controlled by an oligarchy of nobles and the church by an oligarchy of priests, the prevalent theory of politics was steadfastly opposed to monism. Where as conquering people has taken over the government of the conquered, the victors have sometimes been content to restrict their authority to a few essentials (for example, finance, police, and military affairs), leaving their subjects otherwise free from state control. Such, in general, was the character of British rule in India. By contrast the czarist autocracy in Russia during the eighteenth and nineteenth centuries contrived a complete subordination of society to the state. Similar in spirit have been the modern one-party dictatorships—whether Fascist,

Nazi, or Communist—whose efforts to make the functions of the state coextensive with social activity have become a byword.

What happens when a regime of privilege is replaced by one of equalitarianism? Does the latter have a closer affinity with monism or pluralism? The evidence indicates that a sizable extension of the citizen body is likely to be accompanied by an extension of the functions of the sate, though there may be a time lag before the latter takes full effect. The period that can throw most light on this problem is the century from 1830 to 1930. During that time the spread of democracy culminated in many states with the achievement of universal suffrage, and with this was associated a tremendous increase in the functions of their governments. Was this combination of events a coincidence or a case of cause and effect? Without doubt, it was the latter, Generally, the impetus behind the movement to extend the franchise came from a desire to remedy specific ills by political action. Some of these ills were due to differentiations of humanity into classes which determined the breadth of opportunity available to their members. Other ills were of economic origin and stemmed from the union of industrialism with urbanism. Political equality, signalised by the ballot, was desired as a means to social and economic betterment, and the state was then employed as the instrument of equalisation. Hence as new voters were enrolled, political parties formulated programmes to represent their interests, and these were eventually translated into legislative and administrative form. Being composed of people who were poorer and underprivileged, the recently enfranchised were disposed to invoke the powers of the state, since other social institutions treated them as inferiors.

The choice between privilege and equality can be precisely correlated with the next pair of alternatives: authoritarian or controllable government. A system dedicated to the exaltation of a privileged few dares not submit to any procedure of genuine control by the governed. The texture of privilege is stained with the dye of authoritarianism, for in no other way can a minority obtain and enforce the submission of the majority. Those who wield authority are always unequal in relation to those whom they dominate. No less true is the converse. Wherever equalitarianism is substituted for privilege, the governed seek institutional means to keep the power of their officials within bounds. Equalitarianism is no more compatible with authoritarianism than is privilege with accountability.

Turning, however, to the choice between unity of dispersion of power, one finds no definite correlation with either oligarchical or majority government. A few examples will make this plain. In the Middle Ages, when politics was certainly reserved for the few, the structure of authority was loose-knit, while powers were highly dispersed. The church struggled with the state. The localities resisted the centre. The nobility defied the king. On the other hand, various modern oligarchies, especially those of Nazi Germany and Fascist Italy, have been totally centralised and integrated. The same contrasts may be observed among equalitarian systems. Whereas government in the United States was constructed according to the principles of federal decentralisation and the separation of branches, the British system evolved with the predominance of central over local authority and of the cabinet over the other institutions at the centre.

The same can be said concerning the size of the state and its possible effect on the enlargement or contraction of citizenship. A comparison of ancient city-states with modern nations demonstrates that either obligachy or its opposite can flourish indifferently in states of Lilliputian or mamoth size. The size of the political unit has no direct bearing on the internal distribution of rights and influence.

The Accompaniments to Monism and Pluralism

Let us apply the same method to the second of the great issues. The preference for a state of limited or comprehensive functions has been discussed in relation to the alternatives of privilege or equality. How are the other choices affected by the adoption of either pluralism or monism? Suppose we look at some contrasted examples. Medieval society was emphatically pluralist, alike in principle and practice. The same society exhibited a government both in church and state that was not responsible to the governed. Pluralism by itself, therefore, is no certain gurantor of freedom. On the other hand, as ninenteenth-century America proves, pluralism and freedom can be mixed in one compound. The same can be told of experiments in monism. There are classic instances of a monistic state combined with a controllable government. Such was the Athenian *polis* in its heyday. Such is contemporary Britain, where a parliamentary majority may legally do anything, but is ordinarily circumspect in using its theoretical powers. Similarly, in New Zealand, the state is all-powerful within society, yet the government is emphatically subject to popular control. But monism can also be harmonious with dictatorship. Indeed, the most notorious dictatorships of this century make state and society indistinguishable. One could hazard the hypothesis that, because the modern dictatorship arises for nationalistic or economic reasons, or from a desire to accomplish a cultural revolution rapidly (Kemalist Turkey, for example), authoritarian regimes today are less likely to tolerate social pluralism than in the past. Beyond the line where the boundaries of state action are drawn, opposition may develop against those in power.

The other aspect of power, its unity or dispersion, has a more obvious connection with monism and pluralism. There is an understandable tendency for a monistic state to construct authority on a centralised and integrated plan. Where a state assumes the responsibility for overseeing other associations and their activities, it is less practicable to have a governmental structure in which the branches are too independent and the localities too autonomous. Traditionally, therefore, a monistic state like Britain has had its powers both centralised and integrated. In a pluralist state, on the other hand, both separation of branches and devolution from the centre are suited to the prevailing character of a government whose functions are limited. Where the activities to be conducted are fewer, there are fewer chances of overlap, duplication, or conflict between agencies and their programmes. Hence there is less demand for a unified focus of power. Moreover, as American experience in the twentieth century testifies, a government of restricted scope, if impelled by economic or military necessity to expand its activities, must simultaneously modify its previously accepted canons of separate branches and federal-state dualism. The United States today contains more evidence than 50 years ago of unification among branches and levels of government, because more is done by every branch of government at every level and these additional activities would collide unless they were somehow coordinated.

Whether the size of the state influences the functions it undertakes is more difficult to deterine. On this point, history suggests some tentative hypotheses but no conclusive verdict. The classic case of a state whose expansion covered a huge area and population is the Roman Empire. Rome successfully organised an administrative apparatus, legal code, and military machine to unify its diverse and scattered provinces. It was much less successful, however, in uniting the people of its empire with a common loyalty. Deliberate efforts were made to employ religion for this purpose. But when little headway was made with the official ritual of the Olympian deities, or the worship of Mithra, or the defication of emperors, Constantine turned to the Christian faith to inspire a unity of sentiment that was otherwise lacking. The effect of his action, however, was to substitute dualism for monism, and thereby to reduce the scope of state activity. Hence the problem of extending the size of the state outward was solved only by diminishing the sphere where the state could operate inward.

Similar in a sense has been the experience of the United States. The process of peopling a continent from the Atlantic to the Pacific, from the forty-ninth parallel to the Rio Grande, was accompanied by the organisation of society along pluralist lines. The circumstances under which the state expanded its territory and population in North America were ill suited to a monistic view of the role of government in society. Elsewhere, however, there have been instances to the contrary. The growth of European Russia was associated with the establishment of a powerful state that embraced and absorbed the entire social order. Later, when czarist power spread across central Asia to the Pacific, the same all-pervasive state controlled and directed the expansion. The change in scale never resulted in modifying the monism of the Russian *vlast.*[1] However, in drawing this contrast between the United States and Russia, one should remember that the expansion of the United States, though it encountered opposition, did not face a hostile neighbour of equal force on the same continent. The consolidation of the Muscovite state, on the other hand, was achieved in the teeth of prolonged and repeated warfare against nearby powers (Poland, Sweden, Prussia, Turkey, the Tartars, and so forth), and the military stamp left an ineradicable imprint on Russian government in the form of complete state domination of society, which the Communists continued with more pervasive methods.

If large states then can be either monistic or pluralist, what about small ones? There is some evidence to indicate that, as the size of the unit of government decreases, the number functions performed by the state in society increases. At any rate, the smallest territorial unit in the history of the West, the Greek *polis,* was characterised by comprehensive state control. So little was that control questioned that Plato and Aristotle do not even include in their political theory a discussion of the possible or desirable limits of state activity. Nor is it hard to understand why monism should bring advantages to smaller units. Where a state is composed of a small population in a small area, it is simple, effective, and inexpensive to organise the activities of society under one institution only. In such a community many, if not most, of the inhabitants can have direct face-to-face contact. If separate institutions are created for governmental, religious, economic and other purposes, their members are likely to be the same persons reassembled in different guises. In a little state, pluralism would seem superfluous; only in larger units does it make sense.

How the Remaining Issues Combine

The third issue—the choice between dictatorial or responsible government—was considered above in its relation to the extensiveness of citizenship and of governmental functions. But how do the rival conceptions of the source that validates authority affect the problem of whether powers are better unified or dispersed? Between these pairs of alternatives there seems no positive correlation. The United States and Britain are countries in whose political systems the authority of officials is derived from the will of the governed. Yet the structure of power is highly dispersed on the American side of the Atlantic and highly unified on the British. Apparently, then, it is not directly relevant to the politics of freedom to inquire whether the mechanics of government conform to the one design or the other. The same alternatives may be found in regimes of authoritarianism. In the medieval period the mass of the populace was expected to obey the established authorities. Nevertheless, those authorities were subdivided into numerous fragments. In the modern dictatorship unswerving obedience to the leader is the duty of the masses. But authority in this case is solidly compacted, and the colossus that doth bestride the state reveals on its surface no seams or fissures.

Whether the size of the state has any connection with authoritarianism or its opposite is the next question. At first glance, size appears immaterial, since governments of small, medium, and huge states have belonged to either variety, some being controllable and others irresponsible. Sparta, Spain, Germany, and the Soviet Union have provided examples of one kind. Athens, Switzerland, Britain, and the United States illustrate the opposite. Mere size, however, is not the only factor. In a world of many states, size is relative. A state may be safe or insecure according to the kind of neighbours it has and their friendliness or hostility. Irrespective of size any state that feels threatened[2] or that harbours aggressive intentions will emphasize the need for military organisation, which influences the character of the government in an authoritarian direction. The so-called "garrison state."[3] applying to government the discipline of a barracks, can often[4] be explained in terms of relations between states and not as the phenomenon of a single state standing in isolation.

Finally, to complete the circle of correlations, two issues remain whose effects on each other must be discussed. Can any connection be traced between the size of a state and a preference for a dispersed or unified structure of power? To answer this, one must recall[5] that relations between levels of government are not the same as those between branches functioning at the same level. The problem of centralisation is not identical with that of integration, and the size of the state bears more immediately on the former than on the latter. It needs little elaboration to show that, the smaller the state, the less the likelihood of decentralisation.[6] Indeed, in the city-state virtually all government is conducted at one centre. Conversely, as population and territory increase, the sheer growth in size creates complexities and adds to the difficulty of communications. Regional diversities are likely to become pronounced. Differences of soil, climate, and resources will lead to divergent economic interests. Expansion may be accompanied by the absorption of mixed cultures with hankerings for autonomy. Separatist tendencies will be a by-product of bigness—witness the attitudes of the old South to the United States, of the Ukraine to Russia, of Western Australia to the Australian Commonwealth, of Manchuria to China. No matter what the internal character of its government may be in other respects, any large state must permit a measure of decentralisation. Neither Washington nor Moscow, neither Brasilia, Delhi, nor Ottawa, can undertake the entire government of the sprawling territories under its jurisdiction. Understandably, therefore, federalism is found in some of the world's largest states.

As contrasted with the problem of centralisation, the choice between integrating and dispersing the structure of governmental power is not so obviously linked with size. States with tightly integrated institutions have run the gamut of size, from diminutive to huge. It is questionable, however, whether the same can be said about the separation of branches and its application to states of different magnitude. Two famous instances of governments embodying the principle of separation are the republics of Rome and the United States. But it was the tragedy of the Roman Republic, and also a fundamental reason why the century from 133 B.C. to 31 B.C. suffered from prolonged constitutional crisis and spasmodic civil war, that the checks and balances between the branches of the Roman government were unsuited to the territorial expansion of Rome's imperial power. When the Senate clashed with the consuls, and the home authorities conflicted with a proconsul in an outlaying province, civil turmoil and military weakness resulted. Hence, in order that an empire might be governed, the emperorship arose to integrate the powers at the centre.

How does this apply to the United States? Has the expansion of the American Republic imposed any strain on the traditional separation of government into three branches? Undoubtedly it has. The adjustments required by the depression of the early 1930s certainly evoked the need for closer cooperation between presidency, Congress, and Supreme Court. Still more acute have been the tensions arising in the aftermath of World War II. The assumption by the United States of a position of international leadership made it necessary to pursue long-range policies and shoulder long-term commitments in conjunction with other governments. For this purpose not only harmony between the president and the Congress, but also agreement between the major parties, was required. The results were substantially good until the bipartisan foreign policy foundered in 1949 and 1950 on the issues of China and Korea. Simultaneously a new problem was precipitated to the forefront of American politics. The dissension between President Truman and General Mac-Arthur, climaxed by the latter's dismissal, involved more than the supremacy of civil over military authority. For the first time the American Republic faced the same question as Rome confronted in the cases of Sulla and Caesar, and Britain in those of Clive and Hastings in India: How does the home government control a strong-willed commander in a distant theatre?

Thirty-five years later, the threat posed by the "Imperial Presidency" to the American constitutional system became a matter of public concern after the exposure of Reagan's "Iran-Contra" escapade. At that time, officials of the executive branch answerable to the President, namely the Director of the C.I.A. and the National Security Advisor, were engaged with all possible secrecy in a reckless foreign adventure which violated Acts of Congress and contradicted the public official policies of the State Department.[7]

The issue at stake here is basic: Is a President to be a law unto himself? No democracy in the past ever succeeded in reconciling the exercise of massive strength abroad with the maintenance of restraints at home. It is that contradiction which in recent decades has strained the U.S. Constitution to its limits.

Not only is it reasonable to expect some major structural changes, but desirable to have them. The government of a democracy rests on the assumption that those who represent the majority should hold office but should be continuously and publicly confronted by their critics. This has the merit of focusing responsibility for action on one side, for dissent on the other. However, while it is essential in democratic politics always to have two or more organised parties, it is of dubious wisdom to divide between them simultaneously the authority for actually taking decisions. Because of the different electoral procedures and length of terms of the president and the two Houses of Congress, it is possible for one party to run the executive branch while the other controls the legislature, as has regularly happened since the 1950s. Such a division, which can aggravate conflict of policy and divergence of outlook, may cause harm in domestic matters because it is likely to lead to either inaction or unsatisfactory compromise. In foreign affairs, too, the consequences can sometimes be injurious to the national interest.[8]

For it is incorrect to say, as a fact or as a wish, that politics ends at the water's edge. It does not, and in certain cases it should not. Many crucial problems of our time, such as a respect for human rights, overleap national boundaries. Some of the issues on whose future solution our civilisation depends cannot be settled within the confines of the present-day nation. They require negotiation between the governments of many states. On these matters there is frequently as much room for legitimate disagreement between equally loyal and dedicated citizens as there is on problems strictly internal in scope. In countries with vast commitments in the world beyond their borders, the political parties, to the extent that they differ in philosophy, may appropriately stand opposed on both the strategy and tactics of foreign relations. For that reason, the machinery of government can be seriously clogged, if political rivals control its different branches. A strong case exists for unity of decision and fusion of responsibility between the legislative and the executive, especially in the conduct of diplomacy. But equally strong is the need for vigilant and constructive criticism by an informed opposition, which has a continuous incentive and responsibility to expose the majority's mistakes.

THE GREAT ISSUES APPLIED TO DEMOCRACY, TOTALITARIANISM, FASCISM, AND COMMUNISM

This analysis may suggest some ways of applying the techniques used in this book. In the introductory chapter, I argued that the political process can be more clearly understood if its complexities are unravelled in terms of its component issues. Politics has been presented as an arena of controversy about permanent problems which permit alternative solutions. This conception allows for various applications, which can now be discussed. Thus, the great issues can be the framework for comparing the political characteristics of broad historical periods, for comprehending the rival systems of the modern world, and for explaining the distinctive features of contemporary politics. Let me review these themes.

In the political conflicts of our century, the rival systems have been described as democracy, totalitarianism, fascism, and communism. Each of these connotes both concepts and institutions. Each is necessarily all-inclusive, since it comprises the whole political system. For that reason each is difficult, if not impossible, to define briefly. In lieu of definition, however they can be identified and compared by reference to their solutions of the great issues.

Take democracy first.[9] There are two issues which permit only one solution if a state is to be democratic. In regard to citizenship, a democracy must be equalitarian, allowing a fair opportunity for all to participate in the conduct or control of their government. To the extent that they are denied this right, the state falls short of democracy's ideal. Further, in such a state the source of authority must lie in the governed, who need effective means for bringing their representatives or officials to account. This is another way of saying that the essentials of democracy are equality and liberty. Fused together, these form the bedrock on which the foundations of democracy must always rest. With regard to other issues, democracy is neutral. It has been associated with either pluralism or monism, with a concentration or dispersion of power, and with any size of territory or population.

Totalitarianism is indifferent to the size of the state, but on the other four issues its requirements are specific. It results from combining privilege, monism, authoritarianism, and unity of power. When these are compounded, the sum represents the most complete (that is, total) domination of society by the state and of the state itself by a few.

Fascism and communism are not easy to define or compare. For one thing, fascism did not take the same form in Italy under Mussolini as in Germany under Hitler or in Spain under Franco. For another, the realities of communism have deviated so much from the principles of Marx that one must be careful to state whether the theory or the practice is being discussed. On the issue of citizenship, a fascist state proclaims that, because of human inequalities, participation in government is reserved for the few.[10]

Marxist theory is equalitarian, but communist practice, as initiated by Lenin and developed by Stalin, was oligarchical and reestablished a society with sharp differentiations of rank and reward. The functions of the state know no limits in fascist theory, since it is the state that embodied the supremacy of the nation to Mussolini and the supremacy of the "Aryan race" to Hitler. In practice, however both regimes encountered opposition from the religious quarter and has to live with a church they could not crush. Monism was more complete in the communist state, where private ownership of the means of production was virtually eliminated (which is not the case under fascism) and where the church (except in Poland) was subservient. Paradoxically, however, it was Marxism, whose doctrines produced the most powerful state of all, which proclaimed that the state would wither away when socialism was achieved! Both communist and fascist systems, when they came to the problem of the source of power, were similarly authoritarian in theory and in practice. Each aped the other in establishing the dictatorship of a single disciplined party ruling the masses by a mixture of propaganda and coercion. Likewise, the concentration of power was pushed to the same extreme point by all these regimes. As to the size of the state, however, fascism and communism were different. The former was inherently nationalist. Communism in principle and by preference sought to be international, since its fundamental concept of the proletariat leaped across national boundaries. Yet, as Tito's Yugoslavia demonstrated, and as other communist governments manifested in varying degrees, communism too could be as permeated with nationalism as other systems.

Historical Perspective on the Great Issues

The analysis of states in terms of the five great issues may serve another purpose. It can be applied to the successive broad periods in the political history of the West: the Graeco-Roman city-state, the Roman Empire, the Middle ages, the nation-state. Which solutions of the great issues were prevalent in each period?

The Graeco-Roman City State

Citizenship at that time was severely restricted in the oligarchies but was considerably extended in democracies like Athens. Nowhere, however, was it perfectly equalitarian, since slaves and women were relegated to an inferior status. The functions of the state were everywhere considered coextensive with society. Examples occurred of authoritarian and of responsible government, of the unity and of the dispersion of power. Typically and ideally, the size of the state was the simple *polis,* but the largest cities were atypical and tried to found expires.

The Roman Empire

This state moved steadily from privilege toward juridical equality, though the latter was never granted to women or slaves. Initially, the functions of the state were unlimited, but limits were accepted when Christianity was adopted. Under the Republic, an unsuccessful attempt was made to locate authority in the governed. Later, power was vested in the emperor through his command of the army. Powers were centralised when the state was small; decentralised, when it expanded. At the centre. powers were dispersed under the Republic, but were integrated into one power in the empire. In size, Rome was the giant of antiquity, forming an antithesis to the *polis*.

The Middle Ages

In the eyes of God, all were equal. In earthly practice gross inequalities prevailed and politics was an arena for the privileged. The functions of the state were drastically curtailed by its copartnership with the church. Government was authoritarian in fact, though theories to the contrary persisted. Power was decentralised and dispersed to the maximum degree. The unit of government was as large as Christendom in the ecclesiastical sphere, but was localised on the temporal side.

The Nation-State

This period commenced everywhere with the rule of privilege, but many states have been moving toward a broader equalitarianism. The early nation-state was allied with monism in the guise of sovereignty. In the nineteenth century, however, the challenge of economic change led to doctrines of dualism and pluralism. The structure of government in nation-states has been either unified or dispersed. They have varied in size because of the difficulty of making nation and state coterminous, and several have contradicted their own principles by building empires.

THE UNIQUENESS OF TWENTIETH-CENTURY POLITICS

How has our own age sought to solve these issues, and what solutions can be expected in the twenty-first century? A world depression, two world wars, and the revolutionary ferment of the last 50 years are evidence that this century is one of crisis. When the nature of the crisis is clarified in terms of the great issues, our age appears to possess a unique character unparalleled earlier. The modern world is undergoing three major transformations simultaneously—in the relations of person to person, of state to society, and of state to state. In each of these spheres a drastic change of scale is occurring. The drive toward equalitarianism involves more people as political participants. Pluralism has been yielding to increased state activity. Meanwhile, under the stress of technological innovation, with its economic and military by-products, new units of government are being sought as replacements for the nation-state. It is this threefold expansion—the fact of new government, both bigger and smaller, doing more for more people—that makes contemporary politics distinctive and gives our problems a complexity without precedent. Any one of these changes would be hard to undertake with success. But when all three occur together, and when each impinges on the other two, the task of finding a solution is much more formidable. Never before has humanity confronted simultaneously the triple need to establish more equality and more functions of government in states of new magnitudes. What is more, this is not occurring in one corner of the globe, or even on one continent. Tomorrow's solutions, if they are to work, have to be projected on a scale as wide as the earth itself. Eventually they must embrace all humanity. To produce the ideas, the institutions, and the inspiration that will encompass such changes presents a political challenge to match the physical revolutions of electronics, nuclear power, and space rockets. Nor is there anything predetermined about the character of the solutions or the methods that will be used in reaching them. Any prediction of future trends, therefore, is hazardous. Nevertheless, the alternatives can be reviewed and their implications spelled out.

EQUALITARIANISM TODAY

The age-old choice between privilege and equality has assumed a new form in the twentieth century. The social consequences of industrialism, which brought more people into closer contact in crowded cities and required literacy and further education; the invention of improved and speedier communications; the spread of the printed word by the press and magazines; and the extended range of eye and ear through radio, motion pictures, and television have ushered in an era of mass politics, so that the power that drives the wheels of government depends on what beliefs millions accept and what facts they have been told and happen to remember. The masses of mankind are much less the passive subjects of politics than in the past. Instead, they are becoming active participants. Their participation, however, can be organised in alternate ways. Tremendous though it be, the change of scale has not removed the choice between privilege and equalitarianism. What it has done is to augment the difficulty of achieving either solution. The competition between democracy and communism was a struggle between rival systems for the same objective—the allegiance of the mass of humanity.

The promise of communism was to pulverize the existing order and eliminate its social and economic inequalities. But the result, because of the monopoly of power by one party, was to reestablish a new type of privilege to which political power provided the entree. The chief concession that communism made to equalitarianism, and a major difference between Soviet Russia and that of the czars, was that communism recruits its privileged oligarchy from a much wider segment of society. The promise of democracy, on the other hand, is to cut the ties between political power and privilege by offering the masses alternative leaders and programmes through two or more parties, thus preventing the formation of a permanent caste. The impact of the numerical increase in participants produces a different response in the two systems. The one-party state has attempted to organize its millions by demanding conformity and discouraging dissent. Outwardly this method gave an appearance of power by its display of solidarity. Inwardly, however, the intolerance to new ideas put the brakes on progress. The democratic state organizes its inhabitants by tolerating multiformity and leaving scope for political competition. This is a source of strength, because new thoughts may be freely expressed and discontents can receive an airing. But there are some attendant risks. Conflict between groups may delay and even prevent discussion; private interests, uncontrolled, may capture public power; or two large organisations (for example, Democrats and Republicans, or a corporation and a trade union) may cease to function as rivals and, instead, by monopolizing power together, may exclude a genuine alternative.

If millions are organised politically and are to stay loyal to the system, performance means more than promise. For communism, a major difficulty was the discrepancy between what it professed—liberation and equality—and what it practiced—intolerance and privilege.[11] The rigidities of the one-party system with its power monopoly made it difficult for the underprivileged to challenge their masters. The latter, in order to explain the contrast between their sayings and their doings, and justify perpetuation of their dictatorship, propagated the view that they faced a hostile world which sought to destroy them. This exemplifies the dictum that "politics as a practice, whatever its professions, had always been the systematic organisation of hatreds."[12]

Democracies, too, depart at times from their own professed principles, and permit substantial discrimination against women and against racial, religious, ethnic, or economic groups in their midst. Serious difficulties arise when a democracy fails to apply in other sectors of society the equalitarianism it insists on in politics. Thus, in Britain during the nineteenth century the equalitarian tendencies expressed in broadening the franchise ran counter to the privileged status of the aristocracy and the general stratification of people into upper, middle, and lower classes. Similar were the consequences produced by industrialism, allied with laissez-faire notions, in the United States and Britain. By the time World War I broke out, gross inequalities prevailed in the distribution of property and income. Indeed, the contrast then existing between the political power of the many and the economic power of the few supplied a repetition of Aristotle's view that democracy is a struggle of the poor against the rich. During this century, therefore, democracy has tackled and continues to confront a pair of associated problems; how to transfer the fundamentals of equalitarianism from politics to the rest of the social order, and while levelling up, avoid an excess of levelling down which would destroy incentive and deny recognition to talent. Suffice it to say that the democratic state has accomplished much in the last hundred years, but has plenty left to do.

The same verdict—that gains have been made, but much remains undone—can be rendered in the sphere of race relations.

This problem constitutes an aspect of equalitarianism fully as crucial as the economic or social aspects. Indeed, in many communities the ordering of relations between different races is the central problem on which everything else hinges. It is the attitude toward race that governs economic development and moulds the ethos of society in Hawaii and Brazil, in South Africa and South Carolina. In both domestic and international politics the spokesman for racial exclusiveness are doomed to be the faction leaders of a losing minority. They can never be the representatives of a majority. This hodls true alike within the United States and the United Nations.

A further form of discrimination which has yet to be eradicated is as old as the dawn of history. This is the discrimination against one-half of the human race. It has been practiced persistently by the male sex at the expense of the female in virtually every culture. Today, throughout most of the world, these traditional modes of inequality continue with but little change. In certain societies, it is true, women have received equality in legal status and in the right to vote and to hold office. Even in this respects however—and certainly in most matters pertaining to employment and careers, to social freedom and education—either inequalities persist, or such equality as has been conceded turns out to be more formal than real. Seldom does a women of equal, or even superior, abilities stand the same chance in life as a man. The double standard is with us still.

THE TWILIGHT OF PLURALISM

It is no accident that the age of "the common man" and woman has witnessed everywhere an expansion of the functions of government, and that the politics of equality has provided an impetus toward monism. In the nineteenth century the nations that were foremost practitioners of laissezfaire in the relation of politics to economics, and of pluralism in the relation of the state to society, were of two kinds. Britain then led the field in industrialisation; the United States had a vast territory to people and develop, and such was the distribution of property that private associations could finance an economic transformation with substantial independence of the state. In this century, however, circumstances have fundamentally altered. Intensified competition for foreign trade among industrialised states; the vanishing of the frontier in the not so New World; domestic political pressures for aid to the underprivileged; the need for regulation of overmighty private groups; and finally the mobilisation of entire peoples for victory in war and readjustment afterward have aggrandised the state and made the twentieth a century of monism.

Because a society in rapid flux requires a central focus for organisation, the latter-day advocates of pluralism have been placed on the defensive and forced into retreat. Some, like G.D.H. Cole, who was a pluralist when he argued for guild socialism, or Harold J. Laski who wrote as a pluralist until the depression of the 1930s, reversed their positions and accepted the logic of monism. Others maintained their original view, but with increasing difficulty. Robert M. MacIver, for instance, admitted the need for society to be unified, but refused to acquiesce in the state as its unifier. Instead—as a Greek playwright whose plot had become too tangled used to bring in a deity to extricate his characters in the last scene, or as Adam Smith relied on unseen hands to bring harmony out of competition[13]—he introduced his ideal of "community." This is a sense of belonging together which people are supposed to feel in sufficient force to prevent a plurality of associations from flying assunder. But how community is realised and made articulate is unclear, especially since MacIver did not concede that it should be organised and expressed through any association with power to override the rest—which would, of course, be monism.

Other pluralists modify their basic theory and make such concessions to the state that, after denying admission to monism at the front door, they let it creep in at the back. Thus Friedrich. A. Hayek, who denounced socialism and planned intervention by the state in economic matters, advocated planning *for* freedom and insisted that powerful private monopolies and combines must not be allowed to stifle genuine competition.[14] Inevitably, however, this ideal, to be enforced, would require a stronger state and more governmental regulation of the economy than fitted Hayek's premises. Other pluralists distinguish between the internal structure and the external activities of private associations. They agree that the state should have the power to intervene in external conflicts (for example a strike or lockout in a major industry) that disturb the peace and prosperity of the whole society. Then they perceive that the policies pursued externally by a big business firm or a big union may be connected with the character of its internal structure. Oligarchical tendencies, whether incorporate management or in trade union control, may sometimes lead a business executive or union boss on the path of aggression so that he or she may maintain dominance within the organisation by winning victories over opponents outside. Consequently, the pluralist may admit that there is a case for the state to prescribe the conditions that the government of a private association must satisfy. But all these expedients lead to the same conclusion. Any pluralist who holds that society is or should be a unity, or who recognizes the need to mitigate public clashes between private groups, must eventually admit the fundamental point of monism that society requires a coordinator, and must then face the political corollary that the state qualifies for that task more appropriately than any alternative organisation. The most genuine pluralist is the anarchist, who wants to be rid of government altogether. But that philosophy has never found a workable formula for its ideal of spontaneous, voluntary cooperation.

PROBLEMS OF THE MONISTIC STATE

A state which embraces monism avoids the weaknesses by which pluralism is beset, but confronts other problems. Monism may assume one of several guises. In its extreme form, as envisaged by Plato, the state settles the difficulty of rival associations by eliminating them and absorbing their functions. But the notion that a single institution could serve all the needs of twentieth-century society, though a logical possibility, is no more practicable, in view of the scale and complexity of the requisite organisation, than the opposite extreme of anarchism. Of workable monism there are two alternatives. Once is for the state to enforce its control over other groups by permitting no more than one association to serve each major need and interest. Thus organised, society would possess a single system of public education permeated by only one philosophy, a single state-established church intolerant of heterodoxy, a single state-directed economic structure professedly abolishing struggles between occupations and classes, and so on. Monism of this sort, unlike the Platonic variety, is not confined to the realm of speculation, since it is the goal to which the modern totalitarian regimes aspire.

The third kind of monism tolerates a variety of associations for each human need. Thus, if people are free to worship as their consciences dictate, society will contain numerous religious faiths with different creeds. If opportunities exist for a person to learn various skills and move from job to job, or to own property and invest in a choice of enterprises, divergent economic interests will arise which reinforce themselves by establishing alternative associations—corporations, trade unions, cooperatives, and the like. Under such circumstances, the principle of toleration or, in its wider sense, freedom has the result of dividing society into competitive groups. People who are pulled apart, however, by economic institutions, by organised religion, or by cultural traditions, can be reunited through citizenship. In that case, as the monist sees its functions, the state serves to bind society together. It then becomes irrelevant whether one is agnostic or Catholic, Jew or Protestant, black or white, male or female, manufacturer or employee, farmer or teacher, provided that all are equal citizens who share the same basic rights and duties, and owe the same allegiance. Thus on the political plane, by sharing citizenship, human rights, and governmental services in common, individuals can acquire a sense of belonging together and may achieve the unifying focus they otherwise lack.

To attain this goal through the politics of monism depends on avoiding certain pitfalls. For one thing, the possibility of unifying society by the state is qualified by the size of area and population to which the jurisdiction of a single government extends. When continents and people are parceled out among nation-states, the solidarity that each state achieves within its borders stops abruptly at international frontiers. The nation-state system unites the nationals of a state, but its boundaries separate them from nationals of other states. Pluralists point out, however, and with truth, that social relationships, though most numerous among persons of the same state, reach further afield. Religion is a bond between the citizens of many countries. Trade relations create a common interest between the producers of one nation and the consumers of another. Scientific, professional, and cultural bodies draw their membership from the practitioners of different lands. The present boundaries of society are wider, therefore, than the boundaries of politics.

States in Space

We have seen that the state emerged historically[15] to organise some basic services in response to universal needs. To give protection, maintain order, administer justice—for such functions as these are state created and governments instituted. It follows then that, wherever such activities are organised, the political process is *ipso facto* at work and the seeds of the state are being sown. In this present age every eye can see that the same tendencies which ushered in the nation-state are again operating to create its successor. For ensuring security and prosperity, we have found our present units too small to be effective. Therefore, we turn for salvation not to national power alone but to international arrangements, not to sovereignty but to allainces, federations and mutual commitments; not to the exclusive interest of a single state but to a wider community of interests. In the liquidation of the older imperialism, we observe the disappearance of colonial systems, the recognition of new and often unsteady governments, and a need to reunite political clusters which have split into fragments. Some of our urgent problems are soluble only on a scale of territory and population larger than even the greatest of nation-states now contains.

Another crop of problems has sprouted from a fertile field of political controversy. Some of these are age-old conditions which only now are beginning to receive proper attention; others are unprecedented in human experience. The former include those continuing examples of social injustice, of human inhumanity, to which I referred earlier—racial prejudice, religious bigotry, discrimination against women, and the gulf between haves and have-nots. Certain of these stigmata on our civilisation—for example, the contrast between affluence and poverty—are even becoming more acute. But, the significant new feature is the attitude now prevailing toward such conditions. Too many people either ignored them in the past, or if they were aware of them, felt apathetic. This is no longer the case. Today there is not only awareness, but also concern—although admittedly the feelings of the concerned run the gamut from empathy with the underprivileged to hostility and fear.

Some novel problems, however, have risen recently to beset us, which contain potentialities for eventual disaster. First is the population explosion, which threatens to engulf the planet with a tide of humanity and, if unchecked, will surely lead to mounting misery and recurrent wars. Coupled with this is the ever-present possibility of nuclear annihilation, since weapons that could exterminate our species are now lodged in human hands. Third is the increasing burden of expenditures for armaments, which become more complicated and more costly and yet have made nobody safer. Next is the continuing pillage of our physical environment: the poisoning of air, land, and water, the reckless and wanton destruction of our habitat. Finally, we are afflicted by the onrush of technological innovation—the revolution which more and more subordinates us to the imperatives of our machines and has the social effect of enmeshing us in huge, impersonal bureaucratic systems which tend to deaden and dehumanize the spirit.

The cumulative result is more than merely to transform our society. Whether we like it or not, we are undergoing a social revolution. Once again, the human race is adrift from our wonted moorings. We feel ourselves floating on the ocean of an uncertain fate. We know not into what vortex its currents may plunge us. Is it any wonder then that this century thus far has been the most violent in all history? From rage or ignorance or despair, people react with passionate brutality—hoping either to unleash or to block the process of change.

And what implications does this have for government? One point at least can be affirmed with certainty. No social revolution of these depths and dimensions can occur without a consequential revolution in our government system. Since the changes sketched above are global in scope and universal in character, no state and no species of politics will remain unaffected. Is it possible to discern the outline and direction of this revolution? And how is it related to the great issues that form the subject of this book?

Doubtless, the political responses will vary along the lines mentioned in the opening chapter.[16] Some will abandon the effort to understand or control. They will resign themselves to submitting to the dictate of events. In that case, as Emerson warned, "things [will] be in the saddle and ride mankind." Others, however, will seek to apply their reason and their faith to assist us in becoming the masters of our fate. It is to these that I address myself.

One aspect of the contemporary revolution in society is the basic alteration in the scale and size of the problems we confront. Just as conditions that had once been local became national, so now have many of the latter passed into the international domain. But another seemingly contradictory process is at work. Conditions long assumed to be national are now being redefined as subregional or even local. Let us explore these twin tendencies more closely, for their elucidation may offer clues to the solutions we seek.

For many centuries the community to which people belonged in fact and to which they felt attached was their immediate locality, bounded by the short radius of day-to-day contacts. This was true for practically everybody during the history of the *polis* and of the empire-state. The advent of the nation-state, however, broadened the boundaries of political identification as it also enlarged the frontiers of human transactions. Centralised governments emerged. They wielded powers that strongly affected life and well-being, and they supplied services and performed functions on which more individuals came to depend. In a sense that was by no means rhetorical, community and nation became increasingly coextensive.

The revolution now taking shape under our eyes has precisely the effect of breaking that connection. It is dissolving the links of the old-style community while it creates new relationships whose boundaries are as vague as they are varied. Because of such relationship, communities are emerging in fact (objectively, that is) before the subjective attitudes and loyalties have been readjusted. Hence the stresses and tensions, the dissent and demonstrations, the alienation and ambivalence, by which humanity, both young and old, is racked asunder.

We can visualize what is happening as a set of concerntic circles. Quite a few circles would be needed at this time in history; and two of them, comprising both old and new relationships, would appear considerably more problem-ridden, and therefore more important, than in the past—and local community and the community that cuts across national frontiers. Both these aspects of our contemporary society were mentioned earlier, albeit separately. Now let us observe their connection. At the international level, problems have emerged (the supply, control, and price of oil, for instance) which can no longer be resolved by a single government acting along, but only by agreements among a group. Obvious examples of this occur in the military and economic spheres, where, to put it bluntly, national solutions are no solutions. When the range and extent of a problem is international, international policies are required—and, with them, their ultimate corollary: supranational institutions.

Simultaneously, however, at the local level—traditionally much despised and generally ignored—people find that life itself is now affected or afflicted by dangers which also are ungovernable by present means. Social injustices give rise to protests and then to civil commotions; these disturb the local peace and may threaten life and limb. At the same time, our cars and factories pollute the air we breathe, while domestic sewage and industrial waste poison the water of our rivers and oceans. Then, too, millions live in swarms which are ever more congested. Cities have expanded into metropolitan complexes embracing suburban clusters and a sprawl of satellite towns. Residents of these towns may travel over 50 miles to work—plagued, more often than not, by substandard commuter railroads and congested highways.

How can we cope with such situations rationally and intelligently? Obviously not through the governmental machinery that has been traditional for the last hundred years or more. It cannot be asserted too emphatically or too often that this social revolution has doomed the sovereign, centralised, independent nation-state. That has become outmoded and obsolete because it is now too small for some of the problems humanity must solve and too large for others. Not only are its foundations eroding, but its roof is caving in. Many of its powers must be redistributed by delegation, both above and below. The world cannot handle its emergencies of over-population, underdevelopment, and poverty, except through supranational agencies. Nor can it remedy the ills of congestion, pollution, inadequate transportation, and urban ghettos without recreating the community of the local region. Because of the social problems which require ordering by government, I predict an eventual backlash against the tax payers' revolt of recent decades. The total volume of governmental functions is likely to increase, not decrease. What will change will be the allocation of functions at the various levels.

For the future, therefore, if we are to survive as a species—and nothing less is at stake—we must devise unprecedented institutions for these unprecedented conditions. We should be willing to experiment with new layers and levels of government simultaneously; our concepts of citizenship must be readapted both to the smaller and more intimate and to the larger and more extensive. The individual will henceforth be a member of several communities, ranging from local to global, and our machinery of government—state boundaries included—must follow the geography of the problems. Unless it does, solutions will never be forthcoming. Expressed in terms of the great issues, all this signifies a change in the solutions to the fourth and fifth issues preferred during the last hundred years. We may expect in the future to see a flight from centralism along with the evolution of supranationalism.

THE METHODS OF POLITICAL CHANGE

Contemporary trends are unmistakably leading toward more equality, more governmental functions, and large states. But what happens to the remaining issues when changes of this magnitude are occurring? The answer can be expressed in terms of the distinction between political ends and governments means.[17] Of the five great issues, there are the prime movers in relation to the processes of change because they provide the goals for action. Analyse the revolutionary crises of history and you find that the items in dispute have always included one or more of the following: the extensiveness of citizenship, of state functions, and of the size of the state. A major increase or contraction in any of these is likely to set off a chain reaction of consequent changes. The two issues concerning authority—the question of its source and its unity or dispersion—are not themselves the independent originators of political change. They resemble rather what staticians call "dependent variables." Constitutions, institutions, and the distribution of power, to the extent that these are concerned with structure and procedure, are undeniably important, but their importance is most immediately felt by politicians and officials—that is, by the practitioners who operate the system. The mass of the people are most directly interested in the concrete results that government brings in their daily lives and lifetime dreams. They can understand the need for redistributing powers and redesigning institutions when there are substantial goals to be attained for which established methods are unsuitable. Anyone who doubts this should recall the worldwide effects of the economic depression of 1929—1934 upon political systems. A change from dictatorial to responsible government, from unity of power to dispersion of powers—or vice versa—is likely to follow, and not precede, a shift of preference between equality or privilege, pluralism or monism, and a big or small area. Those directing the transition from any of these alternatives to its opposite have often employed authoritarian means, plus a concentration of power, to obtain their results. Especially does this happen when those who were influential under the older regime offer fierce resistance to change or when speed seems to the innovators a condition of their success. Contrariwise, the test of a mature and basically united people is their ability to absorb major changes without resort to dictatorship or loss of liberty.

THE NATURE OF REVOLUTION

In this capacity to absorb great changes, and in the manner of accomplishing them, a significant distinction may be noted among political systems. The role of government in the evolution of society is profoundly affected by the timing of changes as well as by their content. No social order is ever completely static. Most societies generally undergo continuous change which is imperceptibly absorbed. But there are occasions when the rate of change is sharply accelerated, and adjustments are attempted or accomplished with rapidity and urgency. Any kind of change imposes a strain since it involves a departure from settled practices and a dislocation of established institutions. Excessive speed may make the strain intolerable and lead a society to the breaking point.

Changes can differ in depth as well as speed. Some modifications of an existing order may be only surface deep. Others may reach far down and shake the foundations of society. When a party defeats its rival at a free election peacefully conducted, and a new administration and legislative majority replace their predecessors, the top personnel and some of the programmes of government will alter. But the civil service, the judiciary, and most of the policies already in force continue to operate without change. This method of assimilating innovations gradually, and on the whole harmoniously, has become standard practice in democratic states. A deeper change is one that alters not merely the government, but also the constitutional system under which it is organised. The Philadelphia Convention of 1787, for instance, had to reach decisions on more fundamental matters than are ordinarily settled in periodic elections. But the most profound changes of all, inducing the greatest disturbance and most intense controversy, are those that refashion the foundations on which society reposes. The substitution of one form of property for another and basic modifications in ownership and distribution, a major religious upheaval, a sharp challenge to long-cherished cultural values—such movements impinge on entrenched interests and arose the strongest emotions. It is impossible to consummate changes of this sort without producing political repercussions.

The most extreme changes are revolutions. In the light of the preceding discussion, what does this term mean? When one group takes over power from another within the framework of the same constitutional system and by a procedure constitutionally defined and mutually accepted, that is no revolution. But when the constitution as well as the government is reconstructed, then a revolution occurs. If, besides constitutional renovation, society is transformed root and branch, the character of the revolution becomes still more thoroughgoing and the most turbulent disorders usually ensue. Finally, when changes of government, constitution, and social order are simultaneously attempted at breakneck speed, state and society suffer agony and convulsion under the momentum of the driving force. In this way it is possible to distinguish between the major revolutions that have taken place in the last 300 years. The American Revolution from 1775 to 1789 involved a change in government and constitution, but conserved most of the social fabric—its economic system included—in much the same design as before. The English Revolution between 1640 and 1688 altered both constitution and government, settled the issues of Protestant-Catholic and church-state relations, and confirmed the prominence of a new urban commercial class. The French Revolution, which began in 1789, went much further than the English in the ferment—economic, philosophic, and cultural—that it evoked throughout society as a whole.[18] The Communist Revolutions, which took control of Russia in 1917 and of China 30 years later, probed the deepest of the four and attempted some of the most penetrating and intensive overhauls of a social order of which history has record.

All these revolutions, it may be noted, were accompanied by warfare, which in the English case took the form of civil war only, and in the other four cases involved conflict with foreign powers as well. While the constitutions that emerged from the English and American Revolutions successfully provided a peaceful method of governmental change for the future, violence was initially required to lay that groundwork of constitutionalism. The four revolutions whose effects were not confined to the state but spread to society, namely the English, French, Russian, and Chinese, produced the phenomenon of dictatorship with extraordinary powers concentrated in the hands of one man or a tiny clique. Significantly, the American Revolution, which was content to limit itself to a political change without transforming the social order, did not succumb to dictatorship; and while other countries had to resort to Cromwell, to Robespierre and Napoleon, to Lenin, Trotsky, Stalin, and Mao, the needs of the Unites States were more than adequately served by Washington and Jefferson.

DICTATORSHIP IN A TIME OF CHANGE

Besides the cases just cited, there are many recent instances of peoples who spawn a dictatorship while undergoing drastic change. Witness the power acquired for a while by Hither or Mussolini, by Ataturk or Nasser, by Castro or Peron, by Mao or Tito. The frequency of this occurrence suggests some further reflections on the subject of change. Undeniably a community in convulsions is prone to yield to a Directory, a Politburo, a military junta, or the dynamism of a "strong man" whose personality thrusts itself above the leading clique. The reason is to be found in the practical demands and the psychology of crisis conditions. A society deciding major issues faces momentous, and perhaps irrevocable, choices. Collectively its members share the elan, the heightened tension, the sense of adventurousness, and with these the fears and anxieties concerning the outcome, which any period of rapid flux calls forth. It is always more difficult politically to chart a course for change than for conservatism. The former opens many avenues of choice. The latter prescribes one route—continuation, as far as possible, of the status quo.

To minimize the risks and uncertainties of change, and to offset the weakness that division produces, a society in crisis will be urged to submit to a pattern of discipline and thus reassert its unity and solidarity. Authoritarianism will be represented as a source of strength, because it is supposedly efficient, single-minded, and fast moving. In our century many circumstances have appeared to set a premium on such factors. People who seek in warfare an outlet for their aggressions, or who smart under the humiliations of a defeat, have often acquiesced in dictatorship. A long-lasting and widespread economic depression brings loss of savings, unemployment, or bankruptcy to individuals who then lend a willing ear to the advocates of desperate remedies. Or again, a technologically backward community, proud of its ancient memories, faces the challenge of a different culture equipped with superior machines and scientific knowledge. Forced to adapt themselves to alien novelties, yet wishing to preserve enough of their traditional ways so that their identity may not be lost, millions of people attempt to combine the seemingly contradictory policies of heavy borrowing from abroad with a positive reaffirmation of their own cultural distinctiveness. The psychological result in this last case is a stage of ambivalence. The dependent group admires and respects those whose techniques it copies, but also fears and resents them. The political result, not infrequently, is like a state of siege.

This helps to throw some light on one of the most interesting political problems of our century; the common association of dictatorship with nationalism. The building of a nation-state does not, in and by itself, necessitate either dictatorship or democracy. There are, however, two sides to nationalism, which face in different directions. So far as its internal aspect is concerned, nationalism unites people with a common loyalty to their political association. It imparts a sense not only of belonging together, but of belonging together as equals, because nationality does not admit of degrees. In this way nationalism and democracy are compatible, and it is therefore understandable that many political leaders with perfect consistency have been both nationalists and democrats—for example, Lincoln, Mazzini, Masaryk, Viewed externally, however, nationalism asserts the individuality of the group and its separateness from others. When this emphasis on uniqueness happens to be linked with the uncertainties of a time of troubles—due to military or economic reasons or cultural readjustment or a combination of these—the aggressions and frustrations within the group are siphoned into the channels of dictatorship. That has occurred not only in European states which yielded to the embrace of fascism or communism, but also in Latin American and Asian countries, which wanted to catch up with Western technology and at the same time rid themselves of colonialism.

FROM PROTECTION TO PERFECTION

Thus, for all its enlargement of scale, the search for solutions to humanity's political problems will require, both now and in the future, a continuing selection among the same perennial choices and an elaborations of the same basic patterns in presumably more intricate forms. As politics encompasses a wider embrace, the horizons of the state expand and governments assume more duties. It is a far reach from the fortification of a hilltop to walking on the moon, from control of a river valley or a city to the ordering of a planet from participation by a few to equalise liberties for all. The mode and means may vary, but the principles at stake do not. Humanity still must choose, or allow a fraction of its number to make the choices for the rest. The risk is serious, since the penalties for bad government have increased in the same proportion as the potentialities for good. Hitler outdid Attila as a future tyrant could outdo him.

The state originated in our need for protection, which required the organisation of force. A government amasses force initially, and monopolizes it finally, in order to repel any threats, internal or external, to life and limb. But the history of the functions of the state consists in advancing from protection and order to justice and the good life. This does not mean that the state abandons or surrenders its duty of protecting its members. Far from it. The state that ceases to protect ceases to be a state. But, after ensuring the conditions that make life possible, the state must proceed toward the goal of a good life. It is precisely this changeover that presents a supreme challenge to the architects of government. For how does force or power fit in with welfare? The concept of welfare is broad. It embraces economic prosperity, moral well-being, and the whole system of values composing a civilisation. Such considerations transfer the issues of politics from the starting point of physical safety to the terminus of an ethical ideal. The creation of the state resembles the construction of a dwelling to shelter the life of society. A house has foundations to stand on, just as a state is built on our fundamental need for protection. But people do not lead their daily lives in the basement of their homes. The living room is raised some feet above ground level, and here the members of the household develop the relations that can give to life a quality of love, nobility, and taste. And it is, or can be, the same with politics. The function of the foundations is to support the upper framework which houses the political life of humanity and makes us civilised.

That actual states do not reach the ideal is obvious enough. There have been, and continue to be, many governments that build no higher than the basement and force their subjects to stay there. Also, when the warlike politics of an anarchic world compel all states, even those concerned with welfare, to reemphasize the priority of physical protection, humanity rushes to the refuge of the bomb shelter. The state may fail, then, to subordinate the force it must employ to the ethical ideal for which we grope. What was the servant may emerge the master. The power that founded a government can become the means whereby the will of the governing group is forcibly imposed throughout society. In that case, their regime is a tyranny, and when linked with monism, the product is totalitarian. Hence, the crucial test of the would-be monistic state is to keep its stock of power within bounds and sublimate power in the service of the good. Unless this is done, there is no superior merit in monism as against the pluralist alternative. For why flee from anarchy into the embrace of despotism?

The first task, then, is to organise power, yet keep it under control and legitimize it as authority; to unify society through the state, but avoid the authoritarian means and the regimented end. That is the third of the great issues, which offers the choice between freedom and dictatorship. There is no certain way of guaranteeing freedom. It is possible, though difficult, to establish and operate a politically free society. It is not too difficult to suppress freedom entirely by a perversion of power. All that can be prescribed is a set of conditions which, if adhered to, tends to encourage the attainment of freedom and discourage its opposite. These conditions depend on planning a constitutional system that builds the right of criticism and opposition into the central structure of government. Applied in detail, this principle spell itself out into universal suffrage, periodic elections, the coexistence of two or more parties, and opportunities to form new political combinations. Where such requirements are met, liberty is more surely guaranteed than by the pluralist reliance on mutual conflict between private associations and their general rivalry with the state.

POLITICS AND THE GOOD LIFE

But the institutional checks just mentioned, while basic to the politics of freedom, do not ensure the good life. Though liberty may be assisted by procedural arrangements, the purpose of the latter is also to reach decisions about policies. The contents of such decisions, as well as the ways of reaching them, must be encompassed in the philosophy of the state, since the ends accomplished are more significant than the means employed. Hence, the state seeking to integrate society must embody an ethical ideal. Otherwise, instead of the good life taking priority over power, power will steal the priority from welfare—in which case no reply can be given to Augustine's question: What else is the state but a great robber band if it lacks justice? But as it happens, two of the great issues, the first and second, have a direct bearing on the contents of policy. Whenever the state administers a programme, a service is supplied for some or all of its citizens. This evokes controversies over the appropriateness of the service and the designation or selection of recipients. Should the state, for instance, pay and provide for large-scale schemes of low-cost housing? If so, to whom should houses be assigned? Should it embark on programmes of social security, covering all the major hazards, economic and physical, that flesh is heir to between birth and death? If so, who should be eligible for benefits, and how should the financing be apportioned?

Questions like these have other implications for society than that of freedom. They suggest that the state accept some responsibility for influencing the distribution of material goods: that it provide at least a minimum below which no person be allowed to sink, while encouraging all to raise their status above the minimum by their own efforts. To say this is to recognize that social and economic privilege—expressed in a grossly unequal distribution of property, income, security, and living standards—is no more desirable than the political privilege of a limited class or caste. That, in other words, is an affirmation of the principle of equality. How can the state, which assumes the direction of society, organize the race of life so as to mix equality with liberty? It is possible to do this if the state ensures equality for all at the starting tape; if it provides fulfilment to the more talented; and if it guarantees some minimum to each contestant. These criteria satisfy the test of welfare. More than that, by blending the rights and duties of the individual with those of society, they point the way to a conception of social justice. It is only when this is achieved that power, besides being rendered safe by the politics of freedom, also acquires a moral legitimacy. The degree of approximation to this standard is some measure of the level of civilisation that a people has attained. Conversely, a subordination of welfare to powers and the disregard of social justice is an index cf inhumanism.

Finally, it is through this concept that the difficulty stated in the beginning of this book may be resolved. Human beings, as was observed, associate in groups under the contrary impulses of cooperation and competition. But to reconcile the two has always posed a problem. Perhaps the answer is found when liberty and equality are synthesized under the higher concept of the good life. It is in our concern for the human condition that we express our altruism, cooperativeness, and sense of solidarity. It is in the personal achievement of creative growth that each of us display individuality. To maintain both principles in equilibrium and use them constructively in the solution of the great issues, to unite the good person with the good society, is the wisdom of statesmanship. When the power of government is directed in the service of that ideal, the good life emerges into the realm of the possible, and the art of politics becomes a voyage of ethical discovery.

—L Lifson

References

1. A word, not precisely translatable into English, meaning governmental power viewed in its totality. It correspond fairly closely with the Roman concept of the *imperium*.

2. The small state of Israel is one of the most highly militarised in the world today.

3. A phrase of Harold D. Lasswell.

4. Not always, of course. Some garrison states are such because a conquering elite is holding down a larger subject population, for example, Sparta.

5. "Centralism or Localism, Separation of Powers or Integration?"

6. The exceptional case of Switzerland is due to the mountainous geography and cultural dissimilarities.

7. "New Role of the American Presidency and Governorship."

8. On the other hand, it must be remembered that when President Johnson plunged the country into war in Vietanm, the most outspoken opposition came from members of his own party—notably led by Senator Fulbright.

9. On this subject, see my book *The Democratic Civilisation* (New York: Oxford University Press, 1964).

10. Hitler went much further than Mussolini in his racial doctrines and his exclusion of women from public life.

11. George Orwell, *Animal Farm* (New York: Harcourt, Brace & World, 1946) satirizes this inconsistency in the slogan: "All animals are equal. But some animals are more equal than others."

12. Henry Adams, *The Education of Henry Adams.*

13. "Self-Development and selfishness".

14. *The Road to Serfdom* (Chicago: The University of Chicago Press, 1944).

15. "The Primary Function of the State".

16. "The Anti-Eye View of Society", and following sections.

17. "The Use and Monopoly of Force," and following sections.

18. This explains why Edmund Burke, who approved the principles, methods, and results of England's seventeenth-century revolution, was aghast the French Revolution and reacted to it conservatively.

4

Political Science and Social Reality

Social reality describes the nature of society, its parts and the relationship between them. In its operative context, social reality determines all social arrangements and institution, including the state. The latter then guards it by rewarding the conformists and punishing the deviants. Political Science, as a study of state and government, explains this operative context. However, in order to grasp the varied roles and needs of men in society. Political Science has to enter into relationship with all other social science disciplines and to other related subjects. This also underlines the interdependence of various factors in social life.

The discussion of the relationship of Political Science with other allied disciplines highlights the following points.

Political Science is actively influenced and shaped by allied disciplines. This is demonstrated by the growth of subjects like Political Philosophy, Political Sociology, Political Economy, Political Psychology, Geo-politics etc. In all these, Political Science assumes a monitoring role. All this calls for an interdisciplinary approach to the study of social reality.

A GENERAL VIEW OF SOCIAL REALITY

Any view of reality takes into account questions such as: What is the world reality like? What are its parts? How can we describe the world systematically and meaningfully? How can we obtain knowledge of it? What it is like? etc. In other words, any such attempt has to go into the issue of identifying the nature of reality, its different dimensions, its systematic and meaningful presentation. All thinkers have dealt with these issues while presenting their interpretations of reality.

These issues play a similar role in determining social reality. Similar questions are asked and answers attempted. For example, how has society been constituted and what is its nature? What are is parts? What is the relationship between the parts and the whole? How do we identify and analyse social movements? How is a society changed? What should be the ends and the mean?

Social reality has been interpreted in various ways by different philosophers and social scientists. Broadly they can be grouped in the following manner:

(i) the classical perspective—the Greek and the Indian traditions:

(ii) the western liberal perspective—the contractualists (Hobes, Locke, Rousseau); the *Utilitarians (Bentham, Mill) and the idealists (Hegel, Green):*

(iii) the Marxist Perspectives (Marx. Lenin, Mao); and

(iv) the non-Marxist 'third world' perspectives (Gandhi, Nehru, Sukarno etc.)

POLITICAL SCIENCE AND SOCIAL REALITY

Social reality is formed by all those forces that are dominant at a given time and space. Therefore, it can be understood with the help of history, economics, sociology and all the related subjects. For example, to understand Indian social reality, one must take into acount the contributions of history, culture, theories of society and economics, etc. Since human experience is ever changing, differences of time bring about differences in social reality, though there may remain a core in it which does not change. It is like the growth of child into youth, adulthood and old age; there is something permanent along with the changes. Social reality is more complex and depends on the interplay of various forces. But, here also, there is continuity as well as change.

Political Science is intimately related to social reality. As a social science discipline it is concerned with analysing evaluating and directing the course of social reality in a desired direction. The state is a crucial part of social reality and as a science of the state, Political Science deals with the different aspects of social reality.

The state is given a central place in the subject of Political Science. The state affects and is in turn affected by different aspects of the social reality. It protects the existing social reality by rewarding those who conform and by punishing those, who violate its laws. Therefore, Political Science as a discipline studies these interactions between state and social reality.

POLITICAL SCIENCE AND OTHER RELATED SUBJECTS

Man as a composite being, plays many roles simultaneously. He has roles as a member of a family, caste, religion, village/city, as well as of political associations. These roles reflect his multiple needs. Therefore, he tries to reconcile demands arising out of these different roles. His activities cannot be the subject matter of one discipline alone. All social sciences have a complementary role in explaining human activities. Therefore, to grasp the essence of man and society, the boundaries of individual social science disciplines have to be transcended. In the latter half of twentieth century, increasing attention has been paid to this reciprocity between social sciences. Naturally, Political Science too has taken part in this process.

POLITICAL SCIENCE AND CULTURE

Culture combines all the material and spiritual values that contribute to the all-round development of a society. Culture is significant because it, in the words of Dr. Radhakrishnan, 'teaches us great lessons of timeless character' which are not superseded by accidents of history. Thus, culture turns out to be a permanent tradition of wisdom which is continuously passed on the by one generation to another in a society. This greatly helps in shaping people's beliefs and attitudes. As there are many societies in the world, so there are many cultures as well. These cultures often have basic differences with one another. For instance, in an idealist cultural tradition, all social order is thought to have divine sanction. Therefore, culture also is regarded as divine creation. Most ancient cultures, including the Indian, belong to this category. Though there have also been as in the Indian case, non-idealist and materialist cultural traditions in the ancient period. Conversely, in the socialist cultural tradition, culture is viewed as an outcome of the creative activities of the masses for a desirable socio-economic formation. It is, thus, a specific social creation. This difference apart, culture everywhere inspires people to harmonise their respective activities for the development of a liveable society, national or international.

Political Science is greatly benefited by the fruits of culture. Every national society decides for itself specific rules of social living through its culture. These rules get incorporated in the state within its area of functioning. Needless to point out that if there is no culture, there are no social rules and norms, and if there are no rules and norms governing men, there is no relevant framework for state-activity either. So culture is basic to politics. Any understanding of state and politics is impossible without due appreciation of culture. It is in this sense that Political Science, as a study of state, government and politics has to actively take into account the essence of national culture. This relationship can be illustrated by the experiences of our own country. Indian culture generally emphasises tolerance of dissimilarities, unity of ethical and practical elements of life, compassion and harmony among all elements of society. These values characteristically have guided the course of social development in India. The Indian constitution, in course of time, incorporated these values. The preamble to the Constitution endeavours to strike a balance between liberty, equality, justice and fraternity in Indian politics and society.

The Indian Constitution and politics continue to be quite relevant to the society because these values are essentially, the gifts of Indian culture. Politics and society, however, receive severe jolts whenever these values are sidelined or overlooked. Intolerance and disharmony have led to the evils of communalism, lingusitic agitations and other parochial manifestations, which have divided society and posed threats to our democratic political process.

In recent times, the relationship between culture and politics has been found to be so critical that Political Science has developed a theoretical framework to understand what is called 'political culture'. Some useful studies have been undertaken in this field. For instance, Myron Weiner and Ashis Nandy have studied India's post-independence political culture. Similarly, Lucian Pye and Sidney Verba have significantly contributed to the understanding of the American and some European political cultures.

Political Science and Philosophy

Philosophy as 'darsana' is the process of perceiving and appreciating reality, the science of the general laws of being and human thinking. It is one of the basic forms of human and social consciousness. Philosophy raises such important issues as what is the ultimate reality? How and to what extent does the world manifest it? What is the real spirit behind human existence? How does a man meet the requirements of the spirit in his real life situations? How does he reconcile the actuality of life with the reality of spirit? What socio-politico-cultural mechanims get constituted in the process? Under what ideal and real conditions can a society or a state live in harmony? These are some of the fundamental issues of philosophy that have existed and guided the course of human search for identity (both individual and collective) and well-being. To a large extent, philosophy shapes the moral, religious and political outlook of people. Philosophy imparts intellectual discipline to men, while morality gifts to him virtures of purity, nobility and earnestness.

The significance of philosophy is, therefore, obvious in human and social life P.T. Raju has very aptly pointed out that philosophy is "the searchlight of life". Any conscious life is based on sound ideas, and since it is philosophy that facilitates these, Raju very aptly states that "Life apart from thought is a blind movement and thought apart from life is a light that reveals nothing". Philosophy appropriately links life and ideas in a reciprocal manner.

In the light of the discussion initiated about the significance of the dominant themes of philosophy, it can be safely stated that political Science has immensely benefited from philosophy. It is Political Philosophy which provides conceptual framework to

Political Science. Great ideas of Plato, Aristotle, Kautilya, Manu, Machiavelli, Hobbes, Locke, Rousseau, Bentham, Mill, Hegel, Green, Marx and Gandhi among others, have provided the conceptual basis to the study of states and governments of various national societies, irrespective of their ideological differences. It is only in the context of ideas and standards set by philosophy that specific political functions can be properly understood and evaluated. In this sense, philosophy is associated with science. Any disassociation of philosophy from science tends to make science an end in itself. Science, then, loses its relevance. So political philosophy is essential for Political Science. When separated from philosophy, Political Science becomes a science of power, an instrument to capture and retain power by any means, fair or foul. It is reduced to a theory of power politics. Hence, it is necessary to maintain a judicious balance between the two.

Political Science and History

'History' as derived from Greek means "that" which one comes to know as the result of an enquiry, or learning by enquiry. According to another interpretation, it is derived from the verb 'to weave'. A historian is one who selects a number of stands and weaves them into a pattern. Based on such understanding, history turns out to be an intelligible analysis and interpretation of the past relating to men and societies. Sturley, in his. The Study of History, has pointed out that the utility of history lies in its influence on disciplining the human mind by learning from the past experiences of men and civilisations. This disciplining enables men to understand better their own existence which, in turn, leads to greater happiness in their own lives.

History constitutes traditions. It is necessary to note that tadition plays the same role in social life as memory does in human life. Men without memory and societies without traditions are likely to face an identity crisis. Tradition gives meaning to political thinking. It is history of political thought which gives us 'standard' or 'measures' of present day political actions. Whenever political power is discussed Machiavelli can never be left out; if reciprocal' contract is perceived between men and societies, Hobbes, Locke and Rousseau can never be ignored; and if exploitation, social inequities and materialist urges of a society are taken into consideration, the legacy of Karl Marx can never be forgotten. These examples of historical figures significantly influencing all present political thinking can be multiplied indefinitely. History supplies the third dimension to Political Science.

Another level of relationship existing between History and Political Science is illustrated by the use of the historical method in political analysis. Amal Ray and Mohit Bhattacharya, while describing the significance of historical method, point out that" … it enables us to arrive at certain generalisations on the basis of facts garnered from history…. (it) offers us a sense of history, a historical perspective. It teaches us that events are not isolated ocurrences, they are terms in an infinite series".

History, then, offers a wide range of alternatives from which the most suitable one can be picked up by politics. It is in this sense that even for an empirical analysis history presents a grand analytical background. That is why historical accounts of different societies are undertaken for understanding their present trends and relevant issues.

History, on its part, is also indebted to politics and political analysis. In historiography, political issues and conceptual frameworks significantly influence a historian. For instance, no history of modern India is possible without an analysis of the nature of modern Indian nationalism, the ruling mechanisms of the British, the counter persepctives of the nationalist leaders, the broad features of Indias political culture, the constitutional machinery of modern India, the mass-based organisation of the Indian National Congress, the charismatic leadership of Mahatma Gandhi, and the menace of communal politics.

These complementarities apart, it is wrong to overemphasise the intimate ties of History and Political Science. History is not, as Freeman believes, 'past politics' nor politics, for that matter, 'present history'. At times, the two complement each other but quite often, they constitute two autonomous disciplines. Too much obsession with history contributes to inaccuracies and reductionism in political analysis. Whatever is relevant in History may not be relevant to Political Science. For example, the origin and development of musical instruments is not essential to explain political dynamics.

POLITICAL SCIENCE AND SOCIOLOGY

Sociology is the Science of studying the laws governing the development and functioning of social systems; both universal (i.e., society as a whole) and particular (i.e., sub-social or mini-societies). Sociology aims at finding general regualarities in people' social behaviour, thereby developing an overall sociological theory (i.e., a general theory of social organisation, its development and functioning). Modern Sociology highlights that:

(i) human knowledge is significantly related to group, class and culture of different social orders;

(ii) human nature is flexible and, as such, it significantly responds to social and cultural interactions of peoples;

(iii) human race is basically determined by respective physio-cultural attributes of different societies, rather than their biological differences;

(iv) social change is, accordingly, related to group variations and not to their manifest biological differences; and

(v) external surroundings and forces generated by them have an impact on the social and political system. Sociology as a discipline owes much to such theories as Comte, Spencer, Sorokin, Mosca, Pareto, Durkheim, Karl Mannheim, Marx and Max Weber among others.

Sociology is the science of society and society creates State—the subject matter of political science. In fact, functioning of a state is directly related to the nature of its constituting society. It is for this reason that the nature and functioning of the Indian state is different from that of Pakistan or, for that matter, the UK or the USA; precisely because, socio-cultural traditions of India are quite different from those of Pakistan, the UK and the USA. Understanding of these socio-cultural traditions is basic to an understanding of politics and state functioning.

In recent times, intellectual efforts have been made to understand state, government and politics with the help of such informal factors as caste, community, religion, region, culture, etc., all of which are sociological processes and concepts. Emphasis on process is, essentially, derived from sociological analysis. A classic example of a political scientist's focus on process is Arthur Bentley's The Process of Government. Similarly, a focus on socio-psychological analysis, has significantly affected political analysis. In this connection, Graham Wallas' Human Nature in Politics gives us a remarkable analysis of political dynamics.

Sociology too, has been significantly aided by political analysis and the study of various political institutions. For instance, the state in relation to a society has continuously dominated the modes of sociological analysis. Sociologists also regard the state as the highest social institution because of its ability to guide a society and regulate its social behaviour. It should be noted that there have been many overlapping contributions in the fields of social and political analysis. Plato, Aristotle, Montesquieu, Hegel, Marx and Weber among others, have contributed to both social and political analysis.

This reciprocity has given birth to a new discipline—in the form of Political Sociology—which is essentially concerned with social bases of politics, their interaction, their impace on theory-building, etc. Political sociology has contributed to political science such conceptual frameworks as political system, political development, political modernisation and political culture.

It will be, however, wrong to overplay the relationship between Political Science and Sociology. Political Science is, essentially concerned with the state and accompanying processes of community management through power, authority and legitimacy. Sociology has a broader concern in so far as it involves, the study of human and social origins, chronological development and crystallisation of society and its auxiliary institutions. In this sense, sociology precedes politics. In any case, distinctive features of the two disciplines must not be lost sight of.

Political Science and Economics

Economics deals with the relations between people in the process of production, exchange, distribution and consumption of material wealth. It is in this sense that economics forms the basis of social order. Politics mediates the basic interests of various social groups and classes in a pluralist society (e.g. India). By resorting to appropriate policy options and authoritatively allocating the material values in a society, politics caters to the requirements of economics. The two disciplines are, thus, intimately inter-related to each other.

The intimate ties between Economics and Political Science were so deep rooted in ancient times that the classical tradition did not differentiate between economic issues and the political ones. Plato, while articulating his theory of justice concerned of justice in terms of a coordinating excellence capable of harnessing all vital interests of men in the society, including the economic ones. In India, Kautilya envisaged Arthashastra as combing the best of both economics and politics. His very ideas of artha (wealth) included organisation and maintenance of men and materials. In fact, the tradition of viewing economics and politics as a compound equally influenced Adam Smith, who is regarded as the pioneer of modern economics. His Wealth of Nations is as much a work on economics as it is on political science.

The interdependence between Economics and Political Science created the discipline of Political Economy during the nineteenth century. Adam Smith, Richardo, Karl Marx and others were responsible for developing the discipline.

Formally and legally, politics influences, in form or content, the socio-economic aspects of a society and initiates the process of modernisation, progress and development. In a modern state, the state influences economic activities through budgeting, pricing, import-export control, welfare activities, etc. Political analysis owes much to such concepts as socialism which are essentially rooted in economics. Despite these significant overlaps at the levels of concepts and processes, the two disciplines have their distinct identity which must not be overlooked. Economics is largely concenred with money, profit, production, distribution, consumption and exchange, while politics is preoccupied with the concern of power, influence, order, legitimacy, etc. Thus, their areas are quite clearly demarcated. A meaningful social analysis must take this factor into active consideration, while analysing their interdependence.

Political Science and Psychology

Psychology is the science of the human mind and behvaviour. It is by psychology that the explanatory accounts of human motivations and specific actions are accomplished. For understanding man, therefore, resort to psycho-analytical modes is undertaken. It is assumed that specific actions are attributable to the specific working of the human mind. By knowing the persons' psychologically one can better appreciate him socio-culturally. This understanding is, essentially, an advancement over our previous levels of knowledge. As Ernest Barker has pointed out: "If our fathers thought biologically, we think psychologically".

Psychology, while focussing on the working of the human mind and collective social minds in a social formation, deals with individual and social consciousness. This, significantly enables a clearer perception of social traditions. Political Science, based as it is on social traditions and forces, owes much to psychology. The psychology-oriented political analysis was considerably promoted by such writers as Tarde, Durkheim, Le Bon, Graham Wallas and Mcdougall.

Psychology has facilitated a new era of empirical analysis in political studies. Earlier, the idealists such as Plato and Hegel formulated their political ideas on an a priori reasoning (i.e. explaining political reality in terms of an all pervading reason). It was the psychologists who argued that political reality is constituted differently in different socio-cultural systems and is, accordingly, accompanied by a concrete socio-cultural reasoning as well. It is, therefore, necessary to overcome the abstract reasoning of the past in order to better appreciate the culturally-determined specific features of contemporary society.

The latter half of the twentieth century has facilitated a new discipline of political psychology. It has helped in understanding the nature of such complex phenomena as imperialism, colonialism, racialism, etc., besides, providing meaningful insights into the working of both socialism and liberal democracies. An excellent example of the contribution of political psychology in discerning the Indian cultural tradition and politics is available in Ashis Nandy's At the Edge of psychology: Essays in Politics and Culture. He has also studied the impact of colonialism on India in his book entitled: The Intimate Enemy: Loss and Recovery of Self Under Colonialism. At a micro-level, psycho-analytical studies of different political leaders have also been undertaken to understand their concrete political styles and actions. For instance, many studies of Mrs. Indira Gandhi were undertaken during the post-emergency period in India, which aimed at explaining the manifest political actions of the leader with the help of her own psychological attributes. One such example is the work by R.K. Murthy entitled The Cult of the Individual—A Study of Indira Gandhi. Eric Erikson's studies on Mahatma Gandhi and Martin Lurther are notable examples. Sigmund Freud studied human psychology and concluded that the soruce of human behaviour is human psychology.

Many significant politico-cultural studies have developed a meaningful understanding of specific political attitudes of different peoples in different societies. Based on quantitative analysis of human motivations, attitudes, and their bearings on specific political behaviour, such works have enabled us to understand the setting within which different polities and societies function. In this connection, Richard Soloman's Mao Tse-tung and the Chinese Political Culture is particularly remarkable. Other important works include the Princeton volume on political culture and Political Development edited by Lucian Pye and Sidney Verba.

Despite this active interdependence, the distinctive features of Political Science and psychology deserve utmost consideration.

The basic determination of psychology in political matters apart, politics is significantly based on other concerns as well (e.g. society, economy, ecology, geography, etc.). Political Science, as a study of state and Politics must, therefore, concentrate on all these bases of political formation and development. Specifically, the studies on collective behaviour, corrupting influence of power, possessiveness etc. are important in suggesting policy alternatives.

Political Science and Geography

Geography is the science of the earth's forms and physical features and studies their inter relationship with people. Any society in this sense is pre-conditioned by the 'do's and don't's of geography. Physical features such as specific national boundaries, climate, available resources, dependent food-habit etc. decisively act to inform and influence the social character, life-styles and social behaviour of a society. Differing geographical attributes therefore, influence the different constitutions and outputs of, say, India and Britain in world affairs.

The geographical determinants of a society likewise influence the political make-up of a people. In fact, the active influence of geography on politics was found to be so decisive that a new discipline of 'Geo-politics' was developed at the dawn of the twentieth century. Rudolph Kiellen, a Swedish scholar, is credited with coining the term, while Friedrich Ratzel, a German, viewed states as organisms struggling for a living space (Lebensraum) for them. Geo-politics was subsequently influenced by Karl Haushofer who provided a rationale to the Nazi German expansionism. Halford Mackinde propounded his heartland theory for articulating the British expansionism. Similarly, Alfred Thayer Mahan of the (USA), advocated the theory of sea-power.

The historical experience emanating from geo-politics has often been quite conservative and reactionary. It is however, necessary to highlight the basic formative influence of geography on political policy-planning and management. Geographical differences can act to serve as part of an enduring basis of a harmonious world interdependence wherein one country can compensate for its geographic drawbacks, for instance, by entering into trade-relations with the other who would have similar trading motivations and priorities for itself. This alone would constitute one earth' for ourselves.

INTERDISCIPLINARY APPROACH

The 'Monitoring' Role of Political Science

Our discussion of the relationship between Political Science and other allied disciplines brings us to the realisation that, the relationship is actually monitored by Political Science. It is Political Science which borrows from other disciplines in accordance with its own determined requirements to meet the demands arising from different specific social situations. All these disciplines, therefore, essentially play a supportive role in order to best illustrate social knowledge relating to their respective branches. It is Political Science which utilises this knowledge for understanding political reality. The best explanation about this process comes from Aristotle, who regards politics as the 'master-science'. As a master-science it is concerned with impersonal acquisition and use of the available social resources. It is only such knowledge and its rightful application to society that enables a state to become the highest social institution engaged in applying the idea of good to specific socio-political situations Politics in this sense is a coordinating discipline which acts to harmonise all other branches of social knowledge and their social applications. It stands at par with other branches and, as such, coordinates their activities while performing its own functions of articulating power and transforming it into authority in a social setting. The contemporary use of politics, accordingly, employs power for bringing about social transformation in the form of either socialism, welfare state or a combination of the two goals in a single policy (e.g. in India). In any case, politics is not and cannot be an end in itself. It essentially has an instrumental value of including values of harmony and integration in a society.

The 'Monitored' Unity of Political Science

Political Science, thus, characterise a 'monitored' integration of knowledge and its appropriate social application. As society is composed of diverse needs and roles social sciences must, accordingly, try to understand and meet them with the aggregate of commonly pooled knowledge and techniques. This expectation from the social sciences led to an inter-disciplinary approach to social analysis. This approach found its best expression during the post-war period when economists, sociologists, historians, political scientists and psychologists, among, others, joined hands together and launched 'area-studies' to simultaneously study the various aspects of a chosen area. Many useful contributions were made with the help of this approach.

Multi-disciplinary or inter-disciplinary approach has faced many problems, often insurmountable ones, of proper coordination among different disciplinary approaches and techniques, but it is still a very useful way of appreciating and appraising the complex dynamics of a society. The important point is that, since reality is diversely constituted, it must be diversely attended to with the help of different social sciences.

5

The State and Society

States exist because people want the services they can provide. To Know what the states is, therefore, we must look at what its government does. Hence we turn from the citizens it serves to the character of this services. All associations, as we saw, are differentiated by the functions they perform. In the case of the state, these functions admit many possibilities which are debatable since the range of choice is wide. Thus controversy extends beyond what the state does to what it might do. We inject into discussions of the state our preference for what activities properly belong to it. This makes the study of governmental functions both descriptive and normative. For the state is what its functions are, as influenced by our conceptions of what they ought to be.

If we are to choose rationally, we must grasp the issues involved in the debate over what activities are appropriate to the state. Why do we struggle to extend the functions of government or confine them? Since the state evolves within society, how does it relate to other associations? The answer can be attempted by continuing the discussion begun. There, I stressed that cooperation between human beings gives rise to a plurality of groups, and that individuals associate and reassociate in varying patterns according to the aims they share or ambitions over which they clash. The fact that each of us belongs to many groups within a complex society creates a competition among our goals and loyalties. The outward schism between the groups that compose society is reproduced internally by what Toynbee calls "schism in the soul." If people are to live at peace with themselves, if there is to be harmony groups, two requirements must be met. Subjectively, human beings have to feel that what unites them is superior to what separaties them. Objectively, they need some institution to organize those feelings. For the terms *society* to be more than a vague generalisation, something must bind the mixture. Can that "something" be identified?

PLURALISM VS. MONISM

The relations between the groupings in society have been viewed in opposite ways. Some thinkers strees that associations spring spontaneously from the free play of human activity. They are not summoned by fiat, nor do they stem from a single source. In their origins they are independent of one another; and, as the stimuli to associate differ, so do the associations. Therefore, it is concluded, they must be able to operate with the same freedom as allowed them to be formed. Since to be free they must be equal, all should be considered coordinate. No association can arrogate to itself the prerogative of superiority over the rest. The strivings of humanity, it is argued, cannot be folded within the embrace of one supreme good or final end. People reach out for ends in the plural, not for a single end; and as their purposes are plural, so must be the structure of society.[1]

To the pluralists comes the rejoinder of the monists. In their view, society is, or should be, a unity; and for it to be unified, there must be a binding tie. Granted that human drives spontaneously generate a host of groupings; but although independently born, these cannot function independently. As they pursue their aims, groups impinge on one another, creating a need for harmony and order. Individuals are confused by the conflicting claims on their allegiance of distinct and sometimes rival association. The remedy is to discover some higher good which includes and transcends the lesser. Then, one association must be recognised as responsible for attaining it. To this let the remaining associations be subordinated. Thus can society become and remain unitary in purpose as in organisation.[2]

Each of these views is strong where the other is weak. One stresses the role of society as a creative matrix of varied behaviour.

To advocates of this way of thinking, any proposal for central control or unified direction spells death to the kind of society they idealize. Spontaneity, freedom, variety autonomy—these they consider the cardinal virtues of groups and group action; and the society they applaud most is that in which such qualities are maximised. But the price of diversity is the impairment of unity. The more the pluralist exalts and exaggerates the independence of associations, the more "the great society"[3] Vanishes—until, as with the Chesire cat, a face lingers on without a body, then a grin without a face, and lastly the grin fades away.

Contrariwise is the position of the monists. They are all for unity and for the virtues they hope will accompany it—order, harmony, and singleness of purpose. To attain these is impossible, as they see it, unless the many cohere around one focus. Nor does this coherence result from subjective attitudes alone. The unify society, it is not enough for people to feel that they belong together. The sentiment must be fortified with organisation which establishes orderly and harmonious relations between groups by institutional procedures. Though this consummation be devoutly wished by monists, they too encounter difficulties which stem from their positions. For they invite the question whether their insistence upon unity is so excessive that groups, other than the supreme unifying agency, will lose meaning, character, and identity to the extent that their autonomy is impaired. The penalty for unity can be the imposition of uniformity.

Moreover, each of these views confronts a difficulty which is the result of its special position. Both philosophies stand unequivocally against something: the pluralist, against organised unity; the monist anarchic diversity. But, in a constructive sense, for what kind of society does each view positively contend?

The pluralist may argue for a multiplicity of coordinate associations, whose mutual interplay will cancel out the dangers of excessive power by any one group.[4] But, following the potentialities inherent in this logic, you may go further. Approving the subdivision of society into its groups, you may also approve the fragmentation of groups into their individual members. At the logical exteme, therefore, the truest pluralists are individualists. Such thinkers give the primacy to the individual; and in the name of individuality will resist the pressures from the groups in which they combine and the society which would unify the groups. Pluralism, so conceived, is the plurality of autonomous individuals, rather than that of autonomous associations. Conversely, the pluralist may veer in the other direction. Thought conceding the need for individuals to be grouped and organised, one may be dubious about the possibilities of maintaining equilibrium and order among too many associations. Why not then support the idea of a balance two bodies roughly equal in weight and bulk? Distrustful of the monopoly that the monist accepts, one settles for dualism. Two great associations may be more stable than many, and safer than one. Indeed, as the discussion will show, the pluralistic argument for society has in some historical cases assumed a dualistic form.

UNITY THROUGH THE FAMILY, CHURCH, OR BUSINESS

The monist, too, has problems. If you seek an integrating focus for society, you must designate what this should be. Which institution do you select to embrace or oversee the rest? And how can it accomplish that task?

That a choice exists, and that the answers is not cut-and-dried, is substantiated by historical evidence. Several social institutions, in fact, have functioned in the role of prime coordinator for society. One of these, at various places and times, was the family. In such a case kinship becomes the determinant of every relationship. Because human beings are connected in certain ways by birth, their other group activities are cast in the mold of heredity. Thus the family serves as the economic unit, where each works for all and receives a share of the total output. The family takes care of its weak, its aged, and its incapacitated. The family provides education, and, for religion, worships its own ancestors. The family determines marital unions by alliance with other families. The family establishes rules and administers its discipline with rewards and punishments. Sometimes it even levies a death penalty on one of its members or wages war upon a neighboring family in the form of a blood feud or vendetta.

Similarly, religious associations have expanded beyond their primary function of worship and have encompassed the general direction of society under spiritual authority, as in a theocracy. When Calvin and Calvinists controlled Geneva in the seventeenth century or when the Jesuits ruled Paraguay in the eighteenth, a church-government regulated the conduct of individuals and groups in minute detail. Religious, no less than secular, bodies can declare and enforce the law by reference to divine sanction; maintain and direct an economic system as proprietors and managers; supervise the family by granting or withholding its rites; educate the youth; organize charities for the needy; and dominate the arts by control over their themes and forms. Religions can likewise launch crusades, proclaim "holy wars," and place armies in the field.[5] Men have bled and died for the Cross, the Crescent, or the *Mogen David,* as they have for Old Glory, the Union Jack, or the *Tricolore*. Nor need one turn to the past for examples. Early in 1979, when Iran's government changed from the autocracy of the Shah to a theocracy under the Ayatollah Khomeini, a steady stream of fulminations issued from the city of Qom as order to true believers and threats to the infidel. Expressing himself as spokesman for the Islamic faith, Khomeini was the ultimate lawgiver on all aspects of Iranian society.

Sometimes the paramount association is economic. A group formed for purposes of manufacturing or trade may discover in a certain *milieu* that it cannot fulfil these functions unless it extends its control over other institutions. Whether Napoleon was right in describing the British as "a nation of shopkeepers," or whether President Coolidge did full justice to his fellow countrymen with the remark that "the business of America is business," the fact remains that society can be integrated not by kinship or religion but by control of productive resources, by entrepreneurial technique—in Carlyle's phrase, by the "cash nexus." Indeed there have been corporations clothed in the full panoply of governments. The celebrated East India Company,[6] which ruled Britain's empire in India until 1858, is a conspicuous example. When business organizes society for business ends, it too can make and apply the law, establish an ethical code, and define the standards of right and wrong in relation to such concepts as "property," "profit," or "labour." By prescribing the conditions, hours, and wages of work, business can make or break the family. By its influence over occupations and careers, it can mould the policies and curricula of education. By paying artists and purchasing their products, it can regulate aesthetic style and taste. Lastly, to promote or preserve a commercial empire, business has mobilised military force and fought its battles at so much *per caput* and for such and *per cent.*[7]

These facts warrant an inference. Because the family, church, and corporation have made efforts of this kind with considerable success, it would appear that, in the absence of a coordinating institution, society contains a vacuum which there is an opportunity to fill. If various associations made the attempt, it is reasonable to assume that a need exists which they seek to satisfy, and that they can then be judged on how well they fill it. That need arises in part from the competition between associations and their rival claims on the allegiance of their members. The relations between groups demand regulation, supposedly by some superassociation. But there is more to it than that. If the unity of society is not an empty phrase, more will be required than a mechanism that merely mitigates the effects of conflict. Since society is built more on cooperation than competition, a case can be argued for promoting harmony between groups.

As a group is more than the sum of its separate members, so is society more than the mere addition of the component groups. Some writers have described the structure of society as federal. This is a helpful analogy if it is understood in two senses: first, that society is not properly a collection of individuals, but rather of groups of individuals; and second, that the groups constitute more collectively that they would separately. Considered by itself, each association is concerned with human interests that are fractional, these fractions being called economic, educational, religious, and so on. Functioning in its primary sense, an economic association performs activities that are economic, a religious association pursues aims that are religious, and similarly with the rest. No one association, if all are coordinate in rank and limited in function, has the responsibility or means to see that these fragments of human life are fused into a whole. In other words, there is no way of ensuring that the economy functions, not as a thing apart, but as the economic aspect of society; that a school or university is no cloistered academy, but a training ground for the use of intelligence in the workaday world; that the particular, in short, be treated within the frame-work of the general.

DEFECTS OF A SINGLE-TRACK SOCIETY

But the monist who seeks an integrated society, though possessing many weapons against the pluralist, still runs a risk. If any association is to succeed in coordinating society, it must evolve from a minor part to the leading role. It must broaden the necessarily narrow interest from which it started into a comprehensive concern for the whole. The question is whether an association will in fact be capable of growing to stature of its wider responsibilities or will instead remain the prisoner of its origins and of the limits they impose. The problem can be illustrated by some examples that are by no means hypothetical. Suppose the institution that tries to coordinate society is the family.[8] A group created by kinship and sustained by living together must then be expected to transfer to other spheres the characteristics of its primary functions. Relations between human beings will correspond to those between husband and wife, or parents and child, or sibling and sibling. Authority will be parental in form. Status within the family circle will determine status within the social circle. Family dictates will be the overriding consideration in the economic realm. Thus the ownership and inheritance of the family homestead, the provision for a son to marry and support a wife, production for subsistence only or for exchange—such matters will be settled by the prevailing conceptions of the family as the unifier of the social order. The great society will become an association of kinsfolk, writ large.[9]

Likewise, when the integrating agency is religious; its theology will extend to every secular activity. If the religion asserts that there is life after death, we shall be told to prepare ourselves in this world of mortal things for the eternity hereafter. The rules of daily conduct will be construed as a lifelong consecration to the

Deity. The Social contacts of the individual will be confined to the ranks of one's coreligionists. Those who do not belong to the established communion—call them heathen, pagan, gentile, infidel, heretic, or whatever—will be society's outcasts. They are "the stranger within thy gates," "the untouchables," "the internal proletariat,"[10] living witnesses of a house divided against itself, with religion as the divider. Holy Writ becomes law in the form of the Gospel, the Torah, the Koran, the Vedas, and the supreme lawgiver is the Holy Man, Prophet, or Son of God—a Gautama, Jesus, Mahomet, or Moses. Within this frame of reference, criticism of authority is equated with blasphemy; opposition itself is sin.

Similar in principle is the result that befalls the economic group seeking to integrate society. In this case the basic elements of the economic order will pervade the social system. Thus the rights that are vested in the ownership of property, and the human relationships arising from it—such factors of production as the control of natural resources, the use of tools and equipment, the structure of the wage system—all this will affect the rest of man's estate. Humanity will be preoccupied with material concerns such as living standards, the distribution of goods, the struggle for acquisition, the maintenance of employment and of purchasing power. The world will be viewed as a market. Language itself will take its connotations from the categories of economics. "Enterprise" will be synonymous with "business"; ideas one seeks to impart will be commodities one "sells"; human beings will be specified as "managers," consumers," "hands." The great society, if it knows no other god than Mammon, will strike the balance sheet of its civilisation in pecuniary terms. For what shall it profit a man if he gain his own soul and lose a whole market?

The point of the foregoing paragraphs can be summarised thus: When an association that originates with a finite function broadens out to the indefinite horizons of society, it tends to apply to its larger task the criteria of its initial limits. To the extent that this is so, its efforts provide society with both integration and straitjacketing. To subordinate all aspects of life and all kinds of groups to the single principle of kinship, religion, or economics can yield an unwholesome monism. If its results then are to be beneficial, the unifying association must meet this test: While retaining its original functions, it must transcend them and change its own character. It cannot integrate society merely by refashioning every other association in its own image.

This survey of the arguments in issue between monists and pluralists and of the problems peculiar to each facilitates a better understanding of the controversy over the function of the state. The analysis so far has indicated that the question of what activities are appropriate to the state is not narrowly political, but broadly social. It has also become clear that two questions are involved, since a choice must first be made between pluralism and monism; and, if the latter is preferred, a second choice must determine which association can best coordinate the whole. The answer to the second question is, in a vital sense, relevant to the first, if no association can fill the role of integrating, the case for pluralism wins by default. If, on the other hand, some one association is competent to do it, then the case for the monist is strengthened.

THE STATE'S RELATION TO SOCIETY

In this controversy the state is directly involved, because one inevitably asks: What activities is government to undertake? Somehow, the relations of the state to our other associations must be defined. If the pluralists are to prevail, they must explain (1) why it is necessary to limit the functions of the state, (2) where to place the limits, and (3) how a society holds together, or achieves integration, in the absence of a unifying agency. In order to win the argument, the monist must demonstrate (1) that society needs unifying, (2) that the state can do it, and (3) that any risks in confiding this duty to the state can be safely forestalled or are outweighed by the attendant advantages.

Both viewpoints have been expressed at various times by those who wished to advocate or resist some manifestation of governmental power. Nor have the rival philosophies been confined to theoretical debate. Under one guise or another, each has been translated into practice and has received concrete expression. Hence the discussion and evaluation of each can be based both on the resoned hopes of their advocates and on the performance that results from their application in practice. Like the family, business, and church, the state has entered this field of controversy because there is an opportunity for it to grasp. If society is ready for integration, the state is as well placed to provide it as are associations based upon kinship, economics, or religion. Or possibly, it is even better placed because of its original, primary function. All human beings want protection. So, all of us depend on the association which provides it. Moreover, the state controls the force which ensures the protection. Though this same force, the government is able at times to impose itself upon the other institutions of society. Indeed the state can be more effectively monistic than businesses, families, or churches because of the sanctions it employs. Those who do not bow to family control may be excluded from the kin group. Those who defy their employers may lose on means of earning their bread and butter. Those who resist sacerdotal authority may be excommunicated. Such sanctions are not completely compulsive unless the victim is left with no other alternative. But in some societies a person may survive without a family, may earn a living in new ways, embrace a new faith, or do without one. Universally, however, the ultimate sanction of the state is a gun pointed at your heart. If the state has a monopoly of the available force, as is ordinarily the case, there is no choice but to submit or die.

Behind the modern debate over the proper sphere of governmental activity stretches a history a history of at least 25 centuries. For that reason the best way to understand current controversies about the functions of the state is to review them in chronological perspective. The story forms a sequence of alternating episodes, with the emphasis shifting from one pole to the other. The city-state of the Graeco-Roman period was primarily monistic in spirit and organisation. The counter doctrine, that the sphere of the state must be limited, was advanced by the Christian church after it became the official religion of the Roman Empire and a partner in the established order. This principle continued to prevail through the Middle Ages, but lost ground with the advent of the Reformation and the emergence of the nation-state. The ethos of the latter at its inception was as strongly monistic as the city-state has been. It remained so until the economic ferment of the Industrial Revolution once more brought into vogue the concept of the limited state, with business now cast in the role formerly played by the medieval church.

The Twentieth century, influenced in this matter as in others by the nineteenth, has both imitated and rejected its predecessor. In the ninth decade of this century, both viewpoints—That which insists on limits and that which does not—are still embattled. Neither is clearly dominant.

The successive periods may be identified roughly as follows:

Period 1 : approximately from the tenth century B.C. to the fourth century A.D. Monistic State.

Period 2 : from the fourth century A.D. to middle of the fifteenth century. Limited State.

Period 3 : from the mid-fifteenth century to 1776. Monistic State.

Period 4 : 1776 to 1914. Limited State.

Period 5 : since 1914. Return to the Monistic State, but with resistance to its domination.

A survey of these periods[11] and a review of their problems will help to explain the advantages claimed for each doctrine and the difficulties attending its fulfilment.

THE GRAECO-ROMAN CITY-STATE: AN EXPERIMENT IN MONISM

In its developed form, the *polis* or city-state-community, such as Sparta in the sixth century B.C. or Athens in the fifth demanded complete allegiance of its citizens. All activities and associations were either controlled or liable to control by the state. Society—the sum total of all groups—was inseparable from the state. Even the Greek language, that flexible instrument for conveying the subtlest nuance of thought, had no word for society any more than it distinguished between state and city. The one word *polis* sufficed for city, state, and society combined. Within this context of ideas, the state was the paramount social institution when and wherever it chose to intervene. Thus, the economic field was subject to political ordering as the public interest seemed to require. Religion consisted of state worship of the patron hero, the city deity, and the pantheon of the Olympians. Many of the cultural achievements which made that age immortal were evoked or produced by state enterprise. Architects, sculpotors, and painters—an Ictinus, Phidias, or Apelles—dedicated their genius to the temples and other civic building constructed by the state for its adornment. It was the public marketplace that served as classroom for the interrogations of Socrates; the citizen's assembly that imspired the oratory of Pericles or Demosthenes; the official festivals and contests that promoted the staging of dramas by the great playwrights.

Nevertheless, although that describes the general tendency, some aberrations or exceptions existed. Certain religious cults, such as the Eleusinian Mysteries, did not belong to official state ceremony. Some creative artists, the lyric poets for instance, produced their works to satisfy an inward urge rather than a public audience. In actuality, not everything was prescribed and ordered by the state, save possibly in Sparta and Crete. But if the state chose to extend its authority to any sphere, there was no rival institution strong enough to resist its advance and no social philosophy delimiting the bounds of state action. Indeed, the magisterial pronouncements of Plato and Aristotle are wholly couched in terms of the omnipotent *polis.* In their major treatises, these two touch on nearly all of the great issues that occupy the forefront of political theory and practice in the modern world. Significantly, though, they omit the questions of the relation of the state to society and the possible limits of state power. The reason for the omission is that such queries did not even arise in Greek experience. It never occurred to Plato and Aristotle to examine an alternative to monism. This they took for granted.

However, a clarification should be noted. Both Plato and Aristotle are monists in the sense that they view the state as supreme among human associations and set no bounds to its activities. But their monism is not identical. Or, to be more precise, the supremacy of the state is manifested differently. Aristotle asserts his monism in the opening paragraph of the *Politics,* where he calls the state the paramount association, embracing all the rest and pursuing the highest good. Yet this conception of the state does not lead him to undervalue, still less to abolish, the remaining associations. These retain their place within the fabric of society and even serve to strengthen the bonds of social cohesion. But if a conflict arises, it is to the state that all are subordinate. Plato differs from Aristotle in his utterly uncompromising emphasis on unity, which he believes is best safeguarded by the destruction of competing associations. All loyalties and affections are to be focused on and drawn toward on centre. If other institutions., such as the family or the ownership of private property, are likely to distract the individual from a single-minded dedication to the public interest, the platonic guardians must have no share in them. The monistic state of Aristotle is one that permits other groups to exist, but stands supreme over them. The monistic state of Plato prefers to abolish the other groups and absorb their functions.

Apart from the preferences of philosophers, however, what were the social reasons why the practice and philosophy of the city-state were monistic? Two reasons suffice. One was the smallness of the city-state. With an area and population so confined, there was little room for parallel, coordinate systems. As the Greeks read the lessons of their own history, they could choose one of two alternatives: unity with order or faction fights with anarchy. Closeness of contact, and the pressure of small-sised communities, bred a view of the state as the paramount social organisation. In the antithesis between the public and private sides of life, Greek spokesmen supported the former. Thus their term for private citizen, *idiotes,* has given us the modern "idiot," and percales could castigate those who took no part in civic affairs as useless to the community.[12] Besides smallness, besides smallness, a second reason for monism was the insecurity which plagued the Greeks in their interstate relations. Not only was there the possibility of war between Greek and non-Greek, but the little city-states themselves were often at each other's throats, and neighbouring settlements were likely to be hereditary foes. Seeking protection from these perils, the Greeks were impelled to rally around the institution whose function was to protect.

If monism was encouraged by the smallness of the unit of government and facilitated by the absence of any association rivaling the state, it would be expected that, when these conditions disappeared, the monistic state would also disappear. Early signs of this possibility were discernible in the first philosophies which emerged after the absorption of the *polis* into the larger units of kingdoms or empires. The Stoics[13] and Epicureans rejected the assumptions of Plato and Aristotle. They a sought to reconcile opposite extremes by finding a place for the individual within the immensity of the universe. Since the politics of the three centuries between the breakup of the empire of Alexander and the consolidation of that of Rome were chaotic and turbulent, many people viewed the state with pessimism, apprehension, or indifference. If the good life was unobtainable through politics, it must be sought in other ways. If the ambitions of governments were prejudicial to the public peace, peace of mind must be cultivated elsewhere. Hence followed a reassessment of the relative priorities of public and private activity, and philosophers now advised that all should compensate for the insecurities around them by seeking security within themselves.

As occurred with equalitarianism, a concept born in the minds of Greeks received institutional form through the acts of Romans. This happened after Rome had succeeded in expanding into an empire and Christianity had managed to capture Rome. Previously, when Rome was a small community beset by unfriendly neighbours, it was subject to the same internal and external forces as the city-states of Greece. No sphere of life was exempt from the power of the state, if there was occasion or demand for its exercise. None of the other groups composing society was in a position to withstand the state or claim an independent or higher allegiance. Family relations, religious cults, economic affairs, cultural advances—all could be brought within the ambit of official surveillance. That situation changed when the Roman Empire expanded to an unparalleled size. The tightly knit organisation of a small community could not be transferred or reproduced across the large-scale dimensions of Rome's conquests. Given the means of communication then available between the central authority and peripheral regions, the extent of the area to be governed precluded any intensive direction of society by the state. As long as Rome's authority was firmly established in the spheres of military power, foreign relations, and finance, in other matters much diversity and autonomy were permitted to the provinces and municipalities.

Along with this change of scale, an empire that eventually stretched from Jordan to Scotland and from the German forests to the Sahara Desert came to embrace a host of religious faiths. Out of the welter of sects, cults, rites, and deities, Christianity emerged dominant. When the Emperor Constantine was converted, the *Imperium Romanum* entered into articles of union with the church. Considered in political terms, this partnership between the Cross and the Eagle brought gain and loss to both. The state gained, because the spiritual influence of the Christian faith could not be employed to unify the allegiance of Roman citizens. But simultaneously the state lost its monopoly. Accepting a partner, it admitted a separate and coordinate body to the citadel of power. The church likewise derived a benefit; but it also incurred a liability. Becoming an integral part of the established order, the church ceased to be a victim of persecution—henceforth it did the persecuting. Indeed it could, if necessary, invoke the secular arm as its ally against heretics and infidels. This power, however, brought disadvantages. Not only might the church be obliged to extend reciprocal aid and support its temporal partner, ever if the latter were, to put it midly, unsaintly; but the church could also become corrupted by its involvement in the preoccupations of its position. Dominance could even bring wealth, at least to the princes of the church, and therewith a tendency to corruption. It was Dante who wrote, with a reference to the supposed Donation of Constantine to Pope Silvester:

> Ah constantine, what evil hast thou sired!
> Not thy conversion, but that price wherewith
> The first rich father thou has paid and hired![14]

THE CHRISTIAN REVOLUTION: CHURCH-STATE DUALISM

Thus was inaugurated a new era in political history. What it signalised was a different solution to the problem of defining the function of the state. Where the old order had been content with a doctrine that set no limit to these functions and made the boundaries of politics coextensive with the range of social conduct, the crux of the new order lay precisely in the effort to delimit the field of politics within the larger area of society and thus necessarily establish an adjacent field, which the state had no right to enter. The earlier concept of a society unified by the monistic state was rejected. It was replaced by the notion of a society split in two, with twin institutions separated by a frontier. Philosophy was now called upon to justify, and statesmanship to operate, a division of spheres. The issues posed by this endeavour were challenging. Reasons had to be discovered for the assertion that dualism was in some ways superior to unity; a line of demarcation had somewhere to be drawn; and finally the separate spheres and the government of each had somehow to be related to each other. These problems in all their amification occupied human ingenuity for over a thousand years.

Whenever it is argued that the power of the state be circumscribed, the proposal takes its specific form from the nature of the association which offers the challenge to monism. In this case, since religion assumed the offensive, it was the church that emerged as an institution coequal with the state. Relations between church and state now became the central issue for political theory and organisation which they had not been before. It is, therefore, to the social doctrines of Christianity, as these evolved from the fourth to the fourteenth century A.D., that we must turn for understanding the theory and tactics of the Dark and Middle Ages.

Like all systematic philosophies, Christianity assumed a view of human nature. Human beings were thought to be composed of two parts, body and soul. The body, an object of sense perception and known through sensory evidence, exists as a member of the world of material things. It is born, passes through the life cycle, then dies. The soul does not belong in the sensory realm. Belief in its existence is granted by divine revelation and must be accepted on faith. Joining the body when life begins, the soul-will depart of the advent of death and is immortal. The soul is therefore on a higher plane than the body and is our most important possession. Hence in the scale of Christian values this world takes second place to the next. The care of the spirit, which is everlasting, has priority over the temporal and mundane. Our greatest concern, while alive on this earth, is to save our souls for eternity.

The dualism which runs through Christian thought and theology is evident in the saying of Jesus: "Render, therefore, unto Caesar the things that are Caesar's; and render unto God the things that are Gods." The same pattern recurs in the treatise of Saint Augustine, *Concerning the City of God,* where an analogous distinction is drawn between two cities, the earthly and the heavenly. People must resist the temptations and avoid the perils of the earth. Let them seek the eternal bliss of the heavenly city by obeying the counsel to be perfect "even as your Father in Heaven is perfect." To apply these attitudes to actual government was the task initiated by one of the early popes, Gelasius I, and continued by various of his successors. Since every person contained two natures, one mortal and the other immortal, the organisation of society—so the argument ran—must correspond to the dualism implanted in humanity by the Creator. The church should be the institution charged with the salvation of souls and the preparation in this life for the life everlasting. The state should have the responsibility for affairs of this world, for the mortal sphere pertaining to the body. Church and state should be constituted as separate authorities, each paramount within its own bailiwick and possessing its own government. But how were the twain, *sacerdotium* and *imperium,* the ecclesiastical power and the temporal, the spiritual and the secular, to be related? The Gelasian answer envisaged them as "two swords' that could not be grasped and wielded by one hand. As God had endowed us with a soul separate from the body, so must church and state exist independently of each other. It would therefore be as wrong for an emperor to exercise spiritual power as for a pope to hold secular sway. What God had put asunder, let no man put together.

It is evident that the application of these formulas depended on the validity of two assumptions: one, that the spheres of the ecclesiastical and temporal jurisdictions could in fact be separated; and the other, that the two institutions would respectively adhere to their coordinate status. Failure to fulfil either assumption would destroy dualism. How did the medieval Christian world meet these tests of its dogma?

THE THEORY OF DUALISM VS. THE CONDITIONS OF UNITY

The separation of the spiritual realm from the secular was more easily stated as an ideal than realised in actuality. The things that are Caesar's may be distinguishable metaphysically from the things that are God's, yet both are physically interwined. Thus there were ceremonies and official acts of that state that were accompanied by prayer or required solemnizing by some religious affirmation. Treaties between rulers, for example, were signed and sworn under oath that called for the presence of the Bible and a priest. Governments were staffed by human beings who possessed souls and who, being Christians, were children of the church. The church could therefore call them to account if their governmental acts violated its canons of Christian duty. By the weapons of excommunication and interdict, the pope could even subdue a temporal ruler, as in the cases of the Emperor Henry IV and King John of England. The long drawn out investiture controversy revolved around the question: Should a bishop be invested with the insignia of his office by the secular authority of the area of the area or by an ecclesiastical superior? Conversely, while the church was involved in various functions of the state, so was the state immersed in matters vital to the church. As its power waxed, the church became an integral part of the established order which the state protected.[15] The church acquired land and buildings and other forms of property. It employed large numbers of people, including serfs. It used the revenues from its possessions for its own needs and claimed to be exempt from contributing to the temporal treasury. If the state failed to maintain internal order, or was unable to protect its territories from invasion, the church ran the risk of looting and pillage. Hence in a thousand ways, lay matters were interlocked with spiritual. The two spheres were separated by an ideological, not an iron, curtain, and its was not practicable to make them self-contained.

Similar difficulties were encountered with the effort to place the two institutions on that footing of equality which the Gelasian theory enunciated. Each of the partners, as occasion permitted or demanded, pressed its attack on the other. Each, at one time or another, struck at the foundations of Gelasianism by attempting either to subordinate one sword to the other or to grasp both with one hand. In this tussle for supremacy between church and state, the initial advantage lay with the church, and the first major blows at the doctrine of Gelasius were dealt by his papal successors. There were various reasons why this happened. For one thing, the theoretical postulates of Christianity were not easily reconciled with the concept of equal jurisdictions. To a Christian the soul was clearly on a higher plane than the body, life in the hereafter more important than the life here and now, eternity more significant than threescore years and ten. Hence in the hierarchy of Christian values the church outranked the state. If churchmen argued that the spiritual sword should precede the temporal, who could gainsay such a contention? Furthermore, independently of theoretical beliefs, practical considerations favoured unity over dualism. This was especially so in the troubled times following the breakdown of the Roman Empire in the West, when Teutonic peoples invaded its territories and carved out new kingdoms. While the secular power was at the worst in dissolution, or at the best in flux, often the sole rallying point for society proved to be the church. If there were instances when popes gratuitously clutched at both swords, there were also times when the church held both through the state's default.

THE PAPAL REJECTION OF DUALISM

The papal attacks on the Gelasian doctrine were occasioned by two of the most prolonged and harassing issues of the medieval period: one concerning the claim of secular rulers to invest bishops with the symbols of their office, the other arising over royal demands that the clergy pay taxes to the state treasury. During the former of these controversies, Pope Gregory VII, Who eventually dominated over Emperor Henry IV, insisted that within the church the bishops were subordinate to the pope and that in church-state relations a defiant ruler could be excommunicated and his subjects absolved from their oaths of allegiance. This was tantamount to claiming for the papacy a power to depose a monarch, employable at the pope's discretion. Implicit in this, of course, was the view that of the two swords the *sacerdotium* was mightier than the *imperium,* a doctrine which, whether justifiable or not, was not Gelasian. But Gregory went further. Mindful of the distinction that St. Augustine had drawn between the city of God and the earthly city, he proceeded to suggest—which Augustine had not—that the city of God was synonymous with the church whereas the earthly city, or kingdom of the Devil, was identifiable with the state—a pair of equations which definitely concluded with debasing the secular sphere in the hierarchy of Christian values!

The later controversy over the taxing powers was, if anything, fiercer and more embittered. On its side, the church reached the ultimate in extravagant contentions as its relative position weakened. The leading protagonists in this struggle were Pope Boniface VIII and Philip the Fair, King of France. Armed with the doctrine enunciated earlier by Innocent IV that the pope enjoyed *plenitudo potestatis* ("total power"), Boniface moved into the logically final ground and expressly rejected dualism. In a bull entitled *Unam Sanctam,* whose initial word stressed unity, the Pope claimed both swords—though the temporal one could be delegated to the secular arm to be wielded at ecclesiastical bidding. This pronouncement sealed the papal rejection of the goal of a divided society.

ATTACK ON DUALISM BY THE STATE

The state's position in this controversy switched as its power changed relative to that of the church. If the temporal authorities were disorganised, as was not infrequently the case during the Dark Ages; if the empire, reconstituted by Charlemagne in A.D. 800, was more shadowy than real, and the emperor was insecure in his authority; if kings were weakened by the pretensions and powers of the feudal nobility; then the secular branch was scarcely so consolidated as to withstand a determined pope. Under such conditions the state was on the defensive which forced its apologists to adhere fairly strictly to the doctrines of Gelasius. Acknowledging the monopoly of the church in the salvation of souls, the state's defenders had to assert that over temporal matters the ruler derived his power directly from God—not indirectly via the pope as an intermediary. In other words, the things that are Caesar's are entrusted to Caesar by divine dispensation. For the powers that be (and this means all of them) are ordained of God. On this assumption, the state could preserve its role as equal partner of the Church.

In the later phases of the conflict, however, especially during the Struggles between Boniface VIII and Philip and between Pope John XXII and the Emperor Ludwig of Bavaria, the weights were tipped in the balance on the secular side. This was due to the cumulative effect of political trends operating within the medieval system, which finally contributed to its downfall. One such trend was the gradual consolidation of monarchical power at the expense of the nobility.[16] Another, associated with it, was the dawning of national[17] sentiments—particularly evident when the French clergy supported King Philip of France on the tax question against the pope at Rome. A third was the political weakening of the papacy because of internal corruption and its lowered prestige in the period of the schism. Thus strengthened, the state was able to launch its own offensive, and therewith attack the Gelasian theory from the opposite flank. Its line of argument contended that the function of the church is to teach and preach. As an institution organised on this earth, the church falls within the category of worldly affairs. hence its property is taxable by the state, while it personnel (the clergy)are merely one vocational group within society and, as such, are subject to the jurisdiction of laymen. Like the contrary attempt of Boniface VIII, this was a rejection of dualism. But the advocate of unification was now siding with the state, which cast itself in the paramount role.

All in all, the medieval experiment must be judged a failure. Dualism did not work. The two spheres were not kept separate. The two jurisdictions did not continue equal and coordinate. The two swords were not brandished in harmony and unison. Too often they clashed. Like a pair of unruly oxen harnessed to the same yoke, both parties sought to be rid of the Gelasian legacy. But the impasse that medievalism had reached by the early fifteenth century marked the end—not of the story, but only of an episode. A new epoch was arriving with new facts and formulas.

THE RECONSTRUCTION OF UNITY

It is characteristic of the political process that, when a trend in one direction has reached a point of excess, a counteraction is likely. Sometimes the latter movement, too, will be developed to excess. With the breakdown of the attempt at dualism came a new effort to reinstate the older principle which predated Constantine's conversion. In place of two spheres, there would be one. Instead of the state performing limited functions which covered a fraction of society, its sphere was now to be as wide as society itself. In lieu of limits, the state's range of action was to be unbounded.

The yearning for unity was an understandable reaction to the insecurities and discords of a divided society. Many were tired of conflicting claims, clashing loyalties, and antagonistic systems. They preferred to accept, with all its risks, a single authority. Unity at least meant that you know whose laws and which commands to obey. Hence it is that Thomas Hobbes, expounding the covenant on which a state and government are founded, urges the concentration of authority: "The only way to erect such a Common Power, as may be able to defend them from the invasion of Forraigners, and the injuries of one another, . . .is, to conferre al their power and strength upon *one* Man, or upon one Assembly of men, that may reduce all their wills, by plurality of voices, unto *one* will..."[18] In keeping with this plea for unity, Hobbes views with suspicion, distrust, or outright antipathy the development within society of associations other than the state, since these may grow from subordinates of the central authority into rivals. Upon them he vents his displeasure in a wholesale indictment embracing "the Ghostly Authority" of the church, the accumulation of too much treasure by a few, the loyalty of an army to an ambitious general, "the immoderate greatness of a town," and also "the great number of Corporations, which are as it were many lesser commonwealths in the bowels of a greater, like wormes in the entrayles of a naturall man." For full measure he adds to his list "the Liberty of Disputing against absolute Power, by pretenders to Politicall Prudence; which though bred for the most part in the Lees of the people; yet animated by False Doctrines, are perpetually medling with the Fundamentall Lawes, to the molestation of the Commonwealth; like the little Wormes, which Physicians call *Ascarides*."[19]

From the colourful language, a clear meaning emerges. Hobbes is pre-disposed against a plurality of associations on grounds akin to Plato's objection to the family and private property. The coexistence of other associations alongside the state he considers a weakness to both state and society because it subjects each individual, as a member of many groups, to diverse affiliations and potentially rival allegiances. The Hobbesian cure-all for the disorders of pluralism is as drastic, uncompromising, and clear-cut as the platonic. All power must go to the state, and, within the state, to its supreme ruling element. Rid yourselves, so runs his advice, of a multiplicity of associations. Rally around the great association. Finally, since few of his readers were rationalists, with a last flourish he inserts the keystone of religious faith into the archway of his "scientific" reasons for the foundation of the state: "Thus is the Generation of that great LEVIATHAN, or rather (to speak more reverently) of that *Mortall God,* to which wee owe under the *Immortal God,* Our peace and defence."[20]

These excerpts from Hobbes have been cited as representative of the new trend because of the rigorous character of their logic. They have the merit of hewing the issue in sharp outline and high relief. But the ideas were not, of course, chiseled in thin air. They were excavated from the rock strata of facts, thrown up into new convolutions by the political earthquakes of the sixteenth and seventeenth centuries. The violence of those circumstances was due to the breakdown of the Gelasian formula and the search for new solutions.

UNIFORMITY OR TOLERATION?

Since the church had been partner or rival of the state for a thousand years, and since church-state relations were in contention, it was this problem that the new era tackled first. The relative strength of the two institutions, already changing with the emergence of nationalism, altered decisively in the sixteenth century as the papacy weakened. In this respect, even more important than the internal decline of its organisation (which could be, and later was, reconstructed) was the defection from Rome of large areas of Western Christendom. The Protestant Reformation, whose influence was felt most in north central and northwestern Europe and more among Teutonic and Scandinavian peoples than among Latins, established in a Christendom already divided between the Roman and Eastern Orthodox rites a Further split within the West. Since that time, to be a Christian in Western Europe or its subsequent colonial offshoots did not necessarily mean acceptance of the Roman rite or allegiance to papal authority. The Catholic Church, whose Greek name literally means "universal," no longer possessed a universal following. The result has been that for five centuries no one church in the West has enjoyed a monopoly of Christianity. Furthermore, when the dissolvent acids of Protestantism commenced their corrosion of the once monolithic church, the same chemistry could operate within the chinks and crevasses of Protestantism itself. The practice of dissent could react upon its instigators; and the divisive process started a chain reaction of sects and schisms. Lutherans, Anglicans, Presbyterians. Baptists, Quakers, Methodists, and others held out to puzzled humanity their many keys to the Kingdom.

The political consequences of a fragmented Christianity were momentous alike for citizens individually and for the state of which they were members. In spiritual matters the individual no longer faced the compulsions of monopoly. The doctrine that "there is no salvation outside the church"[21] lost most of its effect, since there was now a variety of churches, each proffering salvation Excommunication lacked its former terror when there were other communions to join. The interdict, whereby medieval popes forbade obedience to a heretical ruler, became an obsolete weapon.

Skepticism now had full scope in matters theological, since if many churches indicated different roads to heaven, the curious were bound to inquire which route was right.

What effect did this have on the state? In what ways was government impelled to readjust? The political novelty lay in the fact that Christianity, for the previous thousand years a unifying force in Western Europe, now became a disruptive agent. Previously, if a ruler accepted the church as a partner or as the superior, there would at least be relative harmony. But now a Christian ruler had to choose between different churches (it being assumed that one could not be non-Christian or atheist); and, once the personal choice was made, he or she must decide whether subjects could choose differently or must adhere to the same communion. Thus arose the political issue of whether people's religious beliefs were relevant to their citizenship and their allegiance to their sovereign. Could Protestants tolerate Catholics, or Catholics tolerate Protestants, as equally loyal members of the same state? Could Protestant sect even tolerate another? Should the state, confronted with the fact of differences, exercise neutrality and ennoble the tolerance of diversity as an ideal of politics? Or should it require conformity to orthodoxy, if necessary, by imposing it and persecuting heretics? To find answers to these questions occupied two centuries during which throughout Europe blood was spilled, martyrs were tortured and burned, treasure was squandered, savage wars were fought, and bigotry reaped its bitter harvest of bestiality.

One answer—which was everywhere the first attempt, and in some places also the final outcome—proceeded on the assumptions that a persons' religion is relevant to the ruler, that church and state must be identified by merger of their controlling authority, and that heresy is therefore treason. These doctrines were summarised in the terse Latin formula: *cujus regio, ejus religio* ("who controls the region, controls its religion"). Both Protestants, in areas where the Reformation was successful, and Catholics, where the Counter-Reformation held its ground, applied this formula to their adversaries. In England the Reformation was launched when Henry VIII, wanting a divorce, obtained the support of the Parliament for abolishing papal authority over the church, dissolved the monastic orders, and established a national church with himself at its head as "Defender of the Faith." These decisive events produced their aftereffects, as when Henry sought to exact from the clergy an oath of allegiance to himself as their spiritual superior; when Mary attempted to reinstate Catholicism; when policy was once more reversed under Elizabeth I, who authorised a new prayer book and a revised liturgy; and when James II, a century too late, sought in vain to lead England back to Rome and lost his throne to the final assertion of triumphant Protestantism.[22]

The dreadful cost of internecine strife between irreconcilables promoted England at last to apply an alternative answer: that the state, though officially committed to its own orthodoxy, could safely permit its subjects to profess different religious beliefs—always provided that this concession did not diminish their political allegiance. Through the eighteenth century only members of the Church of England were allowed by law to hold political office.[23] But in the 1820s the disabilities of other faiths were removed and all posts, save the monarchy, were opened to their adherents. Gradually, the principle of tolerance, at first a hard-won necessity, was elevated into a virtue. In the United States, from the beginnings of its independent national hood, public guarantees of private religious freedom, as well as a ban upon establishing an official religion, were incorporated into the legal structure of the governmental system.[24] Jefferson in 1786 was the author of Virginia's notable *Act for Establishing Religious Freedom.* Its preamble affirmed that the state stands neutral where matters of faith are involved. "Our civil rights have no dependence on our religious opinions, more than our opinions in physics or geometry." A few years afterward, when the Bill of Rights was appended to the Constitution of the United States, the opening words of the first amendment declared: "Congress shall make no law respecting an establishment of religion, or prohibiting the free exercise thereof."

MONISM AGAIN: THE THEORY OF SOVEREIGNTY

The quest for a fresh formula to govern church-state relations did not lack results. In the sixteenth century a new principle took shape to express the departure from Gelasianism. This is the doctrine, so much touted from that time to the present, called sovereignty. An early exposition of it comes from the Frenchman Jean Bodin, who in 1576 published his *Six Books Concerning the Republic*. He writes: "Sovereignty is a power over citizens and subjects that is supreme and above the law."[25] In this phrasing, as in others, sovereignty is evidently a complex, embracing several ideas. Some of these, since sovereignty has may ramifications, fall under different headings among the five classic issues and will be discussed elsewhere. But one aspect is central to the issue now being considered. In rejecting the view that the functions of the state should be exercised within a limited sphere, sovereignty asserted the limitless range of governmental activity. When sovereignty was pronounced to be one and indivisible, the state was intended to assume (or resume what it enjoyed in Graeco-Roman days) the general direction and supervision of society. The very force of the new insistence on unity was a measure of the reaction against dualism.

But a further clarification is necessary. When a king, like Henry VIII of England, proclaimed himself head of the church, he unified the two spheres and left the church in no position to set bounds to the sphere of politics. If the state was prepared to tolerate religious dissent, however, as later happened in Britain and the United States, did the abandonment of the demand for conformity imply that the state accepted limits to its power? The answer to this question, though arguable, is probably negative. Where the state tolerated diversity, it did so on one important condition. Whether tacit or expressed. A dividing line was supposed to be drawn between matters of public and private concern. The Churches—any number of them—were permitted their freedom, on condition that they confined their activities to worshiping the Deity and teaching religious doctrine. Belief in this field was ascribed to the private conscience, for which reason the state would keep; its hands off. But in the public domain the state maintained its claim to be sovereign, and any church that departed from the private sphere and entered the public arena would run the risk and pay the penalty of grappling with Leviathan. Hence if toleration existed, it did so on political sufferance. The state stood neutral because the stings of the churches were drawn. They, for their part, exercised their freedom on condition of abstaining from political power. Any breach of this condition would call down on ecclesiastical heads the full weight of sovereignty, that is, of secular supremacy.

Thus the wheel had turned full circle. The first experiment in setting bounds to the functions of the state ended in a restoration of the status quo. From the Greek concept of the all-embracing *polis* to the Bodinian or Hobbesian theory of sovereignty, a connecting thread of sovereignty, a connecting thread is woven across the centuries. But the first challenge to the omnipotent state was not the last. So, let us turn to the second attempt and observe how, when, and why the pluralist cudgels were brandished anew.

References

1. For examples of this viewpoint, consult Harold J. Laski, *Grammar of Politics,* 3rd ed. (London: George Allen and Unwin, 1934), pp. 25-28, 37; or Robert M. MacIver, *The Modern State* (New York: Oxford University Press, 1926), pp.7-182.

2. The monists, curiously enough, exhibit contrasts no less marked than the pluralists. Witness Aristotle, in the paragraph with which he commences the *Politics,* and Mussolini in The *Social and Political Doctrine of Fascism.*

3. This is the title of a book by Graham Wallas, published in 1914.

4. Such, essentially, is Madison's conception of society in The *Federalist*, No. 10

5. "Men never do evil so completely and cheerfully," wrote Pascal, "as when they do it from religious conviction."

6. In the course of his *Speech in the Impeachment of Warren Hastings,* 1788, Edmund Burke thus described the company: "The constitution of the company began in commerce, and ended in empire… The India Company came to be what it is—a great empire, carrying on, subordinately, a great commerce… In fact, the East-India Company in Asia is a state in the disguise of a merchant." *Works, 7* (Boston: Wells and Lilly, 1827), 29.

7. Contemporary cases which approximate to this are many of the business corporations in Japan, whose paternalism envelops much of the life of their employees.

8. Some oriental cultures provide examples of the transfer of the family relationship to an entire society. See an analysis of this attempt in Japan by Robert A. Scalapino, *Democracy and the Party Movement in Prewar Japan* (Berkeley: University of California Press, 1953), pp. 120 ff.

9. Many peoples have expressed this idea in the form of a story that they are descended from a common ancestor.

10. This is A.J. Toynebe's phrase in his *Study of History.*

11. This breakdown into "periods" is offered with the necessary caution that any such subdivision contains an element of arbitrariness. The beginning and ending dates are averages, rather than precise points. Few periods, moreover, are all one thing or all another. Usually, contemporary instances of the opposite to the prevalent tendency can be discovered.

12. See the funeral Oration in Thucydides' *Histories, ii,* 40.

13. For the Stoics, see chapter 5, section on "The Classical Roots of the Doctrine of Equality."

14. *Inferno,* Canto 19. 11: 115-17. My translation, In this canto, Dante is attacking the clerics who sold ecclesiastical office and religious favour for monetary gain.

15. *For some evidence on this point, see Tocqueville, Ancien Regime,* part 2.

16. See chapter 10, section on "The Medieval Dispersion of Powers" and "Sovereignty and Absolutism in the Nation-state."

17. "The Cracks in Medieval Unity."

18. *Leviathan,* part 2 (Everyman's Library), p. 89. My italics. (pp.174-75) for his explicit rejection of church-state dualism.

19. Leviathan.

20. Ibid., p. 89. Italics and capitals in the original.

21. *Extra ecclesiam nulla salus.*

22. The principle of the subordination of the church to the state is thus described by G. M. Trevelyan: "Bishop Jewel, the best exponent of the ideas of the early Elizabethan settlement, declared: "This is our doctrine, that every soul, of what calling so ever he be—be he monk,be he preacher, be he prophet, be, he apostle—ought to be

subject to King and magistrates.' The sphere of king and magistrates covered religion. All were agreed that there could be only one religion in the state, and all except Romanists and very rigorous Puritans were agreed that the state must decide what that religion should be." *Illustrated English Social History,* Vol.2 (London: Longmans, Green & Co., 1950), 34.

23. Annually, however, after 1727, Parliament passed Indemnity Acts; exempting from legal penalties those who held public office without swearing the necessary oath.

24. Prior to independence, of course, the leading example of religious toleration, thanks to Penn and The Quakers, was to be found in Pennsylvania.

25. *Maiestas est summa in cives ac subditos legibusque soluta potestas.*

6

Government and the Citizen

Functions of government cannot be separated from rights of persons, except in the sense in which the reverse of a coin can be distinguished from the obverse. On the one hand, the functions of government are a condition of the rights of persons, because they are necessary to the enjoyment of those right and because they exist in order the secure them. On the other hand, rights of persons are a condition of the functions of government, because they are the source and the cause of the existence and action of government.

To claim, for example, a right to the enjoyment of personal security is also to claim a right to protection against any invasion of that security; to claim that right to protection is also to claim the exercise of a function of giving protection; and to claim the exercise of that function giving protection; and to claim the exercise of that function is also to claim an organ, possessing power or authority, by means of which it is exercised. We may accordingly say that government is a service on behalf of rights, and not a power outside their range: 'servitium propter jura, non potestas praeter jura". We may add that the service rendered by government to rights is both a consequence and a part of the general rights of persons. I have a right to the service, and the service is thus a part of my rights, because, and as consequence, of the other and general rights belonging to me as a person.

The same view of the relation between function of government and rights of persons may equally be attained if we follow another line of reflection. The States is, in its essence, a legal association. The made of its action is law. The function of its organs of government is the declaration and enforcement of law. What, then, is the nature of the relation of law to rights? Does it abridge them, or does it contain them.

The answer, as we have already seen, is that law contains right, and indeed *is* rights. Law and rights are simply two aspects of something which is essentially one: law is its 'objective' aspect, or the thing as regarded from outside, and rights are its 'subjective' aspect, or the thing as regarded from inside, that is to say from the point of view of the 'subject' or person concerned. If we look at a sum or system of rights objectively, and regard it accordingly as an object projected outside ourselves or a fact confronting us, we think of it primarily as law; but we also think of it as apportioning both the rights which we ourselves own as persons and the consequent duties which we owe to others, as similar persons, in order that they may own similar rights.

Conversely, if we look at the same sum or system subjectively, and regard it accordingly as existing in us and ourselves as participating in it, we shall think of it primarily as rights; but we shall also think of these rights, with their consequent and correlative duties, as parts and portions of a sum or system which in the gross is law. If law is thus rights, and rights are thus law, a conclusion necessarily follows in regard to the functions of government. The function of the organs of government, in declaring and enforcing law, is also and equally a function of recognizing and guaranteeing the rights of persons. To declare and enforce law is also, and indeed is the same as, to recognize and guarantee rights. We are thus led once more to the conclusion that the function of governments is the service of rights.

There is a corollary to this conclusion. If we think in terms of ownership, we shall say (as indeed we have already done) that the members of a political community are the owners of rights. We may also say, in addition, that along with their rights, and as a consequence and a part of those rights, they own the services required by their rights, and are therefore the owners of the functions of government which serve and secure the actual enjoyment of the rights which they own. The question may then be asked, 'What do the governors own, in their capacity of governors?' Shall we say that they own authority—the authority of declaring, interpreting, and enforcing the law? It is impossible to use such language. The members of the governing organs (legislative, judicial, and executive) certainly exercise authority; but they do not own what they exercise. They exercise authority as the appointees, direct or indirect, of the community which owns it, and which owns it as a consequence and part of its general ownership of rights. Authority in the sense of a function of government (or rather the sum of its functions) is not something *owned* by governing persons, but something which they *owe*, in virtue of their appointment, as a mode of service of rights. We may therefore conclude that governing persons own nothing as such (though as members of the political community they own rights equally and in common with other members): they owe rather than own. They owe the exercise of the authority which is necessary for the secure enjoyment of the rights of persons: the owe the service, remunerated by pay or prestige or both, of declaring, interpreting, and enforcing the law which is the objective side of rights of persons; we may even say, if we look only at immediate sovereignty, that they owe the service of sovereignty, in the sense of declaring, in the last resort, what the law is and is henceforth to be. All authority, and all the function of government, including the function of immediate sovereignty, are services *owed* to rights.

CLASSIFICATION OF RIGHTS

If rights are thus prior to functions of government, we shall do well to enumerate and classify rights before we examine the functions of government and the methods of their operation. It has already been noticed that there are three principles, or procedural rules, which regulate the distribution of rights among the members of an organised community: the principle of Liberty, the principle of Equality, and the principle of Fraternity or Co-operation. They preside together, and in common, over the whole of the distribution of rights; but we may none the less regard each of the three as having a particular connection with a particular set or cluster of rights, and as regulating particularly the distribution of rights in that set or cluster. We may accordingly seek to classify rights under the three heads of Liberty, Equality, and Co-operation. In doing so we shall not only be concerned with the full legal rights which are already recognised and guaranteed by law: we shall also extend our view to include the nascent rights which are being convassed in the process of social thought, and which, as they become a part of the common conviction of the political community, and come to be formally endorsed by the organs of that community, are ultimately turned into legal rights in the full sense of the term. The reason for this extension of view is that it is necessary to an understanding of that growth of the functions of government which is a feature of our times. It is the growing-pains of rights which cause the growing labours of government. We may begin our classification under the head of Fraternity

We may begin our classification under the head of Fraternity or Co-operation, reserving to the end the rights which come under the head of Liberty. It has already been noticed that the French jurist Duguit, using the term 'solidarity' or 'mutuality' in lieu of the older term, enumerates three particular rights with which the principle of fraternity is particularly connected—the right of education, the right of public assistance, and the right of employment—and that on this basis he would impose corresponding duties on 'governing person' to provide these rights. The view of Duguit is suggestive, but it is also extreme. It is too narrowly economic—and too closely connected, at that, with a particular brand of economics—to offer any safe guidance. We shall do better to interpret fraternity in the sense of a general co-operation, which is not merely economic, but as wide as the general life of society; and on this basis we may proceed to argue, as indeed has already been argued. that there are two main rights which fall under this head, and two corresponding function of government. The essence of both of the rights is that men need, and ought to enjoy, a common or public equipment of services and resources, which goes beyond the equipment that individual effort and the effort of voluntary groups are able to provide, and which can be provided only by the common co-operation of all. We may regard this equipment as twofold, or as being both material and mental; and this is why we may hold that it issues in two different rights. The one is the right of persons to enjoy collectively a common or public equipment of *material* necessities unattainable except by the co-operation of all, and ranging from means of public transport and methods of public sanitation to schemes of national insurance and plans for the national development of national economic resources. The other right is a similar right of person to enjoy collectively a common or public equipment of what may be called *mental* necessities, ranging from schools and places of learning to galleries, museums, libraries, and the like, and thus including not only the facilities needed for public education but also those that are needed for the general national enjoyment of the accumulated treasures of culture.

Under the head of Equality the jurists and thinkers of France, basing themselves on the Declarations of 1789 and afterwards, have enumerated four rights—the right to be treated equally with others, and on the same footing as others, in the eye of the law and in all legislative acts; the right to be treated equally with others in matters of justice and in courts of law; the right to be treated equally with others in matters of taxation, so that each man pays the same proportion of his means as is paid by others; and, finally, the rights to be treated as equally admissible with others to public honours and offices of employment. These four rights are all rights of the citizen in respect of the exercise of governing authority: they are claims, acknowledged and recognised by law or general custom, that governing authority should deal equally with all, alike in its legislation and its jurisdiction, its imposition of taxes and its distribution of honours and offices. But the progress of social thought has given a wider sweep to the notion of equality and to the nature of the rights which it involves. We have learned to think not only of what may be called political equality in relation to the action of governing authority, but also of economic and cultural equality, in relation to the general life of the whole of the organised community; and we have accordingly come to believe that there are further which ought to be added to the rights of political equality. These further rights are still, as it were, in process of construction: they are emerging from social thought, and beginning to pass into the common conviction of the political community;

but the proper nature of their form, and the exact extent of their dimension, have still to be determined by the continuing process of social thought and by the method of tentative experiment. They are rights which men are beginning to claim, not in relation to governing authority and the distribution of its incidence, but in relation to one another: they are rights to a greater measure of general equality between man and man, partly in economic status and the distribution of economic possessions, and partly in educationl opportunity and enjoyment of the general treasures of culture. These new and nascent rights of equality are obviously linked with the similar rights which have already been suggested under the head of co-operation. The greater the provision of material and mental necessities in the form of a common or public equipment in which all alike can share, the greater will be the achievement of equality on both the material and the mental plane. But in addition to common and equal sharing in the stock of common or public equipment there is also needed a greater measure of equality in the enjoyment of individual status, in the possession of individual equipment (or 'private property'), and in the opportunity of individual access to the benefits of education and general cultural development.

The rights which came under the head of Liberty are all the greater, and the more numerous, because Liberty is a multiple principle. Within the State, and apart from the area of Society (which has also a social liberty of its own), there are, it has been suggested, three divisions are the political, the civil, and the economic. We may accordingly classify the rights which come under the head of Liberty according to these three divisions.

The rights of political liberty generally include the right of the citizen to participate in the election of the legislature, and thereby, indirectly, to share in the choice of the government. When the jury system exists, along with a system of unpaid magistrates drawn in large numbers from the general public, the rights of political liberty also include the right of the citizen to participate in the administration of justice and to form, in a sense, a part of the judicature. The right to form political parties, and the right of such parties, when formed, to play a part in the election of the legislature and thereby in the choice of the government, is a sort of border-land right, essentially connected with political liberty but formally a part of civil liberty and a product of the civil rights of freedom of the expression of opinion and freedom of association and meeting.

The rights of civil liberty have been divided by French thinkers into two different groups, distinguished from one another by the historical fact that the one group is earlier than the other. The first and earlier of these groups, already evident in the Declaration of 1789, includes the three rights of personal freedom, personal security, and personal or private property. The second group, gradually developed in the thought and expressed in the legislation of the century which followed the Revolution, includes some half-dozen rights; liberty in the choice and conditions of employment, and in the conduct of trade and industry; liberty of the press; liberty of assembly; liberty of association; liberty of teaching; and liberty of conscience and worship. This historical division of the rights of civil liberty into two different groups may square with the facts of French history, but it does not suit the history of England where no such distinction can be traced, and it cannot be generally applied. Abandoning, therefore, any chronological scheme of division, we may suggest a logical classification of the rights of civil liberty into three different groups, based on the nature and character of the activity concerned. The first group will consist of the rights which come under the head of freedom of physical activity; it will include rights such as personal security (whether from arbitrary arrest and detention, or from torture and inhuman punishment or from arbitrary interference with the privacy of home and domicile), and such, again, as freedom of movement and residence inside a country, along with the right to seek and enjoy an asylum in other countries. The second group will consist of rights which come under the head of freedom of the activity of the mind: this will include rights such as the right to freedom of conscience and religion, the right to freedom of opinion and its expression, and the rights to freedom of meeting and association. The third group will consist of rights which come under the head of freedom of practical activity, or, as we may also say, freedom for the exercise of will and choice in the general field of contractual action; this groups will include the right to the acquisition and disposal of property, the right to marry and found a family on the basis of full and free consent, and similar rights of that order. It may also be made to include a member of rights connected with the choice and conditions of employment and the conduct of trade and industry; but rights of this order, as has already been noted in an earlier part of the argument, are best treated as belonging to a separate class, and are most properly classified under the head of the rights of economic liberty.

The rights of economic liberty were already expressed in some detail in the part of the German Constitution of 1919 which dealt with 'Economic Life', and they have recently found their place in the Universal Declaration of Human Rights. If we seek to formulate them broadly, in terms of contemporary life and the growing demands of social thought, we may suggest that they fall into three main groups. We may regard them as extensions and expansions, into the economic sphere, of the old three rights of civil liberty already declared by Blackstone in England and by the revolutionary thinkers of France in the latter half of the eighteenth century—the right of personal freedom, the right of personal security, and the right of personal property. They are extensions and expansion entailed by the flood of economic development (often termed the 'industrial revolution', though the term is hardly adequate) which began to flow about 1750, and it still flowing swift and deep. The group of rights which is an extension of the old civil right of personal security includes the rights of workers under Factory Act (the first of the rights of economic liberty to be formally acknowledged), their rights under Workmen's Compensation Acts, and their rights, under various acts, to insurance against the risk of sickness and unemployment and age. The group of rights which may be regarded as an extension of the old civil right of personal freedom includes already the right of workers freely to form trade unions and to bargain freely through such unions about the conditions and remuneration of their work: it may also come to include the further right, now beginning to be claimed, to the enjoyment of the status of free partners in the general control and conduct of industry. Finally, the groups of rights which may be regarded, as an extension of the old civil right of personal property may be held to include the right of workers to some share in the capital of the particular industry in which they are engaged .This means their right to acquire, by virtue of the rendering of permanent service, some permanent property in the undertaking for which they work, over and above their weekly remuneration: it means, against, the right to participate in a diffusion of ownership which makes personal property as general in its scope as personal freedom or personal security.

This attempt at a classification of rights may seem to be little more than an academic exercise. But it is, as has already been noted, something more than that. It is the necessary preliminary to any study of the functions of government, which are services owed to rights and can only be understood in the light of the rights they serve. On the other hand, classification is also the creation of compartments; and the creation of compartments, if it may be a help to clear thinking, can also be a danger to the breadth and sweep of thought which not only apprehends but can also comprehend. For one thing we have to remember that the movement of human life does not proceed in compartments. The same general problem recurs, if in different forms, under the different heads of our classification. The future of industry and the development of a fair system of economic rights is at one and the same time a matter of the rights which come under the head of liberty, of those which come under the head of equality, and of those which come under the head of fraternity or co-operation. We cannot think of the problem properly in the limits of one compartment; and we are driven back, in the issue, on that general and comprehensive idea of justice which seeks to reconcile the principle of liberty with that of equality, and both with the principle of co-operation, and which thus controls and co-ordinates the rights belonging to each. There is another thing also to be remembered; or rather there is another aspect of the same general truth. No right is absolute and inviolable, or entrenched by itself in its own inexpugnable iron compartment. The right of personal property is indeed a right; but it is a right which has to make terms, and to enter into combination, with a variety of other rights. Not only has my right to acquire property, as a condition of the development of the capacities of my personality, to be reconciled with the right of others to acquire it, as a condition of the development of the capacities of their personality: the right of each person to such acquisition has also to be reconciled with other rights in other spheres, such as the right of workers to enjoy the status of free partners in the general conduct and control of industry, a right which cannot be simply defeated or abrogated by the right of the owner of property to the free used and disposal of his acquisitions. Once more we are driven back on the general idea of justice by which one sort of right is 'mortised and adjoined' to another.

STRUCTURE OF GOVERNMENT

'Everyone has the right to take part in the government of his country.' The origin and basis of this right have already been suggested at a previous stage of the argument. We saw, at that stage, that discussion is the necessary and vital process of the life of an organised community, and that each and every member is entitled to contribute to this process. To be entitled to contribute to discussion is the same thing as to have 'the right to take part in the government'; for the process of political discussion is the essential activity of government in a politically organised community. The process of political discussion has evolved, in the course of time, a number of organs for its operation. These organs, distinct and yet connected, form a successive series, in which, as in a relay race, each of them hands to another the task of 'carrying on' from the point which it has reached itself. We may distinguish four of these organs, and proceed to trace their connection.

The first of the organs of political discussion is party. Party, as we have already seen, is a social formation which also discharges a political function and has thus, as it were, one foot in Society and one in the State.. Each party is a voluntary association; but each party also formulates a political programme for the consideration and choice of the political electorate, and each party submits to the vote of that electorate candidates for election to parliament who offer themselves as symbols and exponents of its programme. At the first stage or lap in the process of discussion each party discusses in its own counsels the programme which it proposes to formulate; and each, when the programme is formulated, proceeds to discuss and debate it in public, before an attentive electorate, with the other party or parties.

The turn then comes for the second organ, the political electorate. That too is an organ of discussion, at any rate in periods of election (which is not to say that it is dead, or ceases to think and interrogate, in the intervals between such periods); it canvasses and considers the programmes, and examines and cross-examines the candidates, submitted to it for choice; and when it has made its choice, it hands over the further conduct of discussion to the representatives whom it has chosen, trusting them to carry it into far greater detail, and to carry it on with a far greater degree of continuity, than it can possibly do itself.

The third organ then succeeds in its turn to the same double task—the task of conducting discussion itself, and the task of preparing the way for further and later discussion. This organ is the representative body; the core and centre of the whole system of representative democracy; the Parliament which, as its very name indicates, is peculiarly engaged in the activity of 'parley' and constant discussion. But the function of Parliament, like that of the electorate, is a twofold function. It is not only an organ of discussion itself, engaged in a process of constant debate intended to translate a general programme into legislative enactments: it also helps to create, and it continually serves to support, a government which it expects and trusts to carry discussion into even greater detail, and to conduct it even more continuously and intimately, than it is able to do itself.

We thus come to the fourth and last organ in the successive series; the responsible government or cabinet, which is the organ of government *par excellence* (though also, and at the same time, only *one* of a number of organs of government in the wider sense of the word), and which is therefore commonly called '*the* Government'. This government is 'responsible' in the sense that it must necessarily command the support of the representative body from which its members are drawn; but it may also be said to be responsible in another and even deeper sense. It is responsible for carrying the process of discussion to that crucial and final point at which it issues in decision. A responsible government, organised under its head is at once the innermost core of discussion and the originating motor of action. Not that the decision at which it arrives, and the impulse which it accordingly gives, is necessarily final or absolutely conclusive. The decision, on any grave issue, will flow back, as it were, to the representative body for approval and confirmation; it may even flow back to the electorate, either for informal approval by what we call public opinion, or even for formal approval by an electoral vote in a general election at which a proposed decision is made the main or a dominant issue. The process of discussion may thus return on itself; and after flowing from the electorate to the representative body, and from that to the responsible government, it may in turn flow back from the government to the representatives, and then from them to the electors.

There is thus a general system of discussion which operates through a number of organs. The difficulty of this system is to reconcile two necessities: the necessity, on the one hands, that each organ should concentrate on its work with a free vigour and a fresh impetus, as if everything hung upon the conclusion at which it arrives; and the necessity, on the other, that each of the organs should also keep in touch and harmony with the rest acknowledging that they too, as organs of the same general process, have the right and duty to do *their* work, in their place and at their time, and that their right and duty must always be respected. The peril of the system is that one or the other of the organs concerned should lay an exclusive emphasis on the first of these necessities, and arrogate to itself an exclusive and predominant importance. If that is done, the results will in any case be unhappy, because they will necessarily involve a disturbance of the whole system; but they will vary according to the nature of the organ on which an exclusive emphasis is laid as being the organ of discussion *par excellence* and therefore the dominant organ. If it is the organ of party which asserts its predominance, you may have the open tyranny of a single party (whether of the Right or the Left), or the secret tyranny of a cabal which unites the leaders of several parties in an interested coalition and controls behind the scenes both the representative body and the nominal government. If, on the other hand, it is the representative organ which is particularly conscious of its own importance, you may have a parliamentary autocracy, with the enthroned deputies installing and evicting governments as the when they think fit. The system of political discussion is a delicate as well as a difficult system. To remembers, and to seek to observe, the two necessities which it imposes is to face the problem of doing simultaneously two different things which seem almost contradictory: on the one hand, leaving each organ free to act with an original vigour to the full stretch of its capacity; on the other hand, keeping each organ within the limits of its capacity (so that, in the Platonic phrase, it 'does its own business' and no more than its business), and thus keeping all the organs in harmony and co-operation. This is the general problem of representative democracy; and there is no way of avoiding the problem—except by substituting the dictatorship of one organ for a system of discussion divided among several. To do that is to abolish discussion, at any rate as a general process in which all, at some stage, have the right to participate. (There may be left some fragment or simulacrum of discussion within the organ which holds the dictatorship; not that a fragment or simulacrum is anything more than a travesty.) But if discussion be the vital process of the life of any organised community, to abolish discussion is suicide and the end of the common life.

Representative democracy, considered as a system for giving effect to the rights of political liberty, is often defined as a system of government by all, or of government by the people. It *is* that; and yet it is something more than that. The right of everyone to take part in the government of his country is not a simple matter of all men saying, as a single aggregate, what is their will and whats is object of their volition. On the contrary it is a complex matter of all discussing, through a variety of organs which are necessary for the purpose of full and thorough discussion, what is their thought, what is the content of their common conviction, what is the idea which they consider rights and ripe for realisation. Ideas have quality in them, as well as quantity behind them; and while the quantity of wills assembled behind an idea matters, and matters greatly, the quality or value in an idea is also something that matters, and matters at least as much. That is a reason, a fundamental reason, for the time and the pains which we spend on the process of discussion, (It is not the only reason; for we also exercise and breathe our minds, and develop the capacities of our personality, in the course of the process.) We want to get at the quality and value of the ideas presented to us, and we cannot do that without taking discussion through stage after stage, sifting and sifting at each new stage. The courts of law and the methods of justice offer an analogy: there, too, 'the rights of the matter', which are the object of search, are sifted and clarified by a process of inquiry which rises from instance to instance by a progressive refinement. The short cut of an immediate decision is tempting; but the only sure way of arriving is the way of successive stages. The electorate is one sage; but it is only a stage, and a general election is neither the beginning nor the end of the matter. Government by all, in its true and full sense, takes time: it is not only a matter of the voting of all the electors: It is also, and even more, a matter of the deliberation of all the organs concerned and involved in the process of mature and considered decision.

RIGHTS OF CIVIL AND ECONOMIC LIBERTY

We have seen how the rights of political liberty affect the structure of government, and how they issue in 'government by all' in the sense which has just been defined. We have now to see how the structure of government, when it is true to the rights of political liberty, affects in its turn the rights of civil and economic liberty. We have, in a word, to see what manner of fruits it produces: we have to inquire whether 'government by all" will not in its nature be 'government for all'.

It has already been argued that government by all has an intrinsic value, and is, of itself and in itself, something which is for the benefit of all and makes for the common good of all. Considered simply as a process, and apart from any results or product outside the process, it is a way of the development of the capacities of personality. But it has also an extrinsic value; it is also valuable for the results which it produces, and for the new rights—other than those of political liberty, and over and above them—which are added by its operation to the common fund of enjoyment. If we look at the matter historically, we are led at once to the conclusion that during the days of struggle men pressed for the political right of government by the people not as an end in itself, or not only as an end in itself, but because they wished to secure for themselves and their fellows, by the exercise of this right, the enjoyment of other rights hitherto denied, or at any rate confined to the few. The Chartists, for example, were vehement in urging the justice of their six political points; but the ultimate aims of their endeavour were economic aims. If that was true in the days of struggle, it is also true, as experience shows, that the actual achievement of political rights raises at once in the days of attainment two questions of economic rights: the question, first, of the economic rights which ought to follow on political rights by the logic of consistency, in order to secure more liberty for the worker in the course of his work and thus make the economic system correspond better with the political; and, secondly, the question of the economic rights which will inevitably and in any case follow on the acquisition of political rights by the simple logic of facts, or, in other words, as a result of the fact that the mass of the people now have the vote and will tend to use it in order to secure economic rights which they regard as the necessary conditions of economic liberty.

It follows then, alike by the logic of consistency and by the logic of fact, that an extension of the rights of political liberty must involve a similar extension of the rights of economic liberty. When the structure of government is altered, by the extension of political rights, the altered structure of government will alter in turn the economic structure, and it will do so by means of the extension of economic rights. This extension of rights will take two forms. One of these forms is the extension to all of old rights, already recognised as belonging to the members of a section of the community, but not hitherto recognized as belonging to the members of the community as a whole, irrespective of section or class. The other form is a still further extension by the recognition of new rights, not hitherto recognized at all, and their general distribution to all the members of the community. In brief, we have both an extension of the number of those among whom rights are distributed and an extension of the number of the rights distributed.

For the present we may confine ourselves to the extension of the number of those among whom rights are distributed. That rights are for all, and not merely for the members of a single section, is a simple proposition which now seems self-evident; but the actual extension to all even of old and long-recognized rights have been a slow historical process. The width of vision which sees that 'a man is a man for all that', whatever the rank and the guinea's stamp, is a slow historical acquisition. There was long a defect of vision, honest and genuine in its own day, which made men as it were near-sighted, and prevented them from seeing beyond a small and limited circle. Privileged classes, accepting the idea of the general social necessity of different social functions arranged in an ordered hierarchy of ascending degrees or stations, proceeded from that idea to a firm conviction that the masses were confined by the nature of their functions—as ploughmen and artificers—to the one office of manual work, and were not intended, and indeed were not fit, either for the political right of the suffrage or for the civil and economic rights (full personal security, full personal freedom of movement, and the full ownership of personal property) which they themselves enjoyed. We may almost say that they naturally thought in terms of 'two nations', or even of two grades of humanity and two classes of human beings. Three movements of thought, two of them belonging to the eighteenth century and the third emerging in the course of the nineteenth, have radically altered these terms.

The first is the movement of humanitarianism, mainly based (at any rate in England) on the foundation of the Christian Gospel, and inspired by a fervent conviction that the benefits of the Gospel belonged to all and must be extended to all—to the slave, the prisoner, the factory-worker, and whoever else needed the comfort of a recognition of his common humanity and his common human rights. Whether this Christian humanitarianism were Evangelical or Catholic, whether it proceeded from the Low Church or the High, it changed and widened men's view of the distribution of rights, and altered the narrow terms in which they had hitherto thought. The other two movements which have worked in the same direction, however different they may be both from Christian humanitarianism and from one another, are the Benthamite utilitarianism which emerged at the end of the eighteenth century and the Marxian socialism which began to grow from the middle of the nineteenth. The Benthamites, going on the principle of the greatest happiness of the greatest number, and holding that all were capable of happiness of the greatest number, and holding that all were capable of happiness and had therefore the right to enjoy it, attacked the limitation of this universal right by the sinister interests of a privileged few, and advocated a structure of government under which all alike had a voice and a vote and the majority could use their voice and their vote to counteract sinister interests and to enthrone general happiness. The Marxians, going on the assumption (not altogether unwarranted by the history of the past) that the existing structure of government was based on the domination of a small and interested social class, which made law to suit its own interest and thus limited right to its own members, urged that the largest and the most numerous social class, the class of the workers, should acquire domination in its turn, and should then extend and generalize rights by instituting a workers' State in which all would be workers and all would enjoy the common rights belonging to workers. There is an obvious difference between the Benthamites and the Marxians. The Benthamites laid their primary emphasis on the rights of political liberty: They held that the extension of the suffrage was the key to a greater enjoyment of happiness by a greater number of individuals: they expected a peaceable extension of the rights of civil and economic liberty, following easily and naturally on a similar extension of the right of political liberty. The Marxians were primarily concerned with economic liberty: they held that its attainment demanded effort, and even violence: they respected less the rights of individuals than the rights and the status of a whole class. But great as is the difference between Benthamism and Marxianism, the effects of both have been so far similar, that both have tended towards the extension of rights to all, and both have helped to abolish the old assumption of a graded society marked by a graded enjoyment of rights.

RIGHTS AND FUNCTIONS OF GOVERNMENT

The argument has hitherto turned on the extension of existing right to a greater number of persons. We many now turn to consider the extension of the number of rights, or in other words the creation and the general allocation of new and added rights, particularly in the sphere of economic liberty. The distinction between the two modes of extension is perhaps verbal rather than real. Actually the extension of rights to a greater number of persons is, *for them,* the creation of new and added rights. Actually, again, the creation of new and added rights is not so much a matter of the creation of something new as of the broader and more liberal interpretation of something old. The new and added rights in the sphere of economic liberty are really new and extended versions of old and recognized rights in the sphere of civil liberty—the right to personal security, the right to personal freedom, and the right to personal property.

We may begin with the extension of the right to personal security. That right had been recognized, however imperfectly, since the end of the sixteenth century, under the old system of poor relief: and a new recognition was added, from the beginning of nineteenth century, under the system of factory legislation . Still another recognition has been added in the course of the present century, under the system of joint or social insurance. There are thus three stages of recognition (first the poor law, then factory legislation, and then social insurance); but they are all stages of a continuous process, and though we may cherish a vivid sense of the value of the third stage, and associate it particularly with a conception of the 'welfare' State, we have to remember that it is part of a process, and that the whole process has been inspired by the one fundamental idea of the right of personal security. It has become customary to apply the term 'social services' to the developments of this third stage.

But services are secondary and consequential things, entailed by the primary fact of rights, which are the cause and source of all services; and we shall do well to begin any study of the nature of these developments not from the services in which they end, but from the rights in which they begin. From this point of view we may say that our century has been marked by anew and more social interpretation of the right of personal security. This new and more social interpretation has led us to regard the right of personal security as including (1) the right of the worker to be protected against the risks of sickness, unemployment, and age; (2) his right to be so protected by a method of joint or social insurance (producing a joint or social security, and thus broadening and strengthening personal security), under which he is linked with his employer in a partnership of contribution to the cost, and both are linked again in a similar partnership with the State; (3) his right to enjoy the necessary services of government, loosely called 'social services', which the method of social insurance demands. The general result is an extension of the rights of economic liberty under the head and rubric of the right to personal security. But it is also at the same time—necessarily, because an extension of rights is also an extension of services—an increase of the functions of government and an extension of governing authority.

The two results go together: they are indissolubly connected. It is here that we may possibly find a limit, or a principle of limit, to the extension of our rights to the enjoyment of personal security. There is always a cost involved; and its is wise to count the cost in advance. The cost is partly financial, or a simple matter of money: it is partly also spiritual, or a more serious matter of control. The financial cost is that involved in the payment of contributions by the worker, the employer, and the general taxpayer, to meet the expenses of a system of joint or social insurance. The spiritual cost is that involved in the extension of the area of compulsory uniformity and administrative control. The double cost may be well worth the while: what is certain is that it must always be paid. The extension of our rights to the enjoyment of personal security is thus subject to a double proviso: the proviso that the members of the community are ready and able to pay the cost of the benefits which they receive; and the proviso that they are willing to accept the extension of the functions of government, and the increase of administrative control, which are also the price of their receipt of benefits. In a word, new rights are new commodities which, like other commodities have their price, and, like other commodities, must be bought. The commodity bought may be well worth the price; and the liberty gained by the greater enjoyment of personal security may be greater far than the liberty surrendered by the increased acceptance of administrative control. The fact remains that it is always wise to count the cost. Rights are not to be had for the asking, or as a matter of pure gift. There is always a sense in which they are bought; and they are only sure when they are fairly bought by an honest bargain.

We may now turn from considering the extension of the right to personal security, and proceed to consider the extension of the right to personal freedom and the right to personal property —two rights which in their nature are closely interconnected, and which come into question together as soon as we seek to examine the further and fuller extension of economic liberty. The extension of the right to personal security still leaves us with something which may be called *passive;* for though the new system of social security, attained by the method of social insurance, demands the contribution and co-operation of all, workers as well as others, it remains none the less, in its essential nature, a protective system of shelter in which the worker can find a refuge from the risks and chances of the economic process. The question then arises whether there is not also needed some thing which may be called *active*: some system of participation or partnership under which all workers can actively share in the conduct and management of the economic process; some extension of the right of personal freedom, and also of the right of personal property, which will give them a voice and a stake in the undertaking in which they serve. We have already seen that there are two general reasons for answering that question in the affirmative. The first is that you cannot well have, in the same community and at the same time, two separate worlds, one of political democracy and the other of economic autocracy. The second is that, if we assume the general principle that the ultimate purpose of all institutions is the greatest development of the capacities of personality in the greatest number of persons, we are bound to conclude that there must be room for such development in the working of the system of economic institutions which occupies so many hours of the daily life of so many persons, even though the immediate purpose of that system is simply the purpose of producing the maximum of material necessities at the minimum of cost. We may therefore admit, on these two grounds, that there is a presumption in favour of active economic rights; and we are then confronted by the question, 'What is the method, or methods, by which such rights may be secured and guaranteed to all the workers engaged in the general business of production?'

One method which has long been advocated, and partly put into practice, is the method of nationalisation. This means, in effect, that the capital resources of some particular branch of production are taken over by the State, and that the business of production, in that branch, is thenceforth handled, directly or indirectly, by the State which owns the resources. Such a method eliminates, in any range in which it is applied, the right of personal property in capital resources; and it eliminates, along with that right, such elements of value (initiative, variety, and personal responsibility) as are involved in its exercise. That is the price to be paid. On the other hand there may be argued to be corresponding gains which are even greater than the price. In the first place the nationalisation of capital resources makes each worker, in his capacity of a member of the nation, an owner of capital resources, vested as such with a right of property which he did not hitherto enjoy. In the second place it makes each worker, again in his capacity of a member of the nation, an active agent in the conduct of the business of production: indeed, it may even do more, and if there is devolution of the conduct of the business of production on the workers and technicians of each particular nationalized branch, it may make each worker an active agent in his capacity of a member of that particular branch. But it may also be argued that these gains are not so great as they seem to be, and are illusory rather than real. In the matter of ownership, or, more exactly, in the matter of a new and larger enjoyment of the right of property, we have to notice that the ownership is collective, and the right of property enjoyed is not a personal right vested in an individual person. The extension of collective ownership is *not* an extension of the right of personal property: it makes each man not an owner, but (in a State of fifty million members) a fifty-millionth part of an owner. Again in the matter of status, or the new enjoyment of the right of personal freedom arising from the new position of being an active agent in the conduct of production, we have equally to notice that the status is collective, and that the activity of each agent in the conduct of production is merely a fractional activity. When the business of production in the whole of a particular branch is undertaken by the State, directly or indirectly, through the length and breadth of the country, the scale of the undertaking is so vast that the personal activity of the individual worker in the conduct of business is necessarily infinitesimal; and experience appears to suggest that the result is a central mechanism, ponderous and impersonal, in which there is less play for the personality of the worker than there is in a smaller undertaking, even under the system of private ownership of capital. It may thus be argued that the method of nationalisation does not attain the end which alone can justify the means—the end of extending personal and individual enjoyment of rights, and thereby extending the area of the development of the capacities of individual personality.

We may therefore turn to inquire whether another and different method would not be better calculated to promote the attainment of this end. We may begin by assuming the existence, and the continuing right to exist, of personal property in capital resources vested in individual owners. That right, it is true, is not an absolute right of the *Noli me tangere* order. On the contrary, it is relative right (as rights in general are) which has to be properly adjusted to the rights of other persons the problem before us is accordingly a problem of the proper adjustment of the right of the capitalist to those other rights. The right of the owner of capital resources, if it is not an absolute right, is grounded on something more than the mere prescription of continuous possession in the previous course of history. In other words, it is something more than a mere historical right which can only plead the fact that it has been in favour of the claim that it should continue to be. The right of the owner of capital resources is grounded on permanent titles, which belong to the present and the future as well as to the past, and consist in the social and moral advantages which accrue from the possession and exercise of the right. These advantages are various; but they may be classified summarily under three heads. In the first place, the right of the individual owner of capital resources is favourable to the play of personal initiative. It encourages responsibility for taking a personal decision, immediately and directly, at the point where the problem arises; it prevents decision from being centralized in one focus, and therefore mechanized; it remits it to, or distributes it among, a number of separate and living centres, thus following a biological rather than a mechanical pattern. In the second place, the right of individual ownership of capital resources is favourable to variety of experiment and to the method of trial and error. It encourages competition between undertaking and undertaking, and serves, by encouraging such competition, to raise the level of all and to improve the service of each; so that here again it may be said in a metaphor, and in no ignoble sense, to follow a biological pattern. Finally, the right of individual ownership of capital resources, as we have already had reason to notice, is connected with and favourable to that *nisus* toward the development of the capacities of personality which is an essential element of our nature: it provides a way in which we try ourselves out, and become conscious of our capacities by seeing them externally expressed in results. It is easy to exaggerate the importance of such external expression, and to forget that the development of capacity, even if it is encouraged by being expressed in external results, matters infinitely more than any result by which it may be encouraged. But results matter none the less; and men do more, and develop more, when they are moved to action by the incentive of visible results.

We may therefore hold, on the ground of these various advantages, that individual ownership of capital resources has a continuing social and moral title over and above the title of prescription and vested interest. But there is another side to the matter, and it is a side which is still more important. Uncriticised and unadjusted, the right of the owner of capital resources at once does harm to *him* and depresses the workers whom he employs. It does harm to him, in so far as it gives him a power over the lives of others which corrupts; or tends to corrupt, the possessor, as uncriticised power always does: it does harm to him again, in so far as it makes him, or tends to make him, a member of a privileged and almost parasitic class, enjoying results which may not be the results of personal capacity or of personal effort, but of mere inheritance or of pure chance.

Just as it does harm to the owner, so too an uncriticized and unadjusted right of private ownership of capital resources also depresses the worker. It depresses him to the almost servile status of a 'hand' (or, in Aristotle's phrase, 'a living tool') in the undertaking for which he works. It depresses him also to a 'property less being', with no share in the right of personal property, when by the same title of effort and output of personal capacity which the capitalist pleads he too should have his share in the capital of his undertaking. It follows that both in the interest of the capitalist and in that of the worker the State is forced to undertake the function of adjusting and reconciling the right of the owner of capital resources to the workers' rights of personal freedom of status and the enjoyment of personal property. This is a matter, once more, of the general task of the State: the task of achieving a right order of human relations and thereby realizing the reign of justice, by adjusting the rights of one set its members to the rights of another. Hence the particular task is that of adjusting the old rights of the owners of capital resources, long recognized in positive law, to the worker's new rights, or more exactly his new claims to rights, which are now being recognized in social thought and are moving forwards to the further stage of legal recognition.

The method by which the State will seek to perform this task, if it remains true to its own proper nature and continues to follow the line of action which it has hitherto followed, will not be the method of 'Nationalisation,' but the method of 'supervision'. It will not assume the new form of the socialist State, annexing the means and administering the business of general production: it will keep its old form of the supervisory State, still watching and easing the play of rights, as it has always done, but extending the range of its vision and increasing its work of adjustment. Recognizing the right of individuals who are owners of capital resources as a necessary part of the process of production, it will at the same time supervise the whole of the process of production with a view to coordinating this right, belonging to these individuals, with the other rights of other individuals which are also a necessary part of the process. It will see with the eye of its vision individual persons and personal rights, and it will think in terms of such persons and rights; but at the same time it will 'over-see' them and think them over together (which is the true sense of 'supervision'), and it will seek to adjust them accordingly. If we can imagine the State engaged in reflection, and expressing its reflections in speech, it might address itself and its members in words such as these:

'I am by my nature, and I must remain if I am to be true to my nature, a legal association. As such, I am not an agent of production, except where the principle of co-operation compels me to produce some system of public or common equipment (a postal system, or a system of fuel and power, or a transport system) which is needed by all and must be provided by the co-operation of all; but even here I think it best, as a general rule, to delegate the actual work of management to some economic body or board which will manage it simply and separately as a pure matter of business, and thus prevent it from being entangled in my own legal machinery. On the other hand, if I am not an agent of production, I am by my nature the supervisor of the whole process of production; and though it is not my business to manage the work of production, it certainly is my business to lay down the general rules to which such management must conform. That is the line of action which I have long been following. It is now a century and a half since I began to lay down the rules of factory legislation, in order to protect the right of every factory worker to the enjoyment of personal security. My rules have grown and grown. They are based on my two great principles of liberty and equality: they are intended to protect and secure the rights which are involved in the application of those principles; and as the social interpretation of those principles grows, my rules must continue to grow in order to keep in step with that interpretation. Today the interpretation of these principles is beginning to demand from me an adjustment of the right of the owner of capital to the double right of the worker: his right to enjoy a status of personal freedom, by virtue of being treated not as an instrument but as a collaborator; and his further right to enjoy the permanent possession of some personal property, by virtue of being made a partner or 'share-holder' in the ownership of capital. The beginnings of that adjustment have already been made in the course of the last fifty years; I started, for example, as long ago as 1909, as system of trade Boards which gave to workers in unorganized industries an active right of helping to fix the rate of their wages, and thus enabled them to enjoy a status of greater personal freedom. Much has been done since 1909; but there is more to be done in order to improve the status of the worker, and far more to be done in order to increase the diffusion of ownership. It is all a matter for tentative experiment and progressive movement from stage to stage. It is matter of keeping a constant watch on the whole of the process of production: a matter of noting emergent claims for new rights, and how they affect and impinge on the existing scheme of rights; a matter of observing the tentative efforts made by the parties concerned to secure some form of voluntary adjustment between new claims and old rights, until finally, at the end of the watch and the noting and the observing, the time comes for my making of a uniform rule of compulsory adjustment, in the light of all the data collected and all the experience gained. If this is the way in which I act, I shall be acting strictly within my sphere as a legal association: I shall be simply adjusting one right to another—the right of the owner of capital resources to the workers' rights both of status and property—as it always is my duty to adjust rights and to serve thereby as the organ of justice.'

There is a gloss or corollary which follows naturally on this view of the economic function of the State. Whatever the State may do in the way of securing an involuntary adjustment of rights by the method of legal compulsion and in the form of statutory rules, there also exists, and there will always exist, the way of voluntary adjustment by the method of spontaneous agreement between the parties concerned. This way of voluntary adjustment has had a long if chequered history. It has meant the formation of associations of workers, trade by trade: it has meant the long struggle of these associations or trade unions, for recognition and for the right of bargaining and making agreements with the similar associations formed by employers. At first thwarted by the State, and repressed by Combination Acts, but afterwards recognized and even encouraged, these associations have gradually established themselves as permanent social organs, seeking to achieve by social methods a social accommodation between conflicting claims. In themselves, and by the mere fact of their existence and action, they have already given the worker a new and added enjoyment of freedom of personal status which he derives from their collective strength. They have their defects as well as their qualities. The collective strength which can give to the worker a new enjoyment of personal freedom can also be used to insist that each worker shall merge himself and his personality in the collective mass; and the adhesion of these associations of workers, in the mass and in their collective capacity, to a particular political party wedded to policies of nationalisation, has had the disadvantage, whatever its gains may have been of distracting them from that policy of the voluntary social adjustment of rights which belongs to their essential nature, and of turning their attention to the method of compulsory legal regulation through the agency of the State. Yet these may not be the permanent trends; and its is possible to hope, as has already been suggested, that the future may have in store no only negotiation and voluntary adjustment between the associated workers and the associated employers in each industry, but also negotiation and voluntary adjustment, in some form of voluntary 'social parliament', between representatives of the whole body of associated workers and the whole body of associated employers over the whole of the field of production.

This is not to say that the State will tend to become less active in its own work of legal adjustment by general rules. On the contrary it may well become even more active. A country which follows simultaneously the two ways of adjustment between conflicting claims of right—the way of voluntary adjustment by social agreement, and the way of legal adjustment by means of general rules—may become increasingly busy in pursuing *both* of these ways. True, the State will normally wait for the exploration of the way of self-help and voluntary social agreement before it begins to follow the way of public help and legal adjustment. True, again, the State, when it follows that way, will often, and perhaps even mainly, find itself concerned with generalizing, and making compulsory for all, what has already been tried and has already approved itself experimentally in the field of self-help and voluntary social agreement. But that only goes to prove that an increase of activity and experimentation in the social field, far from discouraging, will tend to encourage and foster an increase of activity in the legal field and the area of State-adjustment. The busier the effort of voluntary adjustment the greater will be the amount of material and the volume of suggestion on which the State can act.

The general method of advance which emerges from these considerations is a method which may be called by the name of 'experimentalism'. It is a method which begins with the ventilation of new claims to rights in the field of social thought and the forum of social discussion; with the pitting of these new claims against the old rights which they challenge; and with the demand for an adjustment between the old and the new. It is a method which then proceeds to the stage of social and voluntary adjustment, along a variety of lines and by a variety of experiments which tentatively compete with one another, and are tentatively pitted against one another, in the course of a process of social selection. It is a method which finally arrives at the stage of a legal and general adjustment, ultimately achieved by the State (through the action of its various organs of political discussion), as it works on the data before it and selects for endorsement and registration the solution which commands the adherence of general or common conviction. The whole method is a dialectical method, though it is far from being the method of 'dialectical materialism' "it also is a method which has in its favour biological analogy, though it is far from being a method of natural selection of the fittest, and may rather be called a method of spiritual selection of the best—so far as the spirit of man is able to discover the best. If we call it by the name of experimentalism, which is only a shorthand name with the necessary defects of shorthand, we may plead that we mean by that name the process of gradually feeling a way, through time, be means of discussion, with the aid of the method of trial and error.

This experimentalism, if it may be so called, is something different from 'gradualism.' Gradualism means that you start from, and stick to, a preconceived plan, though you move slowly and with a Fabian cunctation towards its achievement. Experimentalism means that you start from the postulate of the sanctity of human rights—but also from the postulate of the constant growth of new rights (or the constant reinterpretation and extension of old rights) and the consequent need of adjustment between the new and the old—and that you are always seeking to discover, by fresh thought and experiment as you come to each new problem in each new generation, how you can meet the demands of your double postulate. But just as experimentalism is not gradualism, so neither is it opportunism; and just as it is not a plan or 'blue-print,' inherited from some past prophet, for the methodical shaping of the future, so neither is it a matter of immediate and extemporized expedients intended merely to meet an immediate contingency. Its essence is indeed the freedom of the present to shape and determine itself by its own motion, in the light of the situation immediately presented for decision. But it is also the essence of experimentalism that the situation so presented has itself been prepared by thought, experiment, and debate, and is thus, as it were, a 'planned situation', which as such suggests and invites a planned and deliberate decision. There is thus, after all, a plan in the method of experimentalism. But the plan is not a transcendent scheme, preconceived before the beginning of action: it is immanent in the process of action, and conceived by and during that process. To proceed by experiment is to proceed by constant planning, but not to proceed 'according to plan'.

GOVERNMENT ORGANS

The word 'function', in its political application, may be said to have two senses. It has the sense of purpose or aim, as when we say that the function of government is the maintenance of a scheme of law, or the service of rights, or some other such purpose or aim. It has also the sense of a particular mode of action, or a special kind of activity by means of which a government seeks to fulfil its general purpose; and from this point of view we speak of the legislative, the judicial, and the executive function.

In the first of these senses, that of purpose, the course of the argument has led to the conclusion that the fundamental function of government is that of the service of Right. If we look at Right as 'objective', and as expressed in the external form of a body of general rules, we shall say that it is the function of government to render service to Right by translating social thought about the right order of human relations into a system of recognized and enforced law. If we look at Right as 'subjective', and as expressed in the form of rights which belong to persons or 'subjects' as their shares in objective Right, we shall say that it is the function of government to render service to rights by adjusting them to one another and removing obstacles to their enjoyment. In either case, and whether we regard the function of government as the service of Right or the service of rights, we shall say that the function of government is limited; limited by, and to, service, which it cannot transcend, a service which is the cause of its existence and the justification of all its action. On the other hand, justification of all its action. On the other hand, just because it is service, and limited to being service, the function of government is also constantly growing. Since social thought about the right order of human relations is growing thought; since, in consequence of that growth, the system of Right and the rights of persons necessarily grow; since, in consequence of *that* growth, the service owed by government to securing the enjoyment of rights also necessarily grows; it follows that the function of government, even while it is limited to service, must be a growing function. All that has hitherto been said, in the previous course of the argument, about the extension of rights of persons involves a consequent and connected extension of the function of government.

Turning now to the second of the senses of the word 'function' in its political application, the sense of a mode of action or a kind of activity, we may begin by laying it down that there is always one great and general mode of action which government is bound to follow. It is the mode of proceeding by general rules of declared law backed by enforcement. Here again we may notice in passing that government is limited; limited by its general mode of action as well as by its general purpose; limited to acting by the one method of enforceable general rules, and limited therefore to acting in that sphere of acts of external conduct in which alone it is possible to enforce a general rule to means of an act of external compulsion. But within this great and general mode of action, to which government is limited, and by which it is limited, we may now proceed to distinguish particular modes of action, or special kinds of activity. They are commonly held to be three: the legislative, the judicial, and the executive. At this point, however, there emerges something of a confusion of terms. Sometimes the three are described as 'functions'; sometimes they are described as 'powers' (*pouvoirs)*; sometimes they are regarded and described as 'organs'. Before we attempt to consider them, or to discuss in what sense and to what extent they are or ought to be separate, and in what sense and to what extent, they merge or should merge into one another, we shall do well to clarify our terms. What do we mean when we speak of the legislative, the judicial, and the executive, and what is the noun we imply when we use these adjectives?

We may identify, for our purposes, the term 'function' and the term 'power'. A mode of acting, which is the specific sense of 'function', nothing very different from a faculty of acting, which is the specific sense of 'power'. But we must distinguish both of these terms from the term 'organ'. A function or power, such as vision, is one thing: an organ, such as the eye, is another. On this basis we may proceed to argue that while we may sometimes, or even generally, use one organ for one function and one function only, yet there is nothing to prevent us from using one organ for a number of functions, provided that it can perform them, and provided again that they are best performed by being held together and interconnected in that one organ. This may seem to be an abstract and even irrelevant argument. In fact it has a definite and practical bearing on the political doctrine and practice which goes by the name of 'separation of powers' (*la separation des pouvoirs).* This was a doctrine expounded by Montesquieu: it was also an axiom incorporated in the French Declaration of Rights of 1789, which lays it down that 'a society in which the separation of powers is not fixed has no constitution'. But what is this 'separation of powers'? Does it only mean and involve a distinction of *modes* of action, and it that its essence? Or does it also mean and involve a distinction of *organs* of action; and, if so, is each of the different organs confined and limited to one mode of action, so that none of them can possibly act except in a single mode, and each of them is entirely debarred from acting in the mode or entering the province of the others?

Separation of powers must certainly mean a distinction of modes of action. There is a mode of action for legislation, which is distinctive mode with its own technique; a mode at once deliberate and deliberative; a mode which proceeds slowly and proceeds by debate, with 'reading' succeeding to 'reading' and one chamber succeeding to another. There is a mode of action for jurisdiction, which again is a distinctive mode, with its own peculiar technique and its own particular rules of procedure; a mode which is critical rather than deliberative; a mode which mainly depends on a critical appreciation of the relevant rules of law, a critical sifting of evidence, and a critical weighing of the arguments tendered by the rival advocates. Finally there is the executive mode, which is similarly a distinctive mode; a mode which proceeds with rapidity (at any rate in comparison with both the legislative and the judicial mode), and proceeds by way of decision and instructions intended to follow out (*exsequi*) and give effect to the results of the legislative and judicial modes. This distinction of modes is clear; and whether each mode has its own separate and special organ, assigned to it and confined to it, or whether there is less separation of the organs and less confining of each to a single mode, the distinction of modes remains. The legislative mode, with its separate technique, is one thing: the judicial is another: the executive another still. But even if there is thus plurality of modes, there is also, we have to remember, a great and general mode of action which is common to the whole of government, and which blends the different modes in a unity of operation. Whatever the government does, and in whatever particular mode it acts, it always follows the general mode of acting by general rules of law formally declared and regularly enforced. The fact of this unity stands behind the difference of particular modes; and it is obvious that this unity may affect and qualify the extent to which difference and specialisation can properly be carried in the general conduct of government.

If 'separation of powers' thus means a distinction of modes of action, it also means, in any modern system of government, some sort of distinction of the organs of government. In early communities there may exist a single undifferentiated organ (the Anglo-Norman *Curia Regis* was of that order), acting in all the different modes, and simultaneously serving as a legislature, a judicature, and an executive. But in any developed community there will be a plurality of organs. There will be a legislative organ, which may not indeed, be wholly and solely confined to the legislative mode of action, but will certainly be primarily and mainly concerned with that mode; there will equally be a judicial organ, primarily and mainly concerned with the judicial mode of action, but not necessarily confined to that mode; and there will similarly be an executive organ, which may however, be concerned with other modes of action beside the executive. In a word we shall find three organs corresponding to the three different modes of action; but we may find none of the organs so absolutely specialized in its mode of action, or so entirely separate in its province, that it cannot also act in the mode and enter the province of the others.

It may be urged that the system just described, which combines a separation of modes of action (or 'functions' or 'powers') with a competence of each organ to act in more than one mode, is simply an inheritance from the past which is destined to disappear. On this view there has been an evolution from a primitive homogeneity, with little differentiation of modes and none of organs, towards heterogeneity and differentiation. That evolution has brought an increasingly clear differentiation of modes; but it has still left, as a sort of historical relic, a considerable confusion of organs, with each organ still showing signs of an old undifferentiated past. There may be some truth in this view; but it may also be urged, with even more justice, that a system in which each organ proceeds by more than one mode, and is concerned with more than one function, is inherent in the general unity of the operation of government, and is thus far more than a relic. In any case it is certain that such a system is still embedded in modern government; and it is also certain that, far from diminishing, it is constantly tending to increase. Instead of moving toward greater heterogeneity we are actually moving in the reverse direction. The more complicated government becomes, and the greater the service which it has to render, the greater becomes the trend to a unity of operation, and more each organ of government tends to proceed by more than one mode of action.

The judicial organ perhaps shows this tendency less than the other two. Indeed it may be said that the judicial organ is a critic rather than an example of the tendency; in particular it is a critic of what some if its members regard as the encroachments and 'the new despotism' of the executive organ, now reverting, in their view, to the antiquated practice of medieval monarchy, by which the King in Council was a judicial and even a legislative as well as an executive organ. It is natural that a professional feeling should animate the legal profession, and should lead its members to vindicate the principle that a specific function is specifically reserved for the judicature and should not be exercised by other organs. 'The Law', in the sense of the Bar and the Bench, thus becomes the peculiar custodian of the doctrine of separation of powers, at any rate against executive encroachment. But we have already had reason to notice that the judicature itself is an organ which is something more than judicial in the strict sense of that word. In addition to interpreting the law it also in some measure declares it: it has acted in the past, and it still acts in the present, by the legislative mode.

Just as the judicature may thus be said to exercise more than one function, so too may the legislature. The legislative organ in England was originally a body of mixed legislative and judicial competence, proceeding indifferently by both modes; and either House of Parliament is still a Court, if in different ways and different degrees. Moreover, though the legislature does not act as an executive, or by the executive mode, it is everywhere brought into intimate contact with the executive, and it affects, if it does not control or determine, the action of the executive organ. This is not only true—though it is true to a greater extent—in countries which have adopted and follow the cabinet system of responsible government, under which the executive organ is generally answerable to the legislature and dependent on its confidence; it is also true, if in a less measure, in countries in which the executive is independent of the legislature.

Finally, just as the legislature has been increasingly brought into contact with the executive by the modern evolution of government, and has come increasingly to exercise an influence one executive policy and action, so, conversely, the executive has also increased its scope, and has moved, or been drawn, into action proceeding not only by the executive, but also by the legislative and even by the judicial mode. The development of the executive into what may be called a multi-functioning organ (or, in other words, an organ proceeding by all the three modes) is one of the most notable features of modern government. If the growth of the legislative organ, in consequence of the development of the cabinet system, was the notable feature of the eighteenth century, it may be said that the growth of the executive organ, in consequence of the extension of rights and the corresponding extension of services which mostly fall to the lot of the executive, is the notable feature of the twentieth. Today the executive is not only an executive: it is also, at the same time, a legislature, and that in a double sense. On the one hand it suggests and guides the process of law-making by the legislative organ. It does so even under the American system of division of functions between the executive President and the legislative Congress; and it does so even more under cabinet systems such as the British. On the other hand, the executive, apart from and in addition to its work of suggesting and guiding the process of law-making by the legislative organ, also acts itself as a legislature, when it issues supplementary rules of law in the form of 'regulations' and 'orders'. This power of the executive organ to issue supplementary rules of law is particularly evident in the sphere of the social services, and in matters such as housing and insurance; and it is to be noted that the power is often, and indeed mainly, exercised in virtue of a delegation of legislative power, made by the legislature itself, in a law which specifically authorizes an executive minister or ministers to supplement in detail its own more general prescriptions.

The same extension of services (and particularly social services), which has largely caused the growth of this executive legislation, in order to cope with all the detail necessarily involved, has also caused the growth of executive jurisdiction. But such executive, jurisdiction, while it is similar to, is also different from, executive legislation. It is similar, in so far as it owes its origin to a similar, act of legislative authorisation. A law about housing, for instance, which orders the clearing of slums, and therefore entails a decision, in any case of dispute, whether a given property belongs to the category of a slum and is therefore liable to clearance, may authorize an executive minister, as the person most likely to be familiar with the nature of the problem, to act judicially and give a decision. On the other hand, executive jurisdiction is different, in one respect, from executive legislation. When the legislative organ confers a measure of legislative power upon the executive, it takes something away from itself; but when it confers upon the executive a measure of judicial power, it is diminishing not itself, but an organ other than itself. That is one reason, though not the only reason, why the growth of executive jurisdiction is a more serious matter than is the growth of executive legislation.

The notable tendency of the executive organ to become more and more multi-functioning is itself sufficient to disprove the idea that the evolution of government is in the direction of a greater heterogeneity and an increasing differentiation of the various organs of government. On the contrary, the modern tendency would rather appear to be setting in the reverse direction. But though this tendency is a fact, it is also a problem, or a cause of problems. If the various organs overlap, and if some of them may enter the province and proceed by the modes of action which, primarily at any rate, belong to other organs, how is it possible for them to act amicably, without incessant disputes about boundaries and spheres?

Again, if the executive takes to itself, or induces the legislative to allow it to take, both legislative and judicial powers in addition to its primary executive power, will not to the rights of persons suffer from an authority so triply armed, and will not the principle of liberty be endangered by an overgrown and over-mighty executive?

It may be argued that the system works, and that the overlapping organs are able to act in unison, because one of these organs, the organ which is primarily concerned with the primary function of law-marking, is the dominant and therefore the coordinating organ. In other words the legislature, as being the immediate sovereign under the constitution and therefore possessing the sovereign power of making final adjustments, is able to determine boundaries and spheres between the executive and the judicature, and between them both and itself. It may thus be said to secure a unity of operation in a system of different overlapping organs. But there is another factor which must also be present , in addition to the co-ordinating and adjusting activity of the legislature, if a system of multi-functioning organs is to work without friction and without detriment to liberty. Each of the organs, when performing a function or proceeding by a mode additional to its own specific function or mode, should act in the way and according to the technique appropriate to the function or mode thus added. If the executive, for example, is vested with judicial power, and accordingly performs the judicial function and proceeds by the judicial mode it must really and actually proceed by that mode; and discarding the technique of executive action it must adopt and follow, as far as possible, the proper and peculiar technique of judicial action. It must accept the procedure of a public hearing, with a proper confrontation of witnesses according to the regular rules of evidence: it must publish its decision and the reasons for its decision: it must also admit, if it possibly can, the possibility of appeal. The result will be that the distinction of modes will still be observed, even if there is not a separation of organs; and the executive organ, when acting judicially, will cease to follow the executive mode and adopt instead the judicial.

Granted these two conditions—the co-ordinating and adjusting activity of the sovereign legislature, and the observance of the distinction of separate modes even when the distinction of separate organs ceases to be observed—we may accept the contemporary tendency towards the confusion or overlap of multi-functioning organs. But this is not to deny the justice and the propriety, for its time and under its conditions, of the eighteenth-century doctrine of the separation of powers. That doctrine was developed by Montesquieu in reference to French conditions. It was relative to the contemporary French facts of an over grown royal executive organ; of the suspension of any legislative organ, and the substitution of executive decrees for legislative enactments; of the subordination of the judicial organ (the *parlement* of Paris) to the sovereign appearance of the King in person when he sat in a *lit de justice*. Under these conditions Montesquieu could argue, fairly enough, that with the executive claiming to do all things, confusing all the modes, and making its will the canon of Right and controller of rights, it was only possible to clarify confusion and to vindicate rights by asserting the titles of two other organs, the legislative and the judicial to a separate existence and a separate power of acting independently by their own proper modes. In favour of such an assertion he could also plead, fairly enough (even if he was necessarily unaware of the nascent English system of responsible or cabinet government, and of the close connection thereby established between the executive and the legislature), that the government of England was an example of the principle of separation of powers. The case is altered today; but if the facts are different, the principle, in its essence, remains. There is bound to be confusion, and there is bound to be a menace to rights, if it is not in some way, observed. But that way, under our conditions, is now a different way.

Today we have in all countries, at any rate formally if not always in fact, three separate organs which Montesquieu desired. But we have also something more than, and something different from, what he desired. There is in Britain (and there is also in other countries, in various ways and different degrees) an overlapping and an interlacing of the separate organs of government. The legislature does something more than legislation; the judicature does something more than adjudication; and the executive, in particular, does something more than executive action. But we get a co-ordination of what might seem to be confusion by the action of a dominant and sovereign legislature; we preserve a distinction of modes even if we do not maintain a clear separation of organs, and by that distinction of modes we preserve liberty and the rights of persons; and, finally, lest it succumb to the corruption of absolute power, we set bounds which it cannot overpass even to the sovereign legislature.

These bounds of the sovereign legislature are many and various. Some of them have already been traced in the previous course of the argument, and need only be summarized here. In the first place, the legislature, by its nature, is simply an organ of the legal association, or in other words the State; but besides the state and its legislature there is also Society and its social organs, with all the general play of voluntary social activity which proceeds, in the main, independently of the State. Secondly, the legislature, like the whole of government, is limited both by the purpose it fulfils and by the mode of action it follows: the purpose of serving Right and the rights which issue from Right, and the mode of action which consists in proceeding by general rules of law relative to and enforceable in the sphere of external conduct. Thirdly, the legislature is an organ of government acting in and under a general system of democracy, which proceeds by the method of discussion and thus reflects and repeats, at the political level,. A process of debate which is already at work in the social area. Being an organ in such a system it may be said to be doubly limited, first by the play of social debate and the growth of common conviction which are precedent to its own action, and secondly by the existence of other forces and foci of discussion (party and the electorate on the one hand, and the cabinet on the other) which are concurrent with its action, and to which its action must be adjusted in some sort of balance and with some measure of mutual respect.

But there is a still further limit on the legislature which demands our consideration. This is the limit imposed by the development and the activity of political parties. The legislature has not only to respect the system of political parties as a force and focus of discussion parallel to and concurrent with itself. It has also to respect the system as something *within* itself; something by which its motion is *internally* affected and qualified. In an earlier passage of the argument it has already been suggested that the democratic method of government, being as it is in its essence a method of government by discussion, necessarily requires a plurality of parties as a condition and *sine qua non* of discussion. We may now go on to suggest that the legislature, as a representative body reflecting in its own composition the plurality of parties in the national community, is inherently limited by the fact of that plurality, and it bound by the necessity, which arises from it, of attaining such measure of common agreement as is required for any united action proceeding from the whole body. It may be objected that no common agreement is required; that the majority party, or combination of parties, can simply overbear the minority and force it to acquiesce; and that a majority-vote is thus sufficient to ensure the united action of the legislative body. The objection does not hold; and the operation of a representative legislative based on a plurality of parties is more than a matter of counting votes and then doing a sum in subtraction.

Whether the parties are only two, or more than two, they generally arrange themselves in two sides (there may be many *parties,* but there can be only two *sides*)—the side of the party or combination of parties which supports the executive government or cabinet, and the side of the party or combination of parties which opposes that government. The government side, under normal conditions, does not simply outvote and overbear the opposition side; nor is the opposition side always waging a war in which it is always defeated. The two sides are indeed engaged in the conflict of debate; but they are also engaged in the co-operation of managing the nation's business together. The conflict is public: the co-operation, which is unacknowledged and may even be unconscious, is hidden in the background. But it is always there. The two sides must, at the least, attain some agreement about the conduct of the current business of legislation. They must, in a grave emergency, whether of peace or of war, attain some agreement about the conduct of the general business of the nation. But even without an emergency, and even in normal conditions, they must always attain some agreement which goes beyond the conduct of current business and the routine of daily procedure. They must, in regard to all major measures of proposed legislation, endeavour to achieve some sort of compromise which is likely to command the general consent and to be endorsed by the common conviction of the whole community, and which is therefore likely to last even after a change of government, and even when the government side has been succeeded in office by the side now in opposition. This is the price of continuity, and continuity, in its turn, is the price of peaceful progress.

We may accordingly say that the legislature is two as well as one, and that it inherently limited by the fact that the two have to act as one. In other words a joint effort--an effort of construction on the one side and of constructive criticism on the other; an effort which combines contradiction with co-operation—is involved in the double nature of the legislative body. The necessity of this joint effort is an internal limit; and the separation of the two sides of the legislature, thus at once opposed and conjoined, is the return in a new and different form of the old eighteenth-century system of *separation des pouvoirs*. We do not indeed now separate, or seek to oppose and balance, the executive and legislative organ: on the contrary we unite them together in a system of responsible government which brings the executive into the legislature and enables either to affect the other in a constant interaction. But within this union and interaction we retain separation and maintain a balance. We retain a separation of two sides and the leaders of the two sides (the head of the Government and the leader of the opposition): we maintain a balance in the sense that we require both sides and their leaders to adjust their claims and accommodate their policies in a compromise which eventually may command our general consent. Thus the end of the argument on the functions of government is at once in favour of union and in favour of separation. You may unite the executive with the legislature; but when you have done so you must provide some element of separation and balance within that union. Again, and from another point of view, you may set your executive organ to act not only by the executive mode of action, but also by the judicial (in the exercise of executive jurisdiction) and in addition by the legislative (in the shape of executive legislation); but again when you have done so, and when you have thus united three modes in a single organ, you must ensure that there is also separation, and that the one organ uniting the modes nevertheless acts separately, and acts by a separate procedure, in each of the different modes. Union, but also separation—such is the rule which, in this way or that, is always imperative in the discharge of the functions of government.

COLLECTIVISM AND INDIVIDUALISM

We may now return, in conclusion, to the theme of the relation between the functions of government and the rights of individuals. However government may discharge its functions, and however those functions may be distributed among its different organs, they are always, in their nature, functions of service rendered to rights and therefore rendered to persons, *individual* persons, who own these rights as the necessary conditions of the development in action of their individual personality. From this point of view the current antithesis between collectivism and individualism is verbal rather than real. If by individualism we mean a belief in the rights of individual person, and by collectivism we mean a belief in the collective service owed and rendered to such rights by government, we shall see no opposition, but rather a necessary connection. It is possible, indeed, to draw a distinction, as some thinkers have done, between a period of individualism, dominated by the influence of Bentham and his followers and marked by the idea of liberation, which lasted into the third quarter of the nineteenth century, and a period of collectivism, marked by the extension of the idea of protection, which succeeded the period of individualism from 1870 onwards. But the distinction is a distinction of the study; and it may even be said to show a class or professional bias. Some classes or professions might mourn a loss of individual right after 1870; other, and those were numerous, began to enjoy an increase. Generally the whole of the nineteenth century, far from being divided into two different parts, was a century of a single and homogeneous process; a process of the extension of personal rights, which may be called individualism, but a process entailing, at the same time, an extension of the service of government on behalf of those rights, an extension which may be called by the name of collectivism, but is really and in fact the consequence and the other side of the extension of personal rights which is called by the name of individualism.

Individualism is a word which is easily used in different and even conflicting senses. It can be used, and is often used, to denote a doctrine that the State leaves the individual alone, 'letting him do and letting him go' (*laissez faire et laissez passer*) as he himself thinks best. The phrase is a phrase of the French Free Trade economists of the eighteenth century: it originally belonged only to economics, and only to one part of that—the part concerned with commerce. It was a good enough phrase in its day, and it has its value still, in its own restricted field. But it cannot be properly applied to economics generally, or made to include the field of industry as well as the field of commerce: still less can it be applied to the whole broad field of politics. Individualism of the *laissez-faire* order in *that* field, individualism which meant that the State should leave each individual alone in the general business and whole conduct of life, would not only mean dereliction of its duty by the State; it would also mean the destruction on the individual's power to do anything freely or to go anywhere freely. A true individualism, in the field of politics, involves recognition of the State's liberating power, coupled with a recognition of its duty to use that power according to its nature, and therefore for liberation and the removal of obstacles.

Individualism so conceived starts, indeed, from individual personality, and from the inherent title of each individual person to enjoy the conditions necessary to the development of his capacities. But just because it starts from that basis, it cannot end in any conclusion of *laissez faire*, or issue in any doctrine that it is the duty of the State to leave individuals alone. The conditions necessary for the development of each individual person are not to be had for the whistling, and they do not come of themselves in obedience to each person's call. They have to be assembled by a collective effort which is only possible to an organized State. They are assembled for sake of the individual; but he cannot assemble them himself, or be left alone to shift for himself by his own unaided devices. On the contrary, he must be surrounded with service; a collective service which, in union with others, he himself helps to provide for others as well as himself: a service which becomes all the greater, the more fully the conditions necessary for his development are recognized and the more his rights are thereby extended. The State which is based on regard and respect for the worth of individual persons is not a 'let-alone State: it is a State which follows and attends, 'with unperturbed pace', and with a constant office of service. To argue for individuality is not to argue for the unserved and unattended individual. It is rather the opposite: it is to argue for the general legal framework, and the whole system of collective service, which individuality needs for its development: it is to argue for the rights it requires, for the system of Right which is the other side of these rights, and for the service of the State in declaring and enforcing the common conviction about that system.

The argument seems to result in a paradox: 'the greater the liberty of the individual, the greater the interposition of government: the more rights, the more law, and therefore the more the activity of the State in declaring and enforcing law.' The statement of the paradox suggest a reflection. There is always a price to be paid for rights. That price, as has already been noted, is partly financial, or a matter of payment in money; partly spiritual or a matter of payment in the acceptance of control. We need not pause to discuss the nature and the implications of the financial price. That is a matter of economics: of national finance and the balancing of national income and national expenditure. It is the spiritual price which matters most; and the crucial balance to be struck is the balance between the spiritual profit gained in the increased enjoyment of rights and the spiritual loss incurred or involved in the increased acceptance of control. When we seek to strike this balance, we have two calculations to make. The first is a calculation of the gain and loss in the private account of each individual: it is a matter, as it were, of the private bank-book of each; it is a business of reckoning individual gain of liberty against individual loss. The second is a calculation of the gain and loss in what may be called the common account of the whole community: it is a matter of reckoning between classes or sections of the community; it is a business of computing the gain of one class or section, in liberty and personal rights, against the loss of another.

The necessity of reckoning spiritual gain and spiritual loss in the private account of each individual is a necessity which may easily be forgotten; but it still remains a necessity. Men readily accept new rights and the enlargement which they immediately bring: they are less ready to remember the price and the restrictions which may be entailed. The rights comprised in a system of social security are precious; but they are necessarily accompanied by administrative control and regulation, and they necessarily involve the performance of prescribed and compulsory acts in the channels of regular routine. There is at once an increase of liberty and an increase of automatism; and the question is whether the increase of liberty is more than enough to offset the increase of automatism. To enjoy the rights of social security is to be liberated from fears and dangers; to be more of a freeman, and to have more freedom for the development of personal capacity. If the freedom is grasped and used, and if the development is actually achieved, the game is well worth the candle, and the commodity is worth far more than the price. On the other hand there *is* a price. To be liberated from a set of risks is also to be liberated from the responsibility of facing those risks: indeed it is even more, under a system of collective insurance; it is also to be subjected to the control involved in the system. Only if the liberty gained is actively grasped and used; only if it is something more than a passive acceptance of benefits; only then will there be a net gain on the whole of the transaction. The man who is formally made more free by a system of social security must actively use his freedom to make something more of himself if he is to be really and actually more free.

The necessity of reckoning gain and loss between different classes or sections is a still more obvious necessity, daily forced upon our attention by the process of class-debate. The extension of rights for one class may mean the limitation of rights for another; and it is possible that the one class may lose even more than the other gains. But that, in itself, does not necessarily mean that the bargain is bad. The previous distribution of rights between classes may have been unfair and inequitable: one class may have been entrenched in the possession of a superfluity, and the other depressed below the level of bare necessity. If the greatest number are to enjoy the greatest possible development of the capacities of personality, correction is inevitable, and it may be as just (in terms of the sovereign justice which assigns rights equally to each and all) as it is inevitable. The distribution of rights among classes is not a thing fixed for ever. It is a matter for constant adjustment and readjustment, as social thought about justice grows and as the interpretation of the principles of liberty and equality broadens with its growth. But there is still a limit to the process of adjustment and readjustment. It may be fair to ask one class, particularly when in numbers it is a small and limited class, to surrender old rights and responsibilities for the sake to another and larger class, and in order that the members of that class may enjoy new rights and responsibilities. But it will only be really fair if two conditions are satisfied.

The first of these conditions is that the rights and responsibilities surrendered should be used by those who receive them for their own higher development, and not merely accepted as a prizes or trophies. Otherwise there may be no gain, and there may even be loss, in terms of that development of personality which is the final criterion. The other condition is that the class surrendering rights (such as the right to ownership of capital resources and the management of those resources on the basis of personal responsibility) should not be made to surrender so much that it becomes impotent to contribute any energy of initiative or originality of experiment to the development of the national economy and the general national culture or type of civilization. Under any system of organization a national community will always need an initiatory and experimental class which can generate and distribute the electricity of ideas. The recruiting of that class should be broad and generous; and every talent should have an open way into its ranks. But however recruited, and however broad, this class will always require the conditions necessary for the discharge of its electric work; and there will always remain a modicum of right and responsibility when it must necessarily retain if it is to be itself and to contribute its own gifts to the cause of general development. The days of hereditary aristocracy are gone; but there is no numbering of the days of what may be called the professional aristocracy, in the widest sense of the world 'professional'. The more a national community moves towards the greatest possible development of the capacities of personality in the greatest possible number of persons, the more it needs the stimulus which professional skill and managing capacity can give to the whole development of the whole community.

It has been argued that there is no antithesis between individualism, in the sense of a belief in the development of individual personality, and collectivism in the sense of a belief in the collective service necessary for individual development. On the other hand, it has also been argued that though there is no antithesis there is or may be tension—a tension between the 'pull' of individual development and the 'pull' of a collective service which must always be in some measure also a collective control. The two may be complements to one another; but they are complements which need a nice and delicate adjustment There is a principle of polarity in the political nature of man, as there is in human nature generally: a 'quality of exhibiting opposite or contrasted properties', a 'tendency to develop in two opposite directions. In his general nature man has the contrasted properties of privacy and sociability; and though he is one being, and though he needs them both, he is also divided between them, and he also feels the tension between their different pulls. Similarly in his political nature he has the contrasted and yet complementary properties of the individualist who would fain be himself and the collectivist who would merge himself in a fellowship of service; and though he is one being and needs both these properties, he is also divided between them and feels in himself the tension of a 'tendency to develop in two opposite directions. Individualism and collectivism are not the banners of two separate armies, composed of two separate bodies of men. All of us fly them both, and we all serve under both. There is a polarity in each of us, as well as in the whole community to which we all belong. We need not dread the resultant tension. That would simply be to dread life; for life is tension, as tension is life. We have to accept it as it exists, both within ourselves and within the community; and we have constantly to find, in each new conjuncture, the new adjustment which the new conjuncture demands, surrendering neither individual development nor collective service, but endeavouring to find an adjustment which preserves them both and may even make them both mutually serviceable to one another.

There is another polarity, and another tension, besides the tension within the State, between the call of individual development and the call of collective service. This is the polarity or tension between the State and Society; between the community permanently organized in a single legal association, for the one legal purpose of declaring and enforcing universal and uniform rules, and the community organized, or rather constantly organizing itself, in a number of voluntary associations for a variety of purposes (religious, cultural, recreational, charitable, economic, and whatever else may be comprehended under the general designation of 'Social'), which adorn and supplement, and may even stimulate or anticipate, the activity proper to the purpose of the legal organisation. The question which thus emerges, and the tension thus presented, bring us back at the end to the theme from which the argument originally started. What is the province of the State, and what is the province of Society? Is there any definite boundary, or how shall we conceive their relations?

In attempting to answer this question we may begin by asking ourselves whether the goal which is set before us—the securing of the greatest amount of rights for the greatest number of persons; the providing of the conditions for the highest possible development of the capacities of personality over the widest possible range—is a goal which can be simultaneously attained by two parallel lines of action, or a goal to be attained by one and only one. Can the extension and spread of rights 'in widest commonality; be partly secured by voluntary action in the social area, or must it be altogether secured by uniform and compulsory action in the legal area, with a large consequential growth of State-action and a large increase of the functions of government in the necessary service of rights? There is a good case to be made in favour of the first of these alternatives. Voluntary action in the social area is needed as well as, and no less than, the uniform and compulsory action of the organized State in its own legal area. Both are necessary, but the first comes first; and the prior thing, in the order of time (though not necessarily in order of importance) is the voluntary action of Society. We do our best if we do what we can for ourselves, by voluntary social co-operation, before we invoke the action of the State—Which indeed is also ourselves, wherever it is democratically organized, but is ourselves engaged in the making and enforcing of compulsory rules. There is a time for voluntary and varied experiment as well as for the uniform obligatory rule. Indeed the distinction between social action and the legal action of the State is perhaps rather a distinction of time than a distinction of space or area. It is not always the case that one sort of action is concerned with one area or set of subjects, and the other with another area or set: on the contrary, both sorts of action may well be concerned with the same areas or sets of subjects. Rather it is often the case that the one sort of action belongs to one time or conjuncture, the time of the laboratory and the experiment, and the other to another time or conjuncture—let us say, in a metaphor, that of mass-production, when a result of the laboratory is being put on the market as a standardized uniform commodity.

If we follow this line of thought, we shall be led to believe that a reorganisation of the economic process, such as will introduce the principles of liberty and equality into this process, and will therefore secure to all who are concerned in it the rights involved by these principles, may well begin, and may even sometimes remain, as the level of voluntary agreement between voluntary associations (those of the workers and those of the employers), an agreement based on voluntary consultation and issuing in voluntary co-operation. But often the matter will not end there, and there will come a time and conjuncture for acting in a different way and by a different mode. Voluntary social effort, feeling its way, making its experiments, proceeding by trial and error, may discover a best which is so obviously best that it deserves to be made the general rule. In that case the State, which is not the enemy of Society, but rather stands to it in something of the relation in which a solicitor may stand to a family, will register and endorse this best as a rule for general application and enforcement. But just as it is wise to avoid going to a solicitor unless or until you have a case to submit, so it may also be wise to avoid recourse to the State (to which we are perhaps too prone to carry our problems instantly) until social thought and experiment have done their preparatory work. The issue between Society and the State, if we can speak at all of an issue, is not an issue between opposites. How indeed can it be so, when the State is just Society writ legally—Society organized in the form and for the purposes of a legal association? It is either an issue between two alternatives, either of which may serve, but one of which, at a given moment, may serve better than the other, or an issue between two complements, both of which are needed, but one of which is needed as the forerunner of the other.

The conclusion to which we are thus led is not a conclusion in favour of the individualism which means leaving individuals alone, to shift for themselves by their own devices: nor again, on the other hand, is it a conclusion in favour of the form of collectivism under which the State serves individuals so much that they have little or nothing to do for themselves, and thus lose much of their liberty in the very act of their own liberation. It is rather a conclusion in favour of the maximum of voluntary self-help by groups of individuals, voluntarily acting for themselves in the social area; thinking out for themselves, in their own sphere of interest, the requirements and conditions of their own development; and, when they have thought them out *for* themselves, going on to achieve them *by* themselves, and by their own efforts, so far as in their own sphere they can. In one sense this may be called individualism; for it involves a belief in the value of the spontaneous activity of individuals, freely associated for the purpose of shifting for themselves, by their own devices, in a scheme of voluntary self-help. In another sense, however, it may also be called collectivism; for it involves a belief in the value of the concerted activity of collective groups, each knit together by a common interest of all the members in a common object, and each seeking to achieve its object by means of common efforts. But on a broad view the method of voluntary self-help by the concerted effort of a voluntary association is neither individualism nor collectivism, in the ordinary sense of those terms; it is a happy bridge between them. The essence of the method is a spirit of 'voluntary community' which marries *voluntas* to *communitas*; and the essence in turn of that spirit is the power not of force but of persuasion.

The power of persuasion, issuing in the spirit of voluntary community, has studded the world in which we live with a profusion of social institutions. Proféssor Whitehead, in one of the most suggestive of his essays has spoken of the transformation wrought in the problem of liberty by 'a profusion of corporations originated by explicit thought. In his view the development of these autonomous institutions, limited to special purposes, places the problem of liberty at a new angle: and he holds accordingly that the novelty of our days, and the modern method of solving the problem of liberty, 'consists in the deliberate formation of institutions,. Embodying purposes of special groups, and unconcerned with the general purposes of any political state'. His authority and his persuasive power reinforce the argument here advance. The future will largely lie with the development and the activity of a variety of social institutions. What such institutions can do, and what they may ultimately achieve, in the economic field, is a matter already touched upon in the previous course of the argument. But there are other fields besides the economic in which the development of social institutions may contribute greatly to the solution of the ancient problem of liberty. There is, for example, the field of education, which is not and never can be, a monopoly of the State. Education associations—of parents, of teachers, of workers, and of members of religious confessions—are all concerned in the development of educational experiments, and in offering that liberty of choice among types of school and forms of instruction which is essential to the growth of personal and individual capacity. Indeed on a general view, and looking beyond particular fields to the general field of the way of life and the type of civilisation common to the whole community, we cannot but notice that social institutions are active in all its range and over all its extent. 'Our lives are passed from the first not in a monistic, homogeneous circle, but in a number of circles… we live in various social complexes which are in the last resort concentric and each of which has its own intellectual content. These circles and social complexes, each with its intellectual content, and all with their moral aim of mutual aid and common service, are essentially personal unions, enlisting personal interest and eliciting fully the initiative of their leading personalities. The greater the part which they play on that basis and in that form, the greater their contribution to the development of the capacities of individual personality in the community at large, and thereby to the growth of a better way of life and higher type of civilisation. But they must be true to their personal basis, and retain their personal form, if they are to contribute effectively. Social institutions can easily become ossified, no less than political: they can become official organisations, in lieu of personal associations: they can dictate to their members, instead of responding to the lift and surge of their minds. They must constantly be renewed and reviewed: sometimes, when they have served and outlived their purpose, they may even have to be destroyed, in order that something new and better may be able to take their place. It might be a motto for a community: 'Never rest content with your institutions, whether social or political—but least of all with the social: there is a virtue in continuity, but there is no less virtue in change.'

All in all, the question before us is not a question of 'the man *versus* the State', or of individualism *versus* collectivism. There is no point in the question: there is no such antithesis; there is, at the most, a tension, which is as healthy as it is necessary. Nor is the question before us a question of 'society *versus* the State', or of the voluntary principle *versus* the principle of legal control and regulation. There may be more point in that question; but again there is no antithesis, for both of the things thus opposed are needed, and both may be needed equally. Here, however, the tension is greater; and here, as we have already seen, there is a reasonable ground for debating, not so much *what* the State should do and *what* Society should do (both handle equally a number of matters, and few matters can be said to belong exclusively either to the one or to the other), as when and in what conjuncture Society should be the agent, and *when* and in what conjuncture the agent should be the State.

Each mind has a drawing bias, which makes it naturally run in some particular direction. The bias of the writer has always inclined his thought—the more, the older he grows—towards a belief in the value of the social mode of action. With all its imperfections and its possible inefficiencies, it is none the less a mode of action which permits and even demands the free energy of the mind. The movement of the State is the regular revolution of steady and unfailing machinery. The movement of social institutions is a varied and irregular movement, like the movement of trees and plants as they spring from the seed in the ground: here one group, and there another, thrusts up its fresh particular idea into the varied field of social life and experiment. The humming automatism of the State is about us and all our doings, engaged in constant service and constantly intending our good. The varied field is untidy, irregular, unregulated: it has many gaps: it has even more redundancies. But may the time never come when all our life spins round on the revolving wheels of legal regulation.

—E-Baker

7

The Freedom of the Governed

What is the alternative to dictatorship? By what means can the authority of government be made subject to consent? How is it possible to grant powers for use and still prevent their abuse? The beginning of an answer is to reject the doctrine that the government is the source of authority and to embrace the contrary notion that authority derives from the mass of the people who entrust the government with powers to be exercised on their behalf. Although the choice between these two political poles and their resulting forms of organisation is a critical issue of the present century, the decision that confronts humanity is not new. A long tradition supports the view that authority is somehow delegated by the governed to their government, although states founded on this principle have been rarities and continue to be the exception rather than the rule. The assertion of the principle, however, would have had little effect on practice unless institutional means were developed for curbing those in authority. The doctrine that government should be responsible has to be studied in the light of historical efforts to make it so.

THE ATHENIAN DEMOCRACY

In the first democracy an elaborate system ensured that the people, or *demos,* would be self-governing and would control its officials. From the mid-fifth century B.C. to the mid-fourth, Athenian government rested on the belief that all power belonged to the people, who exercised it by a many-sided participation in public affair. The price of Athenian citizenship was activity and versatility. Among a citizen's duties were service in the army or navy, attendance at festivals, and jury work in the courts. Most important of all was his participation at the Assembly's monthly meetings, where he helped to enact laws and decrees, settle questions of high policy, conduct foreign relations, and authorize the finances. The work of the Assembly, however, needed supplementing by administrative officials. These were selected in one of two ways. The Assembly filled by election offices that required special qualifications and expert knowledge. In other cases, where anyone of average intelligence could apply ordinary judgement, the Athenians employed a method distinctive to their democracy—the lot. At the head of a department or agency, they placed a board of citizens picked by lot annually. Such a system served many purposes. It ensured that government was conducted, in a literal way, *by* the people. It contributed to public education by enlarging the direct acquaintance of citizens with governmental problems. Through rotation in office, it spread a sense of civic responsibility.

Certain safeguards were added to forestall the appointment of anybody manifestly unfit and to prevent abuse of power. Before they could assume their posts, those whom the lot selected were made to pass a scrutiny which was both qualifying test and loyalty clearance. Then ten times during the years, at the regular meetings of the Assembly, the populace could vote approval or censure of their officials—censure being followed by an indictment in the law courts, tantamount to impeachment. Finally, when the officeholder's year of service ended, he presented to a special board of auditors the accounts for any public monies of which he was collector, custodian, or disburser. This last requirement—the accountability of the official as enforced by a postaudit—constituted, in Athenian eyes, the ultimate weapon of popular control. When their statesmen and philosophers contrasted their political institutions with those of oligarchy or monarchy, the two features they stressed most were appointment by lot and postaudit. Both practices, in their view, prevented the rise of a bureaucracy as an uncontrollable corps of officialdom.

There was another risk, however, to which Athenian democracy was liable. Where matters of such weight were determined at the Assembly of the citizens, much depended on the judgement displayed by the leading orators. Decisions were reached by majority vote after free and open discussion, and a proposal could be adopted on the motion, not of some holder of public office, but of any private citizen with a popular following. In the absence of further safeguards, policies might be settled or reversed by snap votes; majorities could be incited by ranting orators; the heat of factional fights might inflame the community. To counteract these dangers, of which they learned through bitter experience, the Athenians instituted two more safety devices. One was the drastic expedient called ostracism. When internal dissension between ambitious politicians imperiled the unity of the state, the Assembly could adopt a motion to ostracize. This was followed in two months' time by a special election where, provided at least 6000 participated, whoever received a majority of adverse ballots was banished for ten years, after which he could return and resume all his civil, political, and property rights. A second way in which the Assembly sought protection against divisive leaders and indeed against its own worse judgement was by distinguishing laws of general application from decrees dealing with particulars. No law could be amended or repealed without due notice and procedural safeguards. Decrees also had to satisfy procedural checks as well as conform to law. The Athenians enforced these principles in the courts. Within a year of the passage of any law or decree, its proposer could be indicted on a charge of unconstitutionality, the penalties for which were severe. Thus an all-powerful Assembly attempted to guarantee a government under law.

There is more than experimental novelty and a unique structure to give merit to this Athenian constitution. Its ideals were tinged with realism. The Athenians were not content solely to proclaim the fine-sounding doctrines of citizen participation, official accountability, and rule of law. Such ideas would have been insufficient to mold political behaviour, were they not reinforced with appropriate institutions and procedures. It was the latter that put teeth into theory and made democracy effective. How vital it is to install the necessary machinery, if ideas are to operate in practice, can be better understood by noting the contrast with other systems that neglected adequately to translate some well-meant formulas into hard fact.

THE ROMAN SACRIFICE OF LIBERTY TO EMPIRE

For a contrast, consider the record of Rome. Between the expulsion of the monarchy at the end of the sixth century B.C. and the establishment of the Augustan Principate five centuries later, Rome was a republic. During this period, the Romans accomplished some remarkable achievements. They laid the groundwork for a system of civil and criminal law which is basic to the jurisprudence and legal codes of many modern nations. By the prowess of their redoubtable legions they absorbed within a single empire all the lands and peoples surrounding the Mediterranean. Under the dominion of Rome southern and western Europe, North Africa, and much of the Middle East experienced a greater measure of political unity than that region had known before or has known since. But these organizers of law and legions; these architects of highways, aqueducts, and central heating; these Caesars and Ciceros whose craftsmanship left Rome the eternal city and Latin a universal language—these man could not for all their political talent construct a democracy. The traditions associated with Rome was and is authoritarian. The major concepts that typify the Roman contribution to politics are expressed in these Latin-derived words: "power"—*potestas,* 'authority"—*auctoritas,* empire *"imperium.*

The principles of the republican constitution were potentially democratic. Wanting to avoid a repetition of the tyranny of some of their kings, the Romans deliberately separated powers and distributed them among various assemblies and offices which were a check on each other. From the consuls on down, their officials were elected by assemblies of citizens, and for a year at a time. Legislation, too, had to be voted on by the citizens, whose approval converted a proposed bill into an authoritative law. From this it would seem clear that the Romans intended their government to be subordinate to the governed. But circumstances combined to defeat the intention. The republic seldom enjoyed the luxury of a long peace. Its response to the challenge of nearby peoples launched it on a tide of military conquest. Acceptance of an imperial mission, however, brought an enlargement of size and power for which Rome's earlier institutions proved inadequate. The need for continuous direction of policy and for central supervision of outlying provinces was ill met by the poorly organised popular assemblies and annually changing magistrates.

Only one institution attempted to fill the need, the Senate. But when this body—a tightly knit oligarchy of past and present officeholders and noble families—was itself split through the growing division of Roman society into opposed classes, the state was torn apart by internal conspiracies and civil war. The last century of the republic's existence (133-31 B.C.) was a catalogue of revolution, counterrevolution, and *coup d' etat,* unable to control its commanders in the field, the Senate lay successively at the mercy of Marius, Sulla, Pompey, Caesar, and Anthony and finally succumbed to Augustus. The system founded by Augustus became an autocracy centralised in the person of the emperor, who maintained his position by placating the mob in the streets of Rome and controlling the legions in the capital and on the frontiers of the empire. Only as a memory from the past did the theory linger on that an emperor received his authority in a law conferring the imperial prerogatives at the beginning of his reign. That law, however, was enacted merely out of deference to an ancient form. It altered not a whit the political realities of absolutism.

A striking parallel may be observed in the medieval period. The political structure of feudalism exhibited a glaring contrast between its doctrines—that government is limited by law and rulers are responsible for their actions—and the absence of effective means of enforcement. Though they acknowledged the principle that they should serve the common good medieval governments fought shy of control by the common people. There is a historical explanation for this. The Germanic tribes, which burst the ramparts of the Roman Empire in the fifth and sixth centuries A.D. and sliced its sprawling territories into kingdoms, had formerly developed some institutions of a primitive democracy in the forests of Germany. But the urge that drove them west and south was itself there result of pressure on central Europe from some other peoples farther east—the pressure of Asians, like the Huns, foraging for new supplies of food and plundering as they went. This migration of people, the *Volkerwanderung* had a profound effect on forms of government. A tribe on the march or one that has to repel invaders, must militarize itself it survive; thus it becomes authoritarian. When in addition the Goths, Franks, Vandals, and the rest gradually imbibed the influence of the civilisation they had overrun, they sought to assimilate their own kingdoms to the pattern of imperial Rome. The democratic folkways of the German forests, like the traditions of the Roman republic, thenceforth continued to exist in mythical realm of inherited ideas to which the daily facts gave the lie.

THE MEDIEVAL ORDER: FICTIONS AND FACTS

The medieval world which emerged from the Dark Ages fairly bristled with notions of law as a restrain on government. Being a Christian, a ruler must conform to the law of God. Being custodian of the community's way of life, he must uphold and preserve its immemorial customs, to which indeed he owed his own powers and privileges. But was there anyone to say whether a ruler had in fact violated divine or human law, and if so, how could he be called to account? The possibility of curbing a ruler depended, as always, on the existence of organised opposition. In the Middle Ages, this might spring from two sources.

One of these was the church. If it appeared that a ruler sinned against divine law, the church could direct against him its two powerful weapons—excommunication and interdict. When employed by a masterful pope, these devices could bring to heel a king, like John of England, or even an emperor, as Henry IV. Such clerical resistance to royal or imperial power, though it imposed a limitation on the state, did not necessarily constitute a gain from the standpoint of democratic or popular control. When the papacy won, all that happened was the temporary subordination of secular to ecclesiastical authority, the latter being as authoritarian in spirit and structure as the former. Hence, toward the close of the Middle Ages a movement developed for the reform of church government. Associated with the names of the Italian, Marsiglio of Padua, and the Englishman, William of Occam, this was called the Conciliar Movement because its aim was to place at the head of the church a general council of elected delegates representing not only the clergy but all Christian believers. The Conciliarists came near to their goal at the end of the Great Schism when, in order to heal the breach in the church and overhaul its organisation, two councils were convoked which met respectively at Constance (1414-1418) and Basel (1431-1449). However, in the face of opposition from the pope, the cardinals, and the higher clergy generally, this attempt to democratize the structure of the church failed. The "Petrine theory" of papal power, placing supreme authority in the pope who governs in consultation with the college of cardinals, was emphatically asserted. In consequence, as George H. Sabine has written: "The pope in the fifteenth century established himself as the first of the absolute monarchs, and the theory of papal absolutism became the archetype of theory of monarchical absolutism."[1]

THE STRUGGLE BETWEEN KINGS AND NOBLES

Besides the church the other quarter from which effective opposition to a king could come in the Middle Ages was the nobility. Much of the political history of those centuries consisted in struggles between the nobles and their monarch, each trying to curb the other. When the nobles stood together, they could wribng concessions from a king. A notable instance was the triumph of the English barons in compelling king John to sign the Great Charter of 1215 which reaffirmed their ancient rights and privileges against royal encroachment. Still more successful was the Polish nobility, whose prolonged resistance reduced the institution of monarchy to a weak figurehead. In their case, however, "success" had suicidal consequences, since the Polish state in the absence of strong direction fell easy prey to Russian and Prussian expansion and was erased from the map. Sometimes a powerful nobleman opposed the reigning monarch in order to dispossess him of the crown and place it on his own or a kinsman's head. Usually the rivalries between great aristocrats and their clans sowed a bitter crop of strife and bloodshed. The Wars of the Roses, which for three decades split medieval England into hostile camps, were sparked by the clashing ambitions of the Houses of Lancaster and York, as were the political aims of papacy and empire respectively championed on the Continent by Guelphs and Ghibellines.

From this welter of discord, into which the loose-knit character of feudalism had plunged society, there emerged in one country and achievement which endured. In England during the thirteenth century the institution of Parliament took shape and acquired, at the hands of Simon de Montfor (1265) and King Edward I (1295), the form and functions that differentiated it from the earlier Great Council During the thirteenth and fourteenth centuries that form was set into the definite mould of two chambers, one of which, the House of Lords, contained the higher nobility and higher clergy while the second, the House of Commons, represented the lesser nobles (for example, knights of the shire) and commoners.

The functions of Parliament are a more complicated story. The reason for its existence in the Middle Ages may be found in two circumstances. The "loyal, trusty, and well-beloved subjects" of the king normally had various grievances of which they wished to complain. These could be more effectively voiced and would carry more weight if expressed through a regularised procedure. While subjects needed to approach the king for redressing their wrongs, he had a motive for approaching them, since he wanted their money. Originally the king's government was considered a branch of his household. As any great landowner managed his estates and supervised the affairs of his tenantry, so was a king supposed to govern the realm and protect its inhabitants. Affairs of state were handled by secretaries and other palace officials who in a literal sense were servants of the crown, while the costs of administration were defrayed out of the king's personal wealth. In all this, no attempt was made to separate public from private. Or rather, the concept of public interest had disappeared in the smothering embrace of private relationships. Public officials were court functionaries; the public treasury, a private purse.

Such a situation could continue only so long as the functions of the central government were few and their costs remained small. Everything changed, however, when kings endeavoured to extend their authority to new fields (for example the provision of a uniform, national system of justice) and when they embarked on that costliest of all governmental activities—war. To pacify the Welsh, contain the Scots, crush the Irish, and conquer the French[2] meant retaining and supplying large armies in the field. No longer could a king "live off his own" as tradition expected. He must now ask his subjects to contribute in his service not only their lives but that other dear possession, their money. Here then was a situation with the makings of a bargain advantageous to both sides. If the king were to appropriate his subjects' money without their consent, they would have a new and serious grievance. If he requested them, however, to agree to contribute, was not the time opportune for them to ask him to remedy their wrongs, which might lead to legislative action or changes in executive policy? Further more, when seeking money, the king would have to satisfy the taxpayers who wished to know how equitably it would be collected and for what purposes it would be spent. Hence Parliament received its start in life from the coupling of two original functions—the power of the purse and the need for a public forum for the ventilation of grievances. From these roots there later grew such other duties as the enactment of law, discussion of public policy, and control of the executive.

RISE OF THE ENGLISH PARLIAMENT

Great institutions grow slowly, however, and, like big trees that add a new ring annually, accumulate their layers of precedents. Four centuries elapsed between Edward I's Model Parliament of 1295 and the final victory of parliamentarians over royalists in 1688. What was it that took so much time? The answer lies in a social and economic, as well as a political, explanation. When Parliament was constructed to represent wealth and social superiority, when the dominant interest in the economy was the possession of land, and when the nobles were among the biggest landowners, then an addition to the powers of Parliament with its proportionate weakening of the crown could only mean government of the people by the nobility for the nobility, and it was doubtful whether anything was to be gained by rejecting the king's yoke in favour of that. One the contrary, from the stand-point of the mass of the population there was much to be said in favour of a weak nobility and a powerful king, since when a king abused his power, his oppression was likely to bear hardest on the nobles, the nearest rivals to his preeminence.

The politics of this situation was reinforced by the economic developments of the fifteenth century. At that time the structure of feudalism, centering on the ownership and produce of the land, was challenged by a contrary interest. An expansion of handicraft industries was accompanied by increase in domestic and foreign commerce. Enterprises of this character stimulated and strengthened the craft guilds, associations of merchants and credit and banking institutions. For mutual convenience these clustered within the walls of the trading city[3] (*Handelsstadit),* which was the focal point in the system of production, distribution, and communication. Such cities began to influence the political process. They sought the preservation of order (because warfare disrupted trade) and their emancipation from rural supremacy. On both scores urbanism pitted itself against the feudal aristocracy, whose discords disturbed the peace and whose wealth was drawn from the soil. The monarchy, natural fore of the nobility, was the natural ally of the urban *burghers* or burgesses. The grant to cities of royal charters of incorporation, as in England, enabled them to be self-governing, that is, to be ride of feudal government by the nobles who dominated the countryside. Consequently it was this urban "Middle" class that rallied to the crown, helped to replace the decentralised disorder of feudalism by unified central power, embodied the new concept of sovereignty[4] in the person of the sovereign (a word that became synonymous with "king"), and reaped the economic benefits of the centrally directed policies of mercantilism.[5] In England as in France the monarchy became absolute because there were material interests approving the powers it wielded.

THE REVOLUTION IN ENGLAND

It is the style of political change, as was observed earlier.[6] to proceed from excess in one direction to counter excess in the other. Feudal disunity gave way to royal absolutism, which in turn outlasted its original justification and, by abuses of its own, invoked new opposition . A monarch who was steering a dangerous course—witness Henry VIII piloting the English Reformation or Queen Elizabeth I holding the Spaniards at bay with zigzags of dalliance and defiance—wisely employed the institution of

Parliament for enlisting public support, and Parliament's members, their appetite for authority whetted with each taste, would not willingly be denied a further share once the immediacy of crisis was past. The cooperation between Parliament and the crown, fairly well maintained by Tudor monarchs, broke down under their unhappy successors, the Stuarts. A variety of circumstances turned a rift into a revolution. Chief blunders on the royal side were the decisions of Charles I to dispense altogether with Parliament, to levy taxes without parliamentary consent, and to administer secret and arbitrary "justice" in the Court of the Star Chamber. The price England paid was a civil war (1641-1651). Charles paid by defeat and the loss of his head. Even this example did not deter King James II, 30 years later, from attempting to restore Catholicism to a predominantly Protestant people. Again and aroused Parliament formed the focus of opposition. In 1688 a second revolution was won without bloodshed, the King fleeing with his neck intact. Parliament then invited William of Orange and his wife Mary to occupy the throne and in an Act of Settlement laid down the terms and limits by which the monarchy has since been bound.

Thus was consecrated the first of the modern revolutions which delivered a new birth of freedom. By the end of the seventeenth century England had secured the essentials of political liberty by creating at the apex of its government an institution representative of the governed. In this way the English people established for themselves, and by their example demonstrated to others, a method through which the effectiveness of power could be legitimised with the moral sanction of consent. Then, with parliamentary supremacy assured, the theoretical explanation followed. In 1690 John Locke published his two *treatises of Civil Government*. The first he devoted to the negative task of destroying the fatuous doctrine of the divine right of kings. In the second he constructed a positive theory to take its place. Governments, he asserted may rightfully exercise only those powers to which the people give their consent. Authority is conferred as a trust, being simply "a fiduciary power to act for certain ends."[7] The wishes of the community are represented and formulated by the legislature, which ranks supreme among the organs of the state. Should those in power abuse their trust and a conflict break out between the government and the governed, the latter retain the ultimate weapon of revolution, since they can never surrender the right to save themselves.[8] In any such dispute between the citizen body and authority, no third party can serve as judge. The people are always their own final court of appeal.

The supremacy of parliament, resulting from military victory in the civil war and political triumph in 1688, accorded well with these doctrines—subject to one proviso. It was one thing to assert that the monarchy should henceforth be limited, not absolute, and that Parliament (the legislature) should be paramount over the crown (the executive). It was something else to assume that the dominance of parliament was the same as control by all the people. At the time when Locke wrote, the franchise was limited to property owners who were a small fraction of the population. Nor did Locke propose to change that. Thus the consent of the governed boiled down to the interests of a class. Nevertheless, wittingly or unwittingly, Locke had sown a seed, and there was no stopping its growth. What is more, there were other soils, besides that of England, in which it could take root. This was what an English government learned in 1776.

PRINCIPLES OF THE AMERICAN REVOLUTION

"To secure these rights, Governments are instituted among Men, deriving their just powers from the consent of the governed." The key words in this sentence are "just" and "consent." Jefferson's problem, when he drafted the Declaration of Independence, was similar to that which Locke had faced a century before. He was expounding the right to rebel against authority that was unresponsive to the governed. Since liberty was a supreme good, he wanted a society of free men. These, he recognised, must accept certain restraints on their behaviour and must enforce their rules on offenders. Like the other fathers of the American Revolution, Jefferson was no anarchist. His purpose was not to sweep all government away, but to create authority that could be held to account. How was this to be done? Was it possible to argue for freedom and yet acquiesce in some coercion?

Jefferson began by reasserting that the consent of the governed is the foundation of all legitimate government. Consent alone gives moral sanction and legal validity to the physical force employed by the state. Powers derived from consent, therefore, are just. But what if a government acts in defiance of consent? "Whenever any form of government becomes destructive of these ends," continues the Declaration, "it is the right of the people to alter or to abolish it, and to institute new government, laying its foundation on such principles and organizing its powers in such form, as to them shall seem most likely to effect their safety and happiness."

These ideas have never ceased to yield inspiration. Their expression in this form was a turning point in modern political history, and their subsequent influence has been profound. Yet the concepts enshrined in the Declaration are not free from difficulties, either philosophical or practical. Designed for a solution to existing problems, they inaugurated new ones.

Consider some implications of the doctrine of consent. Besides the ethical force of the argument that consent lends morality to the actions of government, it made sense in the seventeenth and eighteenth centuries to contend that, when people stayed in a community, the fact of their remaining implied their consent to its functions. Englishmen who disliked their government could immigrate across the Atlantic. Colonists who wished, after 1776, to remain under the British crown could move north to Canada. Where there was some freedom of movement, the doctrine of consent was not a pious fiction. It contained some realism. But in the twentieth century, the world is not so open. Millions, having no alternative and being unable to emigrate, must live under a regime to which they do not consent.

Moreover, consent implies agreement, but agreement about what? Is it about procedures (for example, elections, voting, and majority decisions), whereby we assent in advance to abide by any result that emerges from the procedures? Or is it agreement about ends and goals? That is to say, do we agree in preferring a certain social order, a group of values, a civilisation? And do we then regard it as a duty of government not to do whatever would violate such values? In the former case, there can be no restriction on how the procedures are used, provided that a "due process" is followed. In the latter case, the restrictions are definite, since the community is committed to certain goals. These will be modified only as we come to prefer new values or alter the interpretation of the old ones.

Plainly consent, if stated as an absolute, will not be completely realised in practice. Since unanimity never exists in big political issues, somebody's consent has to be forfeited whenever a majority has its way at the expense of a minority. On occasion, it may be in society's interest for the majority to prevail, and for the minority to submit. But cannot majorities also be oppressive? And, if so, is not the minority then entitled to resist? In other words, consent is not the sole pillar of a free society, though it is certainly one of the pillars that are fundamental. Ensuring the freedom of the governed is not the apparently simple process of discovering what the people will and then doing it. On most matters there are many wills. Since human beings, belonging to many groups, have so many interests. Because in actuality the support sustaining a government will at times be that of a majority, at other times that of a minority, the governed need alternately protection by government and protection from it. To assert the inalienable right of a people to regain their freedom by revolution is excellent doctrine. But it describes an ultimate weapon for use in the last resort. Revolution can be a method—fully justified when it is directed against a despotism—of funding a government in the first instance. It is not a means of continuous popular control over regular government activities. For this, something else is required, and it is to the credit of Jefferson's generation that they not only formulated the principles, but also constructed workable institutions which have yield results in practice. The foundations of the later were laid between 1787 and 1803.[9]

SUPREMACY OF THE CONSTITUTION

In the American solution to this problem of giving government the power to serve, but denying it the power to dominate, the distinctive feature is the role assigned to the

Constitution. The English Revolution left Parliament supreme; the American Revolution resulted in the supremacy of the Constitution. How is this ensured? Various measures guarantee that the Constitution will be paramount. It was drafted by a special convention of delegates, with Washington presiding. Its adoption was refereed to the states, all of which, except Rhode Island, elected delegates to special conventions which voted on the issue of ratification. Since going into effect, the status of the Constitutions has remained unique. The preamble announced that "we, the People … do ordain and establish this Constitution," thereby affirming that the government is founded on the popular will. While the people create the Constitution, the latter creates the institutions of government. All these—Congress, President, and Supreme Court, as well as the constitutions of the states—are subordinate to the Constitution of the United States, to laws conforming to it, and to treaties made under its authority, which together comprise "the supreme law of the land."[10]

Besides being asserted, the supremacy of the Constitution must be enforced. How is this accomplished? First, by requiring that all government officials—federal, state, and local, elected and appointed—take an oath or affirmation to support the Constitution. Second, by judicial procedures and penalties, including impeachment, in case any official betrays the peoples' trust. Third, by requiring a special method, distinct from the ordinary process of legislation, for amending the Constitutions' written text. Fourth, by judicial review of legislation, through which any statute enacted by the legislature and approved by the chief executive or repassed over a veto may be challenged as unconstitutional. A case will then be heard in the courts, where the judiciary determine whether the contested statute is to be obeyed as law or treated as null an void.

THE RULE OF LAW

These principles are a special derivation from the broader concept of "the rule of law." The main requirements of that famous doctrine are as follows:

1. Governments shall exercise their powers in conformity with known laws enacted through a regular procedure.

2. No laws shall convert into offenses action that were lawful when they were performed.

3. No one may be convicted on any charge save after a fair trial in open court.

4. The judiciary, when applying the generalities of the law to particular cases, must be independent of external pressure and control.

Such maxims, while arguable on theoretical grounds, have grown from the facts of experience. Each was formulated in contrast with the proven practices of many governments in the past and present. When a state does not enthrone the rule of law, the governed have no adequate protection against the whims of those in power. Tyranny, despotism, or dictatorship exists when a government makes and unmakes the law without permitting public criticism or challenge; when it imprisons an individual without public hearing and an equal opportunity for defense; when judges decide cases under the intimidating shadow of executive power; and when laws are enforced arbitrarily, so as to discriminate on grounds of political or personal favouritism between citizens who deserve like treatment.

The constitution that Massachusetts adopted in 1776 contained the hope "that it may be a government of laws and not of men." That antithesis cannot be taken literally. No legal system can operate automatically without human discretion. Laws, unlike some individuals, are not self-made. Still less are they self-enforcing. Human beings must draft, enact, interpret, and apply the law scaling down the broad classification to the narrow particulars. But though the Massachusetts formula is rhetorical exaggeration, the antithesis emphasizes an important distinction. A state may be organised with curbs on its activities. Or it may flout restraint. In the former case the governments power is harnessed and bridled; in the latter, it is absolute and uncontrollable.

CONFORMANCE OF LAW TO CUSTOM, NATURE, OR UTILITY

To impose the restraint of law on government has been tried in various ways, each with its merits and difficulties. An example is the notion that law is the product of immemorial custom. As the deposits of millions of micro-organisms eventually surround an island with a coral reef, so millions of human acts repeated in habitual patterns construct a ring of custom around a community and its governance. Custom is then a barrier confining officials within limits, and law is the accretion of practices with custom has confirmed. Discover the usages of the past, and you find the law of the present. This done, the duty of government is to preserve unbroken the links which connect the chain of custom. Such a view is adequate to maintain a stable continuity in an imperceptibly changing society. But it ill accords with circumstances of rapid flux when experiment and flexibility are more needed than tradition.

Another device for subordinating the state legal restraint is the belief in a law of nature or reason. Once the assumption is accepted that such a law exists, which is a matter of faith rather than reasons, various consequences can be deduced—for instance, that nature embodies principles that can be understood by reason, that these are universal in scope and eternal in duration, that the state governs well when it assists the individual in conforming to natural law, and that acts which violate such law are invalid. This "higher law" theory, like the doctrine that derives law from custom, is appropriately adapted to a certain goal. By appealing to a higher law (that is, higher than that proclaimed by the state) people may justify resistance to authority or outright revolution, since it is always psychologically necessary for those who resist or rebel to make their opponents, not themselves, appear in the wrong. Alternatively, the higher law doctrine suits the needs of other institutions which fear the state or are its rivals, for these can affirm that humanity does not live by politics alone and that in nature's house there are many mansions. With such reasons, both churches and corporations have welcomed the notion of a natural law.

But its philosophy abounds with unsolved problems. How do we know which principles are natural or what is reason's law? When different interpretations are offered, which is correct? Because of these uncertainties, the practical effects of appealing to natural law can be unfortunate. Those who flee from one type of authority, that of the state and its laws, seek refuge in the arms of another, for example, that of the priest, pastor, or entrepreneur. The law of nature is then respectively translated into the law of nature's God, as clerical authority affirms it, or the natural laws of economics, as some economist expounds them. Alternatively, those who shrink from substituting new authoritarianism for old will escape into the relativism that rejects every interpretation of natural law on the ground that anybody's guess may be right and none can be proven. In this case there is a flight from reason; decisions are reached through force, and the more powerful proclaim themselves the rightful.

A third formula for using law to restrain government is the maxim of Jeremy Bentham and the Unilitarians—that governments must promote the greatest happiness of the greatest number. The Utilitarians were the British reformers of the early nineteenth century who, seeking to modernize their political machinery and legal code, applied to every law and institution the test: What is its utility? Whatever statute or executive act helped to increase the sum total of happiness in the community was considered good. Whatever diminished that stock of happiness must be removed or reformed. A government merited support or opposition according to how it influenced happiness. Such a yardstick subjects the state to a different standard. To appraise a government's action by its degree of conformity to custom or nature means referring to the source of authority. To test an act by its relation to happiness means studying its effects and comparing one set of result with another. Thus the latter approach is empirical. Applied in practice, however, Bentham's formula fails, because it is impossible to measure a quantity of happiness. People have wrangled endlessly about whether a particular governmental action, compare with possible untried alternatives, produces more happiness or less.

CONSTITUTIONS AND CONSTITUTIONALISM

Besides these ways of restraining government by law, there is the more general argument that the state will not tyrannize over its citizens if it is imbued with respect for constitutionalism. What does this mean? A distinction should be made between "constitutionalism" and " the constitution." A constitution is the basic design of the structure and powers of the state and the rights and duties of its citizens. In that sense there is a constitution in every state with an established government—in the United States, Canada, and Britain, as well as in Nazi Germany, Franco Spain, and Stalin's Russia. To say that a state possesses a constitution implies nothing about its democratic or dictatorial character. Constitutionalism, however, is a term with specific implications. It is bound up with the notion of restraining power by the rule of law; it embraces the idea that a government should not be permitted to do whatever its officials please, but should conduct itself by agreed and equitable procedures. The purpose of this restriction on its freedom of action is, of course, to safeguard a fundamental area of freedom for its citizens. For tyranny exists wherever power is total.

Clear though it is that Constitutionalism is incompatible with dictatorship, and that political freedom requires a curb on power, the nature of these limits calls for more discussion. Just as it is one thing to harness a horse and another to hobble it, so it is one thing to control a government and another to cripple it. The difference may be one of degree or emphasis, but it is all-important. It stems from contrasted attitudes toward power. Some are so fearful of its abuses that their picture of constitutionalism is a series of prohibitions. Their rule of law develops into a roll of negatives. To devise checks, controls, restraints, and limitations beccmes the essence of constitutionalism and the prime guarantee of human freedom. But is it really necessary to lean so far backwards? May not this over attention to abuses defeat its own purpose? Since government is indispensable and no one can govern without power, it is evident that constitutionalism should first be concerned with how power must be used, then with the prevention of its abuse. The state should be envisaged as a canal through which political power may flow, releasing its energy for the benefit of mankind, rather than as a dam to hold it back. After all, the first aim of any philosophy of government is to figure out what the state must do, not what it should be prohibited from doing. Nor is it to be forgotten that, while tyrannical governments destroy freedom, other governments may enlarge it. Many of the functions undertaken by the modern state are designed to make opportunities more nearly equal for everybody and to protect weaker individuals from the rapacity of the strong.

But there is a still more basic objection to those who develop their photograph of constitutionalism in the negative and neglect to print the positive. If constitutionalism is approved on the ground that it restrains government, the inquiry is thrown one stage further back. Constitutionalism itself is the result of other factors. What are these? Essentially they are political, which switches the discussion onto another track. Hitherto in this chapter the problem of making government accountable to the governed has been treated in a predominantly legal light—in terms of the rule of law, of legal curbs on power, of constitutionalism—so that political freedom appears as the consequence of a certain legal situation. But this is an illusion, for the image has been turned upside down. Although there is always some interaction between law and politics, it is primarily politics that controls and determines law. It is not the rule of law or respect for constitutionalism that gives birth to a politically free society, but rather the politics of freedom that creates the sanction for constitutionalism and law. What has been called "the firmament of law"[11] is not self-supporting. It is propped up on political pillars. Without them, it would topple.

THE POLITICAL ROOTS OF THE AMERICAN CONSTITUTIONAL SYSTEM

To understand this, let us take a closer look at the government of the United States. The Constitution stands at the centre and is the chief symbol of the American form of government. Drafted in 1787, the Constitution went into operation with the election of the first Congress and the inauguration of George Washington as the first President. In the course of two centuries, this document has evolved in an organic relationship with the country whose needs it serves. The repetition of precedents, arising from similar responses to similar circumstances, has produced a body of custom, and this in turn has grown into living traditions which enfold the written text as the bark surrounds a tree trunk. Moreover, because the Constitution has survived for two centuries and has accompanied the American people from the infancy of Independence to the stature of a super grown power, it has also taken on meanings which are more symbolic than literal. Let us examine some of its complexities.

Because the Constitution is a supreme law and contains a list of judicially enforceable rights, and because of the practice of judicial review of legislation, it has become customary to think of the Constitution as a document to be construed in legal fashion.[12] But this is to overlook the political context which ascribes to law its significance and to judges their status. Under the Constitution the ultimate power is lodged not with the Supreme Court but with the people. It is "We, the people" who "ordain and establish" the Constitution. It is the People's elected representatives who amend it and may express their disapproval of a Supreme Court decision by an amendment.[13] It is the political branches of the government. The President and the Senate, that nominate and confirm appointees to the Court and, by choosing its personnel, influence the trend of future decisions. Where the rule of law exists, it is because a political will wants to have it so.

This point is reinforced by a further reflection. As practising politicians know and students of government soon discover, many features of the American system of government cannot be learned from reading the Constitution. The latter is a compact document, its brevity being one of its merits. On few issues does it elaborate in any detail, and those are mostly concerned with electoral machinery or the procedure for a presidential veto of legislation. For the rest, as a Constitution should be, it is broad in scope and general in its terms. Since the Bill of Rights (the first ten amendments) was added in 1791, the text has been changed only 17 times in two centuries. But the nation has altered beyond recognition. From four million persons living in 13 states along the Atlantic seaboard with an agrarian economy and a precarious military position, this Union has expanded to 250 millions spread across 50 states from the Atlantic far into the Pacific and from the Arctic Circle to the Tropic of Cancer, exhibiting a highly developed industrial technology, administering distant bases and possessions, and wielding a mighty aggregate of military strength. Of these changes there is scarcely a trace in the text of the constitution. But such social transformations cannot fail to affect the basic design of the powers and structure of government and the rights and duties of citizens—to repeat the definition offered earlier.[14] It stands to reason therefore that these effects have been registered in other ways than by the formal method of constitutional amendment. If so, what are they?

The first is legislative enactment. Much of the output of Congress, admittedly, is not concerned with fundamentals. Legislation runs the gamut from private bills that concern a particular person to measures affecting the prosperity and security of the nation and the world. Certain of these statutes, as judged by their subject matter occupy a crucial position in the governmental process. Laws that organize the federal courts, that establish the major departments, that provide a programme of social security, that regulate the franchise or the conduct of elections—these deal with matters no less fundamental than some sections of the Constitution itself. The continuous labours of over 100 Congresses have done much to shape the primary patterns of American government.

The same may be said of the supreme Court. Because the Founding Fathers were writing a Constitution rather than a stature, they drafted many clauses in language so broad as to permit diversity of definition and detail. In countless instances the Court had to supply the guiding principles for Congress and the executive branch to follow. Consider the federal powers over interstate commerce and general welfare.[15] Their terse wording has left room for wide possibilities, as can be seen in the decisions which the Court has rendered. When they interpret these powers—as with due process, equal protection, or free speech—the judges are in effect amending the Constitution by giving its generalities more precision. Judge-made definitions have added essential portions to the foundations which the Constitution laid.[16]

Nor is this all. Many fundamental facts in the American system of government can be explained only in political, not in legal, terms. Some sections of the Constitution have not been applied in practice because political considerations prevented their enforcement. Thus the fourteenth Amendment declares, in section 2, that if a state denies voting rights to any of its citizens, the congressional representation to which its population entitles that state shall be proportionately reduced. Until 1958 no effect was given to that provision because, had it been strictly enforced, both major parties and many states, northern as well as southern, would have lost representation. By "gentlemen's agreement," therefore, the Constitution was tacitly ignored. At long last, however, the Civil Rights Laws of 1957 and 1964 attempted to cope with this problem. The commission created by the Act of 1957 probed for two decades into districts where blacks were systematically prevented from registering to vote and initiated action in the courts against the responsible local authorities.[17]

This becomes plainer when one reflects on other features of American government which have developed into customary political practice and of which the Constitution remains innocent. Many examples can be cited, but none is more revealing than the rise and organisation of political parties. The party system that grew in the nineteenth century was antithetical to the ideals of those who drafted the United States Constitution. Thus the institutions they constructed did not anticipate the emergence of parties, were not designed to admit them, and have not always dovetailed with them in a harmonious fit. What is more, James Madison and other leading spirits of his generation viewed government by parties as an evil, since they habitually described their eighteenth-century equivalents by the unfavourable term *factions*. Modern democracy, however, has taken the parties into the inner sanctum of power, and its political process is now unthinkable without them. Voting for a president by means of a college of electors; the organisation, procedures, and output of Congress; cooperation or friction between chief executive and legislature; the people's choice of policies and personalities; none of these would be as they are if parties did not profoundly influence the result. No small slice of American government is composed of political customs whose content is as important and enduring as what is written in the Constitution.

Hence we need a realistic approach to the problem of explaining what a constitution is and does. The pattern of government in the United States can be compared to a river created by the confluence of four streams. First is the document entitled the Constitution. Second is legislation. The third consists of judicial opinions. The fourth is political custom. A convenient term to embrace the four would be "the constitutional system." This is what underpins the entire structure of government; its strength rests on the bedrock of political power, not on the sands of legal formulas.

THE POLITICS OF THE BRITISH CONSTITUTION

If more evidence is needed to sustain this view it can be gathered from Britain. To many writers on politics the British form of government appears a paradox, especially when compared with the United States. Some striking differences exist between the two constitutional systems. In Britain there is no document analogous to the United States Constitution. Parliament, unlike, Congress, is empowered to make any kind of law it chooses.[18] The courts have no authority to nullify legislation. From the purely legal standpoint, therefore, it is impossible in Britain to specify which rules, procedures, and institutions are part of the constitution and which are not; and a constitutional lawyer, reasoning only from legal assumptions, can never satisfactorily explain the nature of the constitution and its sanctions. Much nonsense has consequently been written about Britain by those who, starting with false premises, arrive at wrong conclusions. Thus de Tocqueville asserted that because of the legal supremacy of Parliament, which may change the constitution at any time by simple legislative act, there is in reality no constitution at all.[19] An odd argument this one, since it involves defining a constitution so narrowly, restricting it to those states where the power of the legislature is limited by a superior law.

Equally odd was the reasoning of A.V. Dicey, the English jurist who distinguished between what he called the law of the constitution and its conventions (that is, customs). The former consists of rules enforced by the courts; the latter, of rules binding through political usage. Political rules are obeyed, he said, because if they were not, a breach of law would follow—which satisfies a lawyer's logic, but is untrue in many cases.[20] For the British constitution is a political instrument, not a legal charter. What the British call their constitution is the consensus, reached by the end of the seventeenth century, about the principles to which their government should conform and the institutions which make it effective. That consensus is political because it embodies the will of an overwhelming majority in favour of a particular structure of government. This will may be expressed in various ways. One is for Parliament to enact a statute, or for the courts to render a decision acceptable to Parliament, in which case a political will is dressed in the outer raiments of law. Another way leaves it to usage to build a set of rules, creating the expectation that what was done under like circumstances in the past will ordinarily be followed in the present. Each method has merits. To write a political agreement into legal form results in greater precision if the wording is detailed and exact, and this may reduce the area of controversy. To leave decisions to the formulation of custom may permit a change to be speedily accomplished in a time of crisis without the need for conforming to legal procedures which can be cumbrous.

THE BRITISH AND AMERICAN SYSTEMS COMPARED

A comparison of the British and American systems permits a more accurate view of constitutions. Misunderstanding of both has given rise to false contrasts and exaggerated distinctions. Thus, the American constitution has been described as written; the British, as unwritten. If taken literally, that is incorrect; if figuratively the meaning is unclear. The truth is that both systems include portions committed to writing and portions that are not. The statutes and judicial opinions, as well as the text of the Constitution of the United States, are written—as if the form were the decisive factor in determining the character of a constitution! That certain topics receive written statement, while others are left to informal understanding, is not of itself a profound difference. What surely matters more is what content receives expression in one medium or the other.

Another contrast calls the British system flexible, the American rigid. The point at issue here is not trivial. It concerns the ease or difficulty of the method by which the constitution is changed. The belief, however, in the flexibility of the one vis-ā-vis the rigidity of the other is a fallacious inference. The British constitution, it is argued, consists of two parts—law and custom. The law may be changed at any time by ordinary Act of Parliament. Custom, too, may be altered by statute, or by the simple device of departing from precedent. In either case, change is possible. The American Constitution however, consists of the document drafted in 1787 and amended 27 times since then. The process of amending the text of the Constitution presents a formidable obstacle to innovation.

The errors and omissions in this argument are numerous. It rests on a myopic view of the American Constitution, excluding from sight the statutes, judicial opinions, and political usages, which in a broader and more realistic sense are integral parts of the constitutional system. It further assume that amendments to the constitution of the United States can be obtained only with the greatest difficulty; that in political reality Parliament will dare to proceed as far as its legal powers extend; and that rules of custom are more readily modified than rules of law. None of these assumptions is wholly correct. When the people of the United States decided after a dozen years of nationwide prohibition that the experiment was unworkable, they adopted the Twenty-first Amendment easily and speedily. On the other hand, the custom that no president should serve more than two terms was maintained for a century and a half with a rigidity which only the menace of Hitler and the greatness of Franklin D. Roosevelt could shatters.[21] As for the use by Parliament of its theoretically unlimited authority, obstacles and limitations do exist—but they are of a political, rather than a juridical nature.

This does not mean that on the subject of rigidity or flexibility the two constitutional systems are indistinguishable. Genuine distinctions may be drawn, but the reasons for them have been wrongly stated. Any portion of a constitutional system, legal or customary, is likely to be rigid if expressed in minute detail and supported by an organised sentiment. Conversely, any provision, legal or customary, can be flexible if its terms are vague or general and if sentiment in its favour is lukewarm or disorganised.

Some examples will illustrate these points. A rigid feature of the American Constitution is the clause prescribing a four-year term for the president and an election for a new term in every fourth year. Never yet in peace or in war[22] have the American people deviated from the requirement of conducting the presidential election at identical and regular intervals. Only by amendment to the constitution could a president's term be shortened or lengthened and a special election held. Rigidity on this point is mainly due to the exactitude with which the Constitution expresses itself. On the other hand, where the wording is general and imprecise, this same Constitution (though "written"!) can prove conveniently flexible. The interstate commerce clause, for instance, has been subject to vastly varying interpretations, each reflecting the changing views of the majority of voters, congressmen, or judges.

The same can be said of the rules produced through custom. I mentioned that the Constitution is entirely silent about parties, yet they have profoundly influenced its operation. Contrast their effect on electing the president and on voting in the legislature. The president is not elected directly by the people, but by members of a college elected in the 50 states for that specific purpose. When people wish to vote for their party's candidate, they vote in fact for others of the same party who then cast their ballots in the electoral college for their party's presidential nominee. Nothing in federal[23] law compels the members of the college to vote for the party's choice. Political obligation, however, requires them to do so. They perform this one duty as expected, whereupon their office terminates.

How different is the voting in congress! Senators and representatives are elected under a party label and continue during their term to be party members. But neither they nor their constituents consider them obliged to vote with the majority of their party on every issue or to support every measure proposed by a president of their own party. Indeed, on many a legislative decision, a minority of Republicans will be found voting with the majority of Democrats, and vice versa. What this means is that the party system requires discipline on the one specific matter of getting its candidate into the White House, since control of the presidency is vital to the power of the party. The parties do not yet, however, regard the enactment of legislation or the acceptance of a president's programme as equally vital. They therefore tolerate some independence in the halls of Congress. Thus rules of custom, like rules of law, may be rigid or flexible according to the precision with which they are formulated and the force of opinion behind them.[24]

THE FRENCH EXPERIENCE

Another comparison confirms the point that control over the government rests ultimately on political sanctions. In the United Kingdom and the United States the constitutions have stood the test of time. And usually they work, because behind them lies the consensus of a community whose union outweighs its divisions. But observe what happens when the picture is reversed. When disunities transcend agreement, not only is it impossible to establish constitutionalism but a constitution itself cannot function properly. Where the needed political underpinnings are absent, the legal super-structure will sag and bend out of alignment. A pertinent example is France. Since 1789 the French have experienced 14[25] regimes, some quite short-lived. The longest, the Third Republic, lasted from 1875 to 1940, but collapsed in military defeat. The average duration for a constitution, through the Fourth Republic, was 13 years. Why was this?

The reasons do not lie primarily in the institutions which the French have tried to operate. As the figures imply, France has run the gamut of constitutional experiments, but none of those adopted thus far gained enough support to endure. This was equally true of legislative supremacy, executive supremacy, and the cabinet system.

During the Third and Fourth Republic, 1875-1940 and 1946-1958, it was evident that the root of the political malady lay deeper than the structure of government. Some attributed the blame to the party system, whose turbulence and inner discords made crisis endemic and agreement abnormal. But the party system was an effect more than a cause. Its own chaotic character was symptomatic of a more fundamental malady, the cleavages within French society, whose number and crisscrossing made widespread and long-term combinations impossible. The French Revolution not only came later than the English, but left deep scars which took time to efface. The representatives of the old order were weakened but not crushed. Aristocrats and others of authoritarian bent despised the unglamorous Republic and its talkative democracy. The army leaders, bred in discipline, saw politics as anarchy. Patriotic as Frenchmen, they were often disloyal to the regime they were supposed to defend. The church, identified with the traditional order, found in the secular state a disturbing competitor and in the accompanying rationalistic philosophies a challenge to its dogma. The economic transformation, which industrialism required, was absorbed more slowly by the French than by Americans, British, Germans, and Japanese. Most French people did not take readily to large-scale organisation. Basically individualistic, they had always been artisans first and mass-producers second. They felt comfortable in the small enterprise, whether in farming, commerce, or manufacturing. When forced into a big organisation, their individualism rendered them mutually discordant.[26]

Then in reaction and resignation, they would finally accept an authoritarian system—witness their army, church, and empire. Large-scale democratic organisation they had not yet devised. In France, therefore, the majorities needed not only for stable government but for a constitutional consensus, were lacking. Negative majorities—that is, a vote against something—were always forthcoming.[27] Positive majorities, in favour of something, were hard to elicit. Under these conditions, the competitive factors outweighed the cooperative. Interests, pressure groups, organisations, and parties struggled among themselves—but without the wider harmonies that keep divisiveness in check. Whether the future will be an improvement, we wait to see. The constitution chosen by de Gaulle for the Fifth Republic has already lasted more than twice as long as the average. It had three conservative presidents in succession, followed in 1981 by a socialist. That is a good augury, since it demonstrates a trend away from multipartism toward a two-party alternation. Moreover, the fact that Left and Right can operate the same institutions may indicate the emergence of a consensus which heretofore was lacking. Should that turn out to be the case, France may at last succeed in extricating itself from the dilemma it faced for so long—either multipartism or Bonapartism.

Once again, does not the French experience illustrate that politics will determine the constitution, the restraints of law, the orderly alternation in power of changing majorities, and all the rest? In the political process reposes our government salvation—or damnation.

THE KEY TO FREEDOM

By what political method can the people control the powers they grant? How can a populace that reposes trust in its officials be sure they will not overstep the limits of their authority? One clue is suggested by the events discussed in chapters. The efforts of medieval popes and modern corporation presidents to curb the power of the state produced competing institutions that rivaled the state in the interests they mobilised and the loyalty they exacted. The peculiar significance of those ventures lay in the attempt to construct within society, but outside the political framework, an association capable of resisting the state. When dualism led to discord, and discord to conflict, the unity of the social order was eventually reaffirmed under the aegis of the political order. The triumphant assertion, however, of the primacy of the state over the rest of society could permit a tyrannical abuse of power, if no corrective existed. The secret of the new solution has been to limit political power not from outside, but from within; to make the state safe for its citizens not by an external but by an inner check.

The method by which this is done is ingenious. It consists of an argument in various stages. Stage one asserts that the state belongs to all its members, whether they are of the government or of the governed. This is a rejection of the authoritarian, elitist view that the rulers are the state and that the people are subjects who belong to them .The contrary belief is contained in the two famous terms, "republic"[28] and "commonwealth." Both have essentially the same meaning: The state belongs to the public who own it as wealth shared in common. The second stage is a corollary of the first. If the state is the property of the whole people, including both government and governed, a distinction exists between the state and its government. The government is not identical with the state. It consists of a few chosen from the whole people who act in the name of the state and on its behalf and for a while dispose of its authority. The implication is that the same state can have a succession of different governments. These may change while the state continues.

But how can the government change and one groups of rulers take the place of another? By a device which is perhaps the most notable of modern contributions to the art of politics: the party system. In itself, the existence of parties is not new. What is novel is the organisation of modern parties, their place in the political process, and our attitude toward them. Two centuries ago parties were viewed with disfavour as a menace to the unity of the state. Because people had conspired to resist despotic kings, part was tinged with the taint of treason. Around the party, because schisms had split the church, hung the whiff of heresy. The name of faction, which a party was often called, was unsavoury in early America, as Washington warned in his Farewell Address.

Since then, the growth of democracy has changed our perspective.[29] While no one would deny that a system of government by alternating parties is imperfect, a superior method of ensuring political freedom has yet to be found. So strong is this conviction in democratic countries that the existence of more than one party has become an essential criterion to distinguish a regime of liberty from dictatorship. For where there is an opportunity of choice, there is some freedom. Where no choice exists, there is coercion. Hence when the nature of the state is appraised, an all important test is whether more than one party is tolerated. When the connection between party politics and freedom is studied, the difference between a two-party and a multiparty system appears far less significant than the gulf between one-party government and any system containing more than one. Indeed if language has any meaning, the term *one-party system* is a misnomer. By definition, a party is a part of the whole and therefore implies the presence of an alternative. To speak of the one-party state is a contradiction in terms. Such a state, whether Fascist or Communist, exhibits a monopoly of power. Its proper name is dictatorship.

THE REQUIREMENT OF TWO OR MORE PARTIES

A system containing two or more parties is a major step in the attainment of political maturity. Historically the emergence of the modern party has accompanied the growth of the modern electorate. Indeed, it was the latter that made the former possible. As the right to vote was extended throughout the nineteenth century, party organisations, which previously had been based mainly on legislative cliques, undertook to attract and mobilize the ever-increasing electorate. Parties then acquired their new character. They became mass organisations, linking together a large body of citizens with their representatives in the legislature; they developed institutions of their own, and to fight and win elections they besought financial contributions. In this way the parties responded to a genuine need. Without them, the millions who comprised the new electorate would have become a disorganised crowd, unable to formulate their aims or debate the vast issues they confronted. By means of parties, the voters obtained a medium that, to state it in no stronger terms, afforded a chance for coherent action and, hopefully, responsible policies.

Nothing in the entire conception of the party system is as crucial as the requirement that there be more than one party. This condition sanctions the right of criticism and opposition as legitimate and necessary element in the political process. The government of Britain symbolizes this situation with a unique terminology. There the ministry is officially styled her Majesty's Government. In like manner the minority party is Her Majesty's Opposition—its loyal duty being to oppose in the name of the crown what the majority is loyally doing in the crown's name. The result of this remarkable concept is that resistance to power—if its methods are peaceful—is brought within the constitutional order. Nor longer need those who seek a change of government launch a revolution. No longer does the prevention of tyranny depend on constructing outside the state institutions capable of opposing it. By the coexistence of two or more parties, the means of curbing an over powerful government is built within the political order. The parties in opposition supply today's equivalent of the captains of industry and finance in the era of unregulated capitalism or the popes and cardinals of a still earlier age. But the relation of the state to society, and the nature of the state itself, are vitally different when the check on the abuse of power exists inside the political order, not outside. Freedom is not primarily the legal concept that jurists depict. Nor is it, as Robert M. Maclver holds, solely the consequence of a pluralistic[30] society. In the modern state, freedom is basically political. It permits and is then perpetuated by a two or multiparty system.

THE INS AND THE OUTS

Saying this, however, does not exhaust the complexity of the relation between a party that governs and one that opposes. The peculiarity of this relationship is that the party in power does not eliminate those opposed to it, and the latter, while opposing, obey the declared will of the majority of the moment. Each side recognizes that it is a member of a system requiring, as a permanent feature, the existence of an opponent. Each accepts the principle of "live and let live" in the knowledge that the system allows each in turn its fair share of power. The corollary to this is that alternation must in fact occur—i.e., at some point of time, those in power leave office and are replaced by those in opposition. The reason why this is essential to a genuine democracy is that the certainty of such alternation imposes restraints on those wielding power for the time being.[31] In addition, if one group holds office continuously for too long, corruption and arrogance set in. When this happens, cynicism pervades the general public and civic morale breaks down.

Alternation cannot occur, however, unless the scales are evenly balanced between the two sides. A free election is not necessarily a fair election: Indeed, we had had evidence since the

1970s of a new threat to democracy. This arises from a combination of factors—the numbers entitled to vote, the cost of campaigning, and the artifice of novel techniques of communication. Already this tendency has reached serious proportions in the United States where the electorate is huge, the interests involved are rich and powerful, and technology is so advanced. Here it is that the politics of democracy now suffers from invasion by the economics of the market. America's commercial culture, obsessed with the need to sell, has relied on advertising to entice potential buyers, and the advertisers have drawn heavily on the research of behavioural psychologists. What results is a massive system of manipulating consumers by blending truth, half-truth, and untruth. For this the most potent of media lies ready to hand. It is television—immediate in impact and, with its fleeting images, escaping critical analysis. When employed in a political campaign by the skilled practitioners of "public relations." Candidates for office and party programmes are packaged and "sold" as are laxatives and deodorants. And all of this costs billions of dollars, which the wealthy contribute. Thus can the oligarchy of the corporate rich prostitute the democracy of the mass.

These dangers, which have become very real, illustrate that general characteristic of the political process which I noted earlier. Conditions generate problems; these receive solutions, which then become problems requiring further solutions. The electoral system, as it evolved during the nineteenth century, contained many flaws which had to be corrected, and eventually were. New flaws are evident now, but built into the system itself is the opportunity for their correction. What is needed is political action to place legal curbs on the power of wealth and bridle the monster of television advertising in the public interest. That in turn will require a consensus between the political parties that the individualist concept of freedom must be tempered by the social value of fairness.

This raises, of course, the very large point that parties, thus prepared to alternate in office do not disagree on everything. Overriding their differences on other matters is a consensus about the basic features of the system to which they belong. This is only another way, however, of describing the Constitution, which, as I stressed earlier, is essentially a political instrument. Its contents include those principles and procedures about which the parties are in the main agreed. Conversely, the parties give their general support to the constitutional system that embodies some of their wishes and guarantees each its place. A revolutionary party is, of course, one that wholly rejects these fundamentals and operates, whether from outside or inside the constitutional system, in order to destroy it.

The situation where parties cooperate in some matters, but compete in others, is precisely the crux of the problem discussed in chapter 2. There, I suggested that individuals and groups are thrown into social relationships by the contrasted, yet complementary, influences of cooperation and competition. The relation between parties and their constitution, and the manner in which government and opposition reciprocally contribute to freedom and to constitutionalism, afford an example of competition within a framework of cooperation. The forces operating at the core of the political process are based on the same principles as give rise to the formation of groups and the development of society itself.

Moreover, the possibility of cooperating and yet competing within the same framework is linked politically with certain requirements as to means and ends. If people are to coexist through constitutionalism, they must abandon violence. Otherwise might prevails—whether this be the majority crushing a minority or a resolute minority intimidating an unorganised majority. Since the 1960s many countries rediscovered amid domestic turmoil a truth that had been forgotten since the thirties, that violence employed by any side begets its counter violence. Once this happens, a community is drawn into a spiralling sequence of conspiratorial coercion, mob reaction, and police repression.

But to prevent recourse to violence, something positive is required. All individuals and groups in the society must be treated according to a common standard of justice in the sense that their basic substantive rights are respected and enforced. Whoever feel that they are denied justice and that the system of government is not responsive to their legitimate claims will be disposed to attack it with violence; that is, they will resort to extra-constitutional means. In that case, "law and order" are imposed by those who enjoy their benefits upon those who do not. Society will avoid disorders only when the order that the power of the state underpins by force is recognizes as universally just—or as capable of achieving justice through flexible adaptation.

FLAWS IN THE "IRON LAW" OF OLIGARCHY

To this argument, however, an objection has been raised which, if valid, strikes at its root. Against authoritarian doctrines that subject the governed to a ruling elite, the principle of freedom proclaims that the governed must and can control their rulers. For this to be realised in practice, the many have to be able to control the few. But can they? Some have denied that they can. There are influential thinkers who hold that all social activity requires organisation; that organisation evokes leadership by a few; that leaders must be in command over their followers; that so it has always been and ever shall be. Vilfredo Pareto is author of the saying: "In fact, with or without universal suffrage, it is always an oligarchy which governs, and which knows how to give whatever expression it likes to the 'popular will'." Roberto Michels formulated what he called "the iron law of oligarchy," Asserting that in every human association power gravitates by an inevitable tendency into the hands of a few. But the force they wield, the fear they instill, the prestige they possess, and the propaganda they spread, the superior few outwit and overawe the mass. "Majority rule." "responsibility to the people," "popular sovereignty," and similar phrases are illusions which cunning rulers offer their unwitting dupes.

This view is backed by enough plausible evidence to have gained may adherents. Nobody would deny that all human institutions abound with examples of oligarchical rule. Scan the records of churches, clerical orders, armies, navies, universities, business corporations, trade unions, governments, political parties, civil services, and you find the same pattern of controlling cliques, power monopolies, and autocratic bossism. Our social history includes, several upheavals against tyrannical authority that were designed to set people free but did not always turn out as planned. The Gospel of Jesus was a challenge to the might of Rome. Its teaching was pacifist and equalitarian; its ultimate political ideal, anarchist. But in a later century the church became wedded to power and then did what it deemed necessary to maintain its power. The French Revolution was initially dedicated to the principles of liberty, equality, and fraternity. Yet its attempts to usher in a new birth of freedom delivered the military autocrat Napoleon. The Bolshevik Revolution was once greeted with the plaudits of many an idealist who hailed it as a landmark in human liberation. But Stalin's relentless rule forged the fetters of a new despotism.

What does this add up to? That the larger part of the government of mankind has been oligarchic? That many a movement conceived in freedom has degenerated into its opposite? This much is true and cannot be gainsaid. When Michels spoke of an iron law, however, he was asserting its universal applicability. In one sweeping formula he sought to summarize the whole range of mankind's experience in constructing institutions to serve their needs. But is it true that all organisations have been, and must be, oligarchic? Apart from two exceptions—the military and civil services, both of which are universally built in hierarchical style from the top down—every institution offers some instances of control by its members. One may grant that democratic governments are imperfect and do not yet attain their own ideal. Nevertheless, to dismiss as a sham the record in countries great and small—in the United States, Switzerland, Great Britain, Norway, or New Zealand—does violence to truth.

The fact that power in any community tends to gravitate to a few and that authority is ordinarily exercised by a minority does not refute the possibility or genuineness of democracy. What makes the vital difference between dictatorship and freedom, between responsible and irresponsible power, is the method whereby authority is acquired, the conditions under which it is wielded, and the manner in which it is forfeited. The nature of power is changed—not merely its external apparatus, but its inner character—when its holders must run the gauntlet of periodic elections and respond to the charges and criticisms of a free press. Nor are such phrases as majority rule and popular control empty of all meaning. A system that invites it citizens to believe in these principles often ends by bringing the beliefs to life, for people will demand of their government that it pay more than lip service to its professions. Moreover, there is the corrosive effect upon the iron law of oligarchy of a two-party or multiparty system. It is not so difficult for a Fascist or Communist party in a one-party state—or any monopoly for that matter—to be authoritarian. But where a choice exists, the knowledge that people may select an alternative is itself a check against oligarchy. A party's rival is likely to create trouble for a controlling clique by encouraging its followers to rebel against their leadership, and such revolts, outside of a police state, are not so easy to suppress. Those who formulated this iron law did not pay enough attention to the mutual interaction of competing organisations.[32] For nothing does so much to keep us free as the chance to choose.

CIVIL LIBERTIES

Where the opportunity exists to choose between two or more parties and to oppose a government within a constitutional framework, certain related liberties are found that negate or mitigate the strength of oligarchy. The state can be subordinated to popular control, instead of the people being subservient to the state, when freedom of association and the right to criticize are preserved inviolate. Without freedom of association one could not organize a group of like-minded individuals as an alternative to those in power. Without the right to criticize, genuine debate of public issues could never be conducted. These rights are in turn buttressed by accompanying freedoms which prevent enslavement of one's person or one's mind. Freedom from arbitrary arrest and secret trail, from seizure of one's belongings or cruel and unusual punishments, these and similar rights protect the liberty of the person. Equally important are the particular rights that add up to liberty of thought in general: the right of access to information and to publish without censorship, the right to read whatever one wishes, and the right of free speech.

For those who cherish the values of a free society, such rights are as indispensable as the air we breathe. The reasons for them are written in clear type in the annals of every police state, old and new, and in the long uneven record of humanity's intellectual progress. There would be no Bill of Rights in the United States today or its equivalent in any other democracy if dissident minorities and individuals had not clashed with past wielders of power in the name of truths they held to be self-evident. There would be none of our modern achievements in pure and applied science, no betterment in our methods of living together in organised society, if some of our ancestors had not been willing at times to express unconventional ideas or challenge the established mores. The memory of Socrates before his Athenian accusers; of Jesus before Pilate; of the destruction of the library at Alexandria; of Roger Bacon, Copernicus Galileo, and Darwin, whose scientific method demolished untruths sanctioned by the religious orthodoxy of their time; of Spinoza excommunicated by his synagogue; of beliefs in sorcery and burning of "witches", of propaganda and persecution as practised by Joseph Stalin, Joseph Goebbels, and the Japanese thought controllers before 1945—these are salutary warnings to prove that the repression of individuals does not determine which ideas shall perish and which prevail.

But though political liberty depends on these accompanying freedoms, it is no simple task to dovetail them in the structure of the state. If a passion for order, pushed too far, can degenerate into authoritarianism, so can a zeal for liberty become license by excess. All rights involve responsibilities, and no right exercise within society is absolute. This is true, for example, of freedom of speech. On the principle that my right to swing my arm ends where the other fellow's nose beings so must the right of free speech avoid infringement of the rights of other. Hence it is appropriate to have laws against libel and slander, or against incitement to violence.

Added to the difficulty of definition is that of enforcement. The rights of a citizen may be invaded by other citizens or by the government. They may therefore require protection by the government or against it. Rights produce their impact upon government, as does government upon rights, through the medium of institutions or agencies. How vigilantly these operate, how they are staffed, what precedents they develop, to what pressures they bow—this can make all the difference between paying lip service to freedom and actually practicing it. Traditionally, the branch of government that has encroached the most on civil rights has been the one whose opportunity is greatest—the executive. That was so under the regimes of absolute monarchy and continues to be true of the modern dictatorship. Naturally, since the executive administers the law and has military force, police, and prisons at its disposal, threats to liberty will always come from this source if such powers be abused.

For that reason, in countries where civil liberties have nurtured political freedom, the other branches—the legislature and judiciary—are often called on to champion the rights of citizens against executive invasion. But institutional history may so vary from one state to another as to place a different emphasis on the respective roles of legislators and judges. In the United States, where the hierarchy of law subordinates a statute to the Constitution, where the Constitution contains a Bill of Rights, and where it is the judges who say what the Constitution is,[33] the courts form the inner citadel in which the defense of civil liberties is conducted. Political factors, moreover, reinforce this arrangement. The courts—and more particularly the federal judiciary headed by the Supreme Court—are generally respected for their impartiality and scrupulousness. The same reputation is not enjoyed by congress or the state legislatures. In general, the legislative branch has shown considerably less zeal to uphold civil rights than the judicial. Not infrequently it endangers them.

Finally, there is the problem of determining the ultimate sanction which guarantees that civil rights will be operative. Though it is valuable to spell out basic rights in classic formulas and constitutional definitions, those are not self-enforcing. Many a constitution has been drafted to include the finest sounding liberties that in practice were not worth the paper on which they were written. Nor does the secret of the defense of rights lie solely in such institutions as courts and legislatures, indispensable though these be. For institutions, like rights, will vary in effectiveness; courts may function under the shadow of intimidation; and legislatures may be maintained as a convenient fiction. The truth is that institutions are strong to the extent that a large enough section of the public feels keenly enough to have them so. Exactly the same applies to civil liberties. If enough people are sufficiently determined to preserve and exercise their rights, those rights will be exercised and preserved and the institutions will then be found to do the job. But where that determination is lacking, no court, no congress, no parliament can fill the gap. The ultimate sanction, therefore, of all civil liberties resides in the source that creates the constitution initially and renders it effective—the political will of the people. Freedom in any society is what the people earn and guard for themselves.

References

1. George. H. Sabine and Thomas L. Thorson, *History of Political Theory,* 4th ed. (new York: Holt, Rinehart & Winston, 1973), p. 305.

2. For example, the protracted campaigns of the Hundred Years' War (1337-1453).

3. Witness the growth in importance of the Hanseatic League (including in its membership Hamburg, Bremen, Lübeck, Bergen, Danzig, and others), the cities of northern Italy (like Venice, Milan, and Florence), and Antwerp, Amsterdam, and London.

4. "Monsim Again:" The Theory of Sovereignty."

5. "Medievalism and Mercantilism."

6. "The Reconstruction of Unity."

7. *Second Treatise of Civil Government,* sec. 149.

8. Ibid.

9. 1803 was the date of the decision in *Marbury v. Madison.*

10. *United States Constitution*, Article VI.

11. Robert M. Maclver in *The Web of Government,* rev. ed. (New York: The Free Press, 1965).

12. A cynic has observed that "a government of laws, not of men" becomes a government of lawyers, not of men.

13. There are several instances of amendments which reverse decisions of the Supreme Court. To wit, the Eleventh, which recorded the indignation of the states at *Chisholm v. Georgia;* the Thirteen, Fourteenth, and Fifteenth, which repudiated the principles of the Dred Scott case; and the Sixteenth, which overthrew the opinion of the Court concerning federal inability to levy income tax.

14. See the section on "Constitution and Constitutionalism," in this chapter.

15. In its list of subjects on which Congress may legislate, Article I, section 8 of the Constitution includes the powers" to regulate commerce . . . among the several States" and "to lay and collect taxes . . . and provide for the common defense and general welfare of the United State."

16. Many doctrines have been enunciated by the Court that, until modified by a later majority of judges, have controlled the legislative and executive branches—for example, the doctrines of "original package," "business affected with a public interest," "the flow of commerce," "clear and present danger," Separate, but equal," and so forth.

17. In the 1980s however, during the Reagan administration the Commission was systematically crippled and became a nullity. Also in those years, the Justice Department adopted interpretations (e.g., on the subjects of affirmative action, bussing and reverse discrimination) which were inimical to racial minorities.

18. With one important exception. Since Britain Joined the European Community in 1973, Parliament's lawmaking power has been subordinated to the requirements of the Treaty of Rome, and British courts must nullify an Act of Parliament that contravenes the Treaty.

19. Alexis de Tocqueville, *Democracy in America,* part I, trans. Henry Reeve (New York: J. & H. G. Langley, 1841), p. 103,

20. See his *law of the Constitution*, 8the ed. (London: Macmillan and Co., 1931), There have been, for example, a few instances of somebody briefly serving as a Minister without a seat in either House of Parliament. This broke Political custom, but not the law.

21. What was a rule of custom eventually became a rule of the Constitution by the adoption of the Twenty-Second Amendment.

22. E.g., in 1864 and 1944.

23. The laws of some states, however, place certain restrictions on presidential electors.

24. Nixon's enforced resignation in 1974 illustrates my point. Charges of illegalities were levelled at his campaign for reelection in 1972. His own guilt or innocence centered on the burglary at the Democratic Party's campaign offices in the Watergate building. Did he know of this in advance? Did he authorize the subsequent attempted cover-up? It took a year and a half for the courts, the Congress, and the press to extract in public the information which proved that Nixon had broken the law. When it became certain that Congress would use it constitutional power to impeach him, he resigned. Thereupon, his successor. President Ford, granted him an absolute pardon.

25. I exclude the Vichy regime of 1940-1944, since that was a puppet government set up in half of France under German military occupation.

26. Signs have increased, however, since the 1960s that certain French business firms have adapted successfully to the requirements of large-scale organisation. The underlying causes lay in the economics of the new technology (especially in electronics, aircraft, and automobiles) and the stimulus provided by the policies and potentialities of the Common Market. The same has been true in agriculture. By 1980 France had many fewer farms and farmers than in 1950.

27. When the Constitution of the Fourth Republic was adopted in 1946, only a minority of the registered electorate voted for it. Those who voted against it, plans the large number who abstained, formed a majority.

28. From the Latin *res publica,*" a public possession.

29. I have discussed this in my work *The Democratic Civilisation* (New York: Oxford University Press, 1964).

30. For the meaning of this term, See Maclver's *The Web of Government* (New York: The Free Press, 1965).

31. Such regimes as those of Japan or Mexico cannot, therefore, yet be considered fully democratic. Various parties do coexist in those

political systems and elections are held regularly. But one party has held power continuously, either alone or in a coalition which it controls. Never yet has the opposition obtained office. As a consequence, the dominant party has become corrupted by its long tenure of office.

32. This holds true even when the competing organisations are themselves structured on non democratic principles. Acton makes the telling point that the modern democratic state evolved neither out of the medieval state nor from the medieval church, but from the struggle between the two. The fact is that, whenever an alternative exists, there is some element of freedom. It is monopolies which are coercive.

33. This is the observation of the late Charles Evans Hughes, former chief justice.

8

The Role of a Modern State

The problem of state interference may be said to be as old as human history. From time immemorial there had always been a conflict between authority and liberty—between the head of the family and the other members, between the tribal chief and the members of the tribe, between the king and his subjects, between democratic governments and the citizens. The nature of government has changed completely from the personal rule of the Pharaos to direct rule by the people as in the Swiss cantons; but the problem of the proper sphere of government and of the individual has remained undissipated nonetheless and according to some, like J.S. Mill, the problem is more acute in democracy.

No fixed principle of state interference can be applicable for all ages, but for our age we may consider some principles about the way the state should act for the establishment of common good and for the best realisation of the potentialities of man.

Our general position is that the state cannot fulfil the various hopes which a twentieth century citizen has for the state without the latter's assuming the role of a welfare organ. There is no need to raise the state to the mystical height as the Hegelians do, nor any necessity to assign to it the ignominous role that Spencer selected for it and that too grudgingly. It is better to utilize it as best as we can for our good, keeping always in mind that we can never dispense with its service even if it fails at times to live up to our expectation. In this respect we fully agree with J.S. Mill's contention that the "proper end of the government is to reduce the wretched wastes due to neutralisation of the best efforts and talents of men to the smallest possible amount by taking such measures as shall cause the energies now spent by mankind in injuring one another or in protecting themselves against injury, to be turned to the legitimate employment of human faculties, that of compelling the power of nature to be more and more subservient to the physical and moral good." We would like to emphasis on Burke's argument that the state "is not a partnership in things subservient only to the gross animal existence of a temporary and perishable nature.[1]" It should aim at much higher moral attainment.

It is argued by some that the state should not interfere at least in the following fields viz., (1) excusively personal affairs, and the likes and dislikes of individuals, (2) family relations and the domestic life (3) ecclesiastical and religious affairs, (4) morality.

Regarding the first point we may say that there is hardly any activity of the individual which will not have a bearing directly or indirectly on others. J.S. Mill is criticised for his arguments to separate self-regarding actions from other-regarding actions. In spite of the atomistic theory of the utilitarians and the individualism of Spencer we find that we do not live in isolation in society.

As regards family matters the state has to interfere to settle disputes arising out of succession to property, compulsory education for the children, enforcement of sanitary regulation in case of epidemic and so on. One may raise serious doubts about the possibility of enjoying any amount of liberty when the state wants to regulate the number of children a man and a woman may have. In one sense the idea of family planning and state support for it, takes away from the people their liberty in their private affairs and no limitation, it is held, can be placed on state interference if even this right is not enjoyed smoothly. But this argument misses the vital point, *viz.,* that one should not take the responsibility which one cannot carry out properly. The parents who go on adding to their number of issues without caring for their maintenance and education, create social problems by giving rise to delinquency and other problems. These underfed, uneducated urchins who develop as half men are great social cancers and the state which has to be responsible for the general welfare or common good of the people cannot take an indifferent attitude. J.S. Mill, though a great champion of the sacredness of self-regarding actions, did not give this right of multiplication to the irresponsible father. This problem has assumed tremendous importance in underdeveloped countries like India where whatever effort is made by the country to improve the standard of living by increased production, greater employment facility and social security is neutralised by the disproportionately large number of mouths produced in a given period. If the state is charged with the responsibility of providing better life it should be given the power to take means to achieve this end. One need not get frightened at this, as we shall later argue that the state should undertake only those measures which are supported by the democratically elected legislature and by a free, frank public opinion. Anyway, the state's abstention from the major area of family precincts does not mean its inability; rather it can interfere whenever it thinks fit to achieve some common interest.

But in the religious field we believe that the state should keep its hands off from it mainly. Belief in God or non-belief in any religion are things which do not affect the life of the state. (Sir James F. Stephen had a different opinion).[2] No state can prove beyond doubt that there is a God or that disbelief in a particular religion is a great hindrance to good citizenship.

Regarding morality we accept MacIver's view that to turn all moral obligations into legal obligations is to destroy morality. The state as he says, is a clumsy instrument to perform certain functions which need individual spontaneity like those duties in a man's life which he performs because of his moral urge.[3] Yet we can say with Green that the state cannot be a non-chalant onlooker while the morality of the people takes a downward course. In modern times it is not wise for the state to wait and see till a morally degraded man commits some crime which would fall within the province of law and only then take measures to set him right. For the morality of the people is linked up with their social values. Many moral crimes are not legal crimes but they may be social crimes, *e.g.*, hatred, jealousy, intemperance or loose moral character, against which the state should take indirect action by education, by the creation of a healthy atmosphere, by giving economic security to life and possession and so on. If one has no faith in a particular religion one is not a great problem to a state on that account alone. But if one has no 'moral scruple, he is a menace to both society and the state. It is difficult to make a good citizen out of a bad, immoral man. A few examples of a Socrates or a Gandhi where a good man is a bad citizen are only exceptions. A good man may be considered a bad citizen in a bad state for the time being but ultimately his moral principle would have great impact on public opinion and laws making them good. So a good state depends on good citizens, but a good citizen can be created out of a good man only. But a man who attaches no importance to moral values can never be an asset to the state in the ultimate analysis, for, as has been well said "morality lies without the constitution but within the state."[4]

The state has the right of censorship and is justified in disapproving obnoxious literature and obscence pictures though it should not always lay down rigid ideas of what constitutes obscenity. The notion is bound to change with the change of time and vary from person to person. Though it is true that those who are on the Board of Censors should not be considered the best judges or guardians of morality in the country yet the men who run the affairs of the state—legislative, executive and judicial—must have power to introduce some uniformity. This is because if there is social degeneration and political insecurity results there form it is these people who will have to share the major part of the blame. Moreover in a democracy if there is a strong public opinion and a truly intelligent and representative legislature, no branch of Government can act in a cavalier fashion. The danger is that morality may be linked up with social vices like polygamy, untouchability, colour bar or suttee. While prohibiting all these, the state officers should generally act under the broad principles laid down by the legislature allowing the officers to use their good sense and intelligence. But in all cases they must be controlled and regulated by the body and whenever needed the sensors themselves should be censored by the people's representatives.

It must however be remembered that in all these fields, viz., the individual sphere, family or morality where the state is to interfere the better method would be to adopt peaceful means of persuasion and education but not the method of force or compulsion. A wise policy would not seek unnecessarily to impose laws that will clash with custom, beliefs or traditions of the people as is done in an autocratic state. Too much use of force without moral education and understanding will make the people hostile to government activities.

Today we do not consider the Government as a necessary evil because with the passage of time it has transformed itself into an indispensable welfare organ. Moreover, the gradual transference of power from the one to the many has also helped to change its nature and role. Suffering and discomfort, unhappiness and want are seen on every hand. Some of these are undoubtedly inseparable from the imperfections of human nature as it exists in its present fallen condition. Yet it has been proved in many welfare status (e.g. Britain, the Scandinavian countries etc.) of our time that conscious actions of the individuals may do much to lessen particular evils. Aristotle was advanced for his time when he prescribed in his Politics that a permanent plan should be set up not only for the relief but also for the prevention of economic privation. Government acting in the name and with the united power of the whole community, has a much greater capacity to grapple with such evils than the simple citizen can ever have. The extreme forms of individualism and socialism suffer from exaggerations. The right attitude towards the state should be that the individual finds his sphere to be no narrower than the state itself, while the sphere of the Government may be logically extended to embrace almost all the interests and actions of every man and woman. This is the theory of organic unity according to which it is absurd to draw a line between two things whose essential nature lies in their connection with each other. The socialistic and the individualistic approaches are in the political world what the forces of attraction and repulsion are in the natural world. They seem opposed, yet neither could exist without the other. The two may be described in the words of Kant as the "unsocial sociability of man"—the fundamental contradiction of human nature which forces man to seek one another's society, and yet cause each one to endeavour "to direct everything merely according to his own mind.[5] While nothing is suffered to remain outside the state, proper provision must be made for every individual to enjoy a full free life within it.

This a theoretical answer no doubt but it is not easy to give any more detail in a theoretical study like ours. We can only say that the actual province of any government is just whatever is entrusted to it by the sovereign legislature as the source of positive law and as the mirror of the demands and wishes of the people. It is not true to argue that the welfare state, planning and democracy are incompatible and that if there is too much planning, democracy cannot function. For, we can cite the examples of Sweden, Denmark and also Britain to a certain extent where planning and welfare works organised by the Government have not led them to the "road to serfdom." Rather these plans have enabled the citizens not only to enjoy life and liberty in a real sense but also to contribute to the strength and progress of the State. Mutilated, deformed and half-fed men are more liabilities than assets to a state.

It is no good to brood over the failures and defects of the democratic system and castigate it. For there is no other system so far discovered which is as good as the democratic. We do not claim that democracy has absolute virtue. Our contention is that we may cure it of its drawbacks. We should not kill it because of its failures. If we ride a motor car, sometimes we are put to much inconvenience by its mechanical defects. But on that ground we do not give it up for ever and travel by the bullock cart. We should make the motor car more perfect and avoid breakdowns. Whatever change is brought in the life of a nation—politically, socially or otherwise—the process must be democratic and physical coercion should have a very limited area of action. Men must always endeavour to improve their condition according to the demands of a new age to which ideal they may approximate but whose total realisation may never be attained because the concept of perfection has no fixed content.

In the early part of the nineteenth century factory legislation was resented but with the change of time public opinion became conscious of the vices of the factory system and people's representatives in Parliament passed laws giving greater scope to the workers.

Similar is the case with private property. Though this institution was considered scared and inviolable from the time of Aristotle down to the first half of the last century, it is not considered so now. It is held that the state has every right to take away property from the people who have it in abnormally greater amount and use it to establish more equitable standards of life. Even in the USA whose constitution guarantees the right to property to the citizens (Amendment XIV), the state has had recourse to such doctrines as the "power of eminent domain."[6] and the "police power of the state"[7] in using private property for the common good and the country's protection. In the communist countries this acquisition of private property has been done by outright confiscation whereas in some other countries like the U.SA. it has been done by giving owners adequate compensation. Perhaps outright confiscation without compensation would make the state an instrument of coercion. It carries with it the odium of force.

We do not support the argument that if the state punishes a citizen for forcefully taking away the neighbour's property it itself should not create the impression of a mightier robber by coveting people's property. This argument is not convincing as there is a fundamental distinction between the state acquisition of property and an individual's grabbing of his neighbour's property. The former is motivated by the desire to promote a common good, the latter by private good. But our objection to this method is that this method apart from giving the state huge powers, may alienate the sympathy of a minority permanently and no democracy can be virile if there is always in it a hostile, revolting minority. We think it is better to control the property, business or industry of the citizens through laws and taxation and to establish state's own factories on as wide a scale as possible to give employment and other benefits to the people. Nationalisation with adequate compensation is also no good as it would mean huge drainage from the state treasury to the owners of property without augmenting the total wealth in the country. But if on the other hand this huge sum is invested by the state to found new factories, schools and hospitals and at the same time laws are passed to regulate the present owners of property, factories or business so that they may not exploit the labourers and consumers, the result would be more beneficial than any doctrinaire method of appropriation. Moreover the mind must be prepared to accept the socialistic system of communal life which can be done only by a gradual process. Miss Follett has rightly argued that "socialisation of property must not precede the socialisation of the will.[8] As we have already said we believe in the democratic process and hence the imposition of socialism by violent, abrupt means does not appear to us right because force perverts aims and does not care for the means. This much we can say that as things stand in the political and economic fields in our time the state has to take the responsibility of providing full employment, education and other social benefits to the citizens because the isolated efforts of the individuals are quite inadequate to tackle the mighty problems of modern life. A wise Government will always see that in the process of doing this it does not transform itself into a totalitarian oligarchy. For, in that case all the good services rendered will be valueless as the people will be reduced to the category of automatons. We must remember that men do not live by bread alone.

The best security to check the natural tendency of the power to become corrupted is to grant freedom of thought and expression and a democratic machinery. If eternal vigilance is the price of liberty the citizen must be ready to sacrifice himself for it. There may be many attacks on freedom of thought, the citizens must face it squarely. To build up that sturdy independence of character and a critical mind there must be freedom of expression. But it is needless to say that this right as also the other rights cannot be absolute. Apart from checking everyone against using indecent or defamatory utterances, no state can guarantee freedom of speech which would create chaos or overthrow the very set up which grants freedom of speech. "Free and frank discussion", said Right Hon. Lord Justice Denning of England, "and criticism of matters of public interest must in no way be curtailed. But there comes a point at which 'every country' must draw the line; and that is when there is a threat to overturn the state by force." "Every society must have the means to protect itself from marauders."[9] In India all the seven rights to freedom under Article 19(1) of the Constitution are subject to "reasonable restrictions" to be decided by the court. Even in the U.S.A. the Supreme Court on various occasions had to curb the right of freedom of expression by establishing maxims like the "clear and present danger" (Sehenk V. United States 1919) declared by Mr. Justice Holmes. This was supported by Mr. Justice Black while giving judgement in Bridges V. California in 1941.[10] Whereas though not fully agreeing with the Holmes formula of "clear and present danger" Mr. Justice Brandeis gave greater weight to the formula of "reasonable ground" in Whitney V. California (1927). In other words according to Mr. Brandeis, "to justify suppression of speech there must be reasonable ground to fear that serious evil will result if free speech is practiced" and instead of "clear and present danger" he emphasised on "imminent" and "serious" danger.[11] Generally speaking we have no objection to accept the opinion expressed by the U.S. Supreme Court in Gitlow V. New York (1925), "that utterances inciting to the overthrow of organised Government by unlawful means, present a sufficient danger of substantive evil to bring their punishment within the range of legislative discretion, is clear."[12] But we think that in the ultimate analysis if the state becomes so corrupt and the majority in the legislature so tyrannical that in spite of appealing through all constitutional means no effect has been produced the citizens must have the right to preach the removal of the government directly and may defy the law of such a government. Here incidentally we may distinguish between the state and the government and without denying allegiance to the state a conscious citizen in this rare case may refuse obedience to the particular law of a particular government. But this is a very dangerous right and should be used very rarely after exhaustion all the other means of redress and this disobedience to the laws of the government should not generally be a violent one.

A government can and should allow very wide freedom of expression which may be used to criticize the government but it may not allow that much of freedom of action because an anarchistic idea, for example, may not create much disorder so long as it travels from person to person but it may cause irreparable loss to the stability of social and political life if allowed to materialize in practice. In this regard certain conditions may be laid down: (i) The dissenting individual or party should be allowed freely to plead every argument against the disputed measure and check ought to be applied only when freedom of discussion has been used as an instrument of obstruction. (ii) The majority should always take sympathetic attitude towards the minority before overruling it by sheer force of numbers and attempt should be made to convert the minority by persuasion. (iii) When force is applied it should be minimum and as the last resort. (iv) The minority ought to acquiesce when fairly beaten; accept the conclusion arrived at as its own; and work for its success, thus rendering coercion unnecessary.[13] There should be always supremacy of the laws and not of the individuals.

Apart from this political question of majority and minority which always presupposes that the two sides are on equal footing in their mental and moral development and that their relation is that between brother and brother, we have to take into account quite a number of citizens who, it should be admitted frankly, are not sufficiently equipped intellectually to be their own guide. It is difficult for a sick man to pursue the good life, it is no less difficult for an uneducated or intellectually backward man to do the same. Without becoming a Carlylean it may be submitted that the state has to play the role of the father in these cases and in addition to the sympathy and the love of a brother there may be the need of the affectionate guidance and care of a father. But on that ground we do not support the Platonic conception that the ordinary man has neither the knowledge, nor the self-discipline to enable him to exercise the powers of Government. Supporting the democratic theory of government we pointed out the exceptions when guidance may be needed temporarily.

Certain factors are responsible necessitating the state to assume greater responsibilities of the citizens which in a sense mean more interference in and control of their lives and liberty. Apart from the need that arose to check the undesirable forces of the Industrial Revolution there are at least three other important factors which have become significant in the twentieth century. They are: Firstly, frequent rise of emergencies like (a) internal discontent, (b) economic crisis, (c) external danger from war or threat of war, etc. Secondly, the concept of welfare state and the impact of socialism after the successful revolution in the U.S.S.R. Thirdly, the defeat of democratic tradition at the hands of totalitarian dictatorships in many part of the world. In the nineteenth century Spencer accepted very reluctantly even the policing duty of the state whereas in the twentieth century Hitler went to the extent of fixing the menu for the dinner table in every house.[14] We cannot deny that in our day too many emergencies occur too often calling for the attention and control of the state. Sometimes the state has to take measures before-hand so that they may not take place. Toal war obliterating the old distinction between the combatants and non-combatants is taking place demanding sacrifice of life, liberty and property of the citizens. Only by a colossal effort of the entire nation managed under a powerful governmental leadership can the nation be saved from complete disaster.

With the passage of time people are becoming conscious that only the state can bring the prospect of a good life and so it is thought desirable not to waste the limited resources of the country in cut-throat competitions, advertisement or over-production. Better to plan them economically according to the requirements of the people. Planned society may mean curtailment of liberty in its abstract sense but if freedom from hunger is the most important freedom, we should not lament the loss of a little abstract liberty whose enjoyment is of dubious value if the stomach is constantly empty, if the mind is uneducated, if the body is exposed to the cold, rain and sun.

We know that too much planning of life will surely land us in the domain of Stalinism or Hitlerism which, instead of developing the latent faculties of citizens would make them barren. That is why we have laid emphasis repeatedly on the importance of creating the democratic tradition, on legislature and on the necessity of a strong, vigilant public opinion. Planning and welfare state do no automatically bring a curtailment of real liberty. Care must be taken to regulate the planners and the executors of plans. And instead of restricting the real liberty these systems will herald the dawn of a new age of well being, real liberty and good life. By giving these the state can justify its continued existence. Political democracy will be an empty phrase if it is not based on economic democracy. There is no gainsaying the fact that by a steeply graded income tax, and excess profit tax, death duties and estate duties, the huge income of a few has been brought down and there are now fewer millionaires say, in England today, than those before the 2nd World War. Yet it cannot be denied that this loss of a few has been more than compensated by the general prosperity and security of life and liberty that the state in England has given to all classes of citizens in the form of Old Age Pension, Unemployment and Health Insurance Benefits, free education, state scholarships, medial aid, legal aid and so on. One may argue that this is the price the rich have to pay to the poor for their security. In a sense it may be contended, as Laski has pointed out, that "it is a proof of the Hegelian thesis that history is the revelation of freedom that constantly widens."[15] Moreover as there is no end to what the state can do, specially in the material field for the betterment of the people, its service is constantly being extended in newer and unexplored spheres with the march of time.

The significances of free democracy is not linked up with the laissez-faire theory or individualism. Historically speaking modern democracies arose after the breakdown of mercantilism and the growth of industrial capitalism. At that time democracy and laissez-faire stood for each other. But the nature of democracy is such that it can "if the trend of opinion ran long enough and strong enough in that direction," said MacIver, "change gradually from capitalism to a thorough going socialism."[16]

The most effective criticism against a planned society is that it creates mediocrity as there is less initiative and imagination in state managed affairs and every thing is done as a routine affair. But this argument has lost much, though not all, of its force today because of the astounding discoveries in science needing exceptionally brilliant brain and imagination as they are in the most planned society of the world, the Soviet Union. It is true that by the order and force of the state only poor quality of literature was produced under the Stalin era. But somehow the Soviet Union has passed that era and proved that at least in science and technology they are in no way behind the achievements of the most affluent society of the world (i.e. U.S.A.). They have done all these in a surprisingly short period unaided by the advanced knowledge of the West except at the initial period after the Revolution of 1917 and at the beginning of the First Plan in the late twenties and early thirties. We do not like to be blind to the coercive aspect and the regimentation, the brainwashing that prevail in a totalitarian state like the U.S.S.R. Our main aim is to combine planning. with freedom and pave the way to progress, material and moral.

Regarding the state's role in the cultural functions of the people it may be pointed out that there is no harm in the state patronizing them. Athens in the best period of her life organised and superintended a considerable variety of cultural functions of her citizens. These functions were part of the way of life of the Athenians and what the state did was to promote them and to give them dignity. At the same time, as Pericles is stated to have remarked, care was taken so that no orthodoxy was clamped on the free cultural life of the people. But these Athenian constitutional provisions as recorded in Aristotle's Athenian Constitution, differ sharply from the constitutional provisions of Plato's Republic and the Laws where Plato wanted to "co-ordinate" the life of the citizens under a rigorous cultural code. He prohibited all arts, philosophies and poetry and opinions which were against his own ideas. Modern dictators find an easy support for their interference in the freedom of opinion of the people in Plato's Laws where poets and writers are asked to submit their works to the magistrates who are to decide if these works are good for the spiritual health of the Citizens. When Stalin asked the writers to write novels and plays glorifying the Revolution of 1917 and praising the system of collective farming and other aspects of the new system he only succeeded in drying up the wonderful source of Russian literature. Therefore we fully realize that art and culture to be creative must come out of the depths of the heart of the people, they can not be created by an executive order. But on that account we do not find any reason why the state should not help a needy artist or a poet or render whatever assistance it can in building up a richer culture of the people, and help them to share the heritage of mankind. But we must stress the point that the state should not impose its own views everywhere, it can disallow only such views as can create immediate, not remote, social or political disorder.

There are three different ways by which the state can interfere, viz., (1) state ownership, (2) government administration, (3) legislative control. They may be secured using different techniques. (a) The state prohibits this and that; (b) it compels persons to do this and that positively and punishes them if they do not do this; (c) the state encourages by giving protection (physical, legal) or help (financial) to those who do certain acts or refrain from doing certain things; (d) the state does something and prevents the people from doing it or competing with the government (e.g. setting aside of a certain field in economic activity for the "public sector" exclusively as in India): (e) the state does something and gives freedom to individuals to do similar things and thus compete with it (e.g. the "common sector" in economic activity); (f) the state may indulge in propaganda (by publishing news, articles, pamphlets, or broadcasting news through radio or giving financial help to associations to do these things for it) for crating the necessary motive in the individuals etc., etc. We think that in modern times the state cannot give its citizens various opportunities and blessings of modern life unless it takes up more or less socialistic or at least welfare programmes of development. Though socialistic or welfare state means greater state control and interference, the converse is not always true—greater control by the state does not mean socialism or welfare, it may be naked regimentation under a totalitarian dictatorship.

Anyway, of the three types of interference state ownership and legislative control appear to us to be better than administrative control and regulation. In administrative control there is every possibility of arbitrariness and the personal interest may influence the step to be taken to secure the general well-being. Mere legislative control of private business enterprise and institution is also not sufficient, for this method can interfere in a negative way through "Do's" and "Dont's". But as we have already argued, in a welfare state the state has to take the great burden of providing employment, medical benefit, education,. Social security, etc., to the citizens. All these cannot be achieved unless the state begins to establish its own institutions and undertakings. In these state undertakings authorisation for such activity must come from Parliament and not from the administrative department. But it is to be noted that we support Parliamentary control and authorisation but not Parliamentary management of state undertakings. The folly of this policy was proved when the Long Parliament in Britain after its open breach with king Charles tried to take the reins of administration into its own hands.

State activity is to be carried in such a way as not to affect private initiative, and the imagination and the will to work of the people. The general nature of state interference should be medicine-like and like good food. Medicine is not needed when the body is fit, but good food is always needed to keep the body fit. Hence sometimes indirectly and sometimes directly the state has to help the individual to stand on his own feet. But the state will defeat its aim if in the process of helping, it allows the feet to grow weaker and weaker and provides stronger crutches to rely on. Perhaps with the gradual progress of civilisation there will be less and less interference in the intellectual and moral field of human activity. Interferences would be restricted to the sphere of material well-being only. On the whole the state is to adjust its means to attain the true end embracing the most despised of individuals and the remotest posterity as essential parts, and embodying social, moral and spiritual interests as well as material once. It must recognize too its obligations to other state and to humanity as a whole.

If the state assumes larger numbers of responsibilities there is a grave potential danger that those who are in charge of the machinery of the state may use it for their own benefit and deprive the people of their legitimate share. Hence we think, the human element is the most decisive factor in a welfare state. Whether a law passed following certain good principles of state interference will have good effect on the people ensuring them greater well-being or not, will depend vitally not on the substance of the law but on the nature and character of those who enforce and administer the law. In India there is the much hated and criticised Preventive Detention Act by which a man may be arrested before he has committed any actual crime and may be kept behind the bars without trial, because of his questionable and anti-social character. Theoretically the aim of the law is not so bad; for, it may be found sometimes that the authorities are not in a position to give any direct or concerte proof of a man's crime yet at the same time may consider him a menace to social peace for his past or present behaviour. So before he causes any damage to society he is put under custody as a preventive measure. But there will be a serious danger to the liberty of the people if the police officer or the party in power taking advantage of this law uses it to satisfy personal vengeance or party interest. Then instead of achieving social peace and harmony it will destroy them along with the liberty and security of the people. The state will gradually move in the direction of medieaval despotism.

On the other hand the deficiency in the words and aims of a law can be made up considerably if the judge while trying cases takes a progressive and humane attitude to social problems and gives verdicts accordingly. The success or failure of a particular principle of state interference will depend sometimes on the explanation and administration of law as these are done by those who are in charge of the law. If they stick to the old outdated notion of right and political opinion (as was the case with the U.S. Supreme Court Judges who nullified one by one all the progressive measures introduced under the New Deal by President Roosevelt, until 1937 when fortunately new judges were appointed and the New Deal became operative) the citizens can never gain in a dynamic world.. So what is important is the training of mind and character giving importance to certain social and individual values. This education should be provided by the state without however closing the doors to the adult educated mind of gather knowledge and information from the wide open world. Now what will be these values according to which education is to be imparted will be decided democratically by the people through organised public opinion and through their representatives in the legislature in accordance with the demands of a particular age.

The problem of the role of the state is so difficult that it is not easy to tell with certainty whether a course pursued by the state will be best suited to met the hundreds and thousands of intricate problems that the officers of the state have to face every day and every hour. Nevertheless the state cannot sit idle or keep quiet. The officers of the state are to use their conscience, reason and initiative while discharging their duties under some broad principles of state interference laid down by the democratic legislature or wanted by the public opinion. Administrative discretion should not be wide and there should be effective checks on the powers of the administration. We cannot ignore the fact that without special knowledge and experience modern government cannot be run by ordinary people as it was in ancient Athens (the system of election of magistrates being lottery there).Hence some aristocratic and bureaucratic element is bound to come into every efficient government and some more powers than those possessed by ordinary citizens are sure to devolve on these officers of the state. But at the same time every one must have the right to invoke the law of the land in his defence against the highest in the land and no official of the state is to be given any chance to oppress the citizen with impunity under any pretext except as directed by the laws passed by the parliament of the People. In this respect the example of the British cabinet system of government can serve the double purpose of (a) specialised knowledge supplied by the permanent civil servant and the (b) democratic control imposed on these civil servants by the democratically elected ministers who are in their turn responsible to the people's Parliament.

We would like to make the point clear that even this Parliamentary check is not sufficient unless the people themselves are conscious of their rights. As we know even in a highly educated and advanced country like Germany Hitler became a dictator using the democratic machinery. We should remember Lord Acton's warning that "power always corrupts and absolute power absolutely corrupts. All great men are bad." To make its policies effective the democratic government should utilize all modern methods of feeling the pulse of the people, should sense the current of opinion and formulate its principles accordingly and after implementing its policies should record the reaction of the people and again reformulate the policies if needed in the light of people's reactions.[17]

In conclusion we may say that state interference should be directed to those fields (1) where private efforts would involve great human and material cost, (2) where the powers and resources of private organisations are too in adequate or where the profit is not sufficient to induce private agencies to work but the need is great, e.g., scientific exploration into the space or the establishment of huge industrial plants. Apart from these we have already said that we do not see any harm if the state without suppressing private organisations establishes its own institutions side by side with the private institutions with the sole intention of doing good to the people. Moreover we cannot deny that the state has the "primary responsibility of safeguarding the whole against the part, and in our world of organised interests this responsibility of safeguarding the whole against the part, has grown ever more comprehensive and more complicated."[18]

We have tried to prove that it is neither possible nor desirable to be guided by any rigid formula of state interference either of individualism or of socialism. It is better to regard the state as a welfare organ and used it for the benefit of the people as a whole without giving special favour to this class or that except on merit or worth. That the state has made mistaken interferences in the past is no proof that it will err again in the future or that its defects are incurable. The past failures may be due to imperfect machinery arrogant and corrupt bureaucracy or to the inadequate information and statistics on which the state had to base its policies. But we believe, with the progress of our civilisation in science and human understanding many of the gaps in the past policies may be filled up by the experience and knowledge gained, by adopting a humanistic approach to solve any problem and by making the administration more responsible to the people through parliamentary and other checks. The question of ultimate value cannot be decided by arguments, it will vary from man to man. Even great logical minds like Aristotle and Locke could support slavery and the exclusion of the Roman Catholics respectively from citizenship and Hitler did the same thing in the case of the Jews though to a modern impartial mind all of them are unjustified. It is then a matter of personal conviction and so there will be doubts in this or that mind about the ethics of each and every act of the state. Yet we cannot help living in the state except in the association of others and therefore we have to find out a workable method by mutual give and take and ask the state to take measures so that our life may be richer, fuller and more beautiful.

—Sisir Kanti Bhattacharjee

References

1. Burke, E., *Reflections on the French Revolution,* p. 143.

2. Stephen, James, *Liberty, Equality, Fraternity.*

3. MacIver, R. M., *The Modern, State,* Bk. II, See. I.

4. M. Kechnie, W.S., *The State and the Individual.* p. 96.

5. Kant, *Principles of Politics*, Translated by Hastie, p. 10.

6. According to Prof. Willis the "power of eminent domain is the legal capacity of Government to take the private property of individuals for a public use upon the payment of just compensation. Eminent domain is the superior dominion of the state over all the property within the state.... Eminent domain differs from Police power in that the police power is not a taking of any right, whether of property or a person from people, but a limitation on the exercise of such rights by the people, although the police power may result in making people lose their property"—Willis: *Constitutional Law of the United States,* pp. 224-25, 716-17.

7. The police power under the U.S. Constitution is very comprehensive. It means the power of the state "to prescribe

regulations to promote the health, peace, morals, education and good order of the people and to legislate so as to increase the industries of the state, develop its resources and add to its wealth and prosperity"—Barbier V. Connolly, *Supreme Court of the United States*, 1885, 113, U.S. 27.

8. Follet, M.P. *The New State*, p. 74.
9. Denning, *Freedom Under the Law*, pp. 44, 5.
10. Strong, *Ibid.*, pp. 853-54.
11. Dowling, *Cases on Constitutional Law*. pp. 941-46.
12. *The Supreme Court of the U.S.A.*, 1925, 268, U.S. 652.
13. M. Kechnie, W.S. *The State and the Individual*, pp. 315-16.
14. Laski, H.J., *The State in Theory and Practice*, p. 100.
15. Laski, H.J., *The State in Theory and Practice*, p. 75.
16. MacIver, R.M., *The Leviathan and the People*, p. 161.
17. MacIver, R.M., *The Web of Government*, p. 330.
18. MacIver, R.M., *Ibid*, p. 350.

9

Nation-States vs. International Order

No unit of government has brought enduring peace and prosperity. The Greek system, by emphasizing the autonomy of each urban-rural cluster, prevented wider unions. Efforts to achieve these by combining freely did not last long, and attempts to enforce unification, though tried repeatedly, provoked opposition and war. Rome, beginning like the rest as a city-state, was the only one to achieve a lasting success in the imperial role, thereby eliminating the independent city-state and imposing the new unit of empire. But even Rome Could not command the world,[1] and the peaces and unity to which she aspired reached their bounds in the north and east. The same was true of the Middle ages when popes and emperors sought the holy grail of universal order. In neither sphere, however, did practice arrive at universality. Each of those experiments groped for a structure within which people could obtain welfare in safety. Each lasted only as long as it fulfilled the need; each collapsed when it could do so no longer.

The change from one unit to another, whether smaller or larger, is revolutionary, and it is a revolution of a deeper kind than those upheavals to which we ordinarily apply the term. To alter fundamentally the size and scale of one's unit of government is a more radical transformation than to substitute one ruling group for another or to introduce a new style of Constitution. That is why this kind of revolution is so rare. Indeed, as was observed in the Western world it has occurred only twice since the institution of the *polis.*

Our age in history, however, in my judgement is the third instance of this revolution. For the nation-state is now retracing the history of its predecessors. It emerged at a time when it was more capable than the medieval system of supplying humanity with security and well-being. But this unit of government, like the rest, is failing to meet these objectives. Consequently, it is now obsolescent and will become obsolete. Our contemporary world shows many signs of being in transition from the outmoded nation-state to some new unit. Seen in historical perspective, the age in which we live is comparable to the readjustment that occurred between the breakdown of the *polis* and the rise of the Roman Empire or between the collapse of the medieval order and the founding of the nation-state. Once more, an experiment is under way to discover the territorial unit best adapted to ensure prosperity and security in the twenty-first century. Since modern internationalism, however, is a reaction to the declining adequacy of nationalism, the discussion must continue where the last chapter ended. What failings has the nation-state revealed? Is some more workable alternative in sight?

Despite the strivings of states to build nations and of nations to organize states, few perfect correspondences exist between nationality and statehood. The world still exhibits instances of peoples united by a common culture language, and religion who aspire to a national consciousness and seek to formalize it in a state of their own.[2] conversely, there are states which include in their jurisdiction a subject people who are unincorporated in the national body politic. In some countries those subjects are a minority; in other—South Africa, for example—they are the majority. Also there are numerous states, some of them very new, which contain inhabitants, but do not constitute a nation. These facts require explanation. Since the nation-state has been in vogue for over four centuries, why so imperfect a correlation between statehood and nationality?

IMPERIALISM AND SEA POWERS

The answer must be sought in histoi ical timing and in a set of economic and military factors all combining in a political result. When the nation-state was born, with it appeared its twin-sea-powered imperialism. How inseparably these were connected is plain to read in the annals of Spain, Portugal, England, France, and the Netherlands. Of course, the practice of imperialism, which consists in the forcible subjection of a community to alien rule, was no novelty. Nor was the employment of sea power, as the Athenians, Phoenicians, Norsemen, and Venetians may bear witness. What was new, however, was political expansion on an oceanic sale. The discovery that the earth was round and could be circumnavigated was quickly put to a use that challenged comparison with Rome. The peoples of Western Europe first mapped the world; then with guns and galleons they partitioned it.

The result was a succession of struggles for maritime supremacy, colonial acquisition, and the wealth to be gained thereby. The first pair of competitors were Spain and Portugal. Between their claims Pope Alexander VI arbitrated in1493. By his award and the Treaty of Tordesillas in 1494 the non-European world was divided. To Spain was assigned the exclusive possession of all that lay more thanv 1110 miles to the west of Cape Verde; to Portugal, all that lay east. Such an award was no more acceptable to Catholic France than to Protestant England, both of which had ambitions of their own. When Spain was humbled by the English victory over the Armada and the Dutch had fought successfully for independence, the Atlantic seaways were open to new contestants. Neither France nor England could take full advantage of its opportunity until internal disunion was overcome. This was achieved in the seventeenth century by the triumph of Catholicism and absolute monarchy in one country of Protestantism and Parliament in the other. Then the two powers were ready to inaugurate their second Hundred Year's War over wide battlefields on sea and land. The epoch that opened with Britain's resistance under Marlborough[3] to aims of Louis XIV closed with Napoleon's downfall at Waterloo. In between occurred the colonial rivalry, extending long and far, wherein France during the Seven Years' War (1756-1763) bowed to the British in India and North America, but revenged itself by aiding the United States in the War of Independence. To the latter setback Britain responded by speeding up the technological revolution of her industries in the struggle against Napoleon, and later by reorganizing her empire on the principle of self-government for the component parts as they matured.[4] Thus, with her nearest military rivals worsted or enfeebled, Britain preempted the nineteenth century.

Secure in the assets of a factory system whose productivity then led the world, and of a navy and merchant marine predominant in every ocean. the people of a small island off the coast of Europe constructed and commanded an empire which by 1914 covered fourth of the land surface of the globe and contained one-fourth of its population. In this climactic episode, sea power, the progenitor of the nation-state, had reached the ultimate. To make it possible, the varied talents of an ebullient age contributed their quotas—victoria, the queenly symbol; Palmerston, the swashbuckling spirit; Disraeli, the imagination and brains; the City of London the financial sinews; Kipling, the ballads; and Gladstone, the out raged liberal conscience in self-rebuke for sins it did not prevent.

CONTRADICTIONS OF SOVEREIGNTY

The success of imperialism, however, and its duration for four centuries involved the nation-state in a fundamental inconsistency. Depending on the angle of view, this unit of government can be considered the opposite of either localism or internationalism. Both of those were characteristic of the medieval period, one receiving theoretical[5] lip service and the other reflecting more accurately the realities of social organisation. Since the nation-state rejected the system immediately preceding neither local autonomy nor international control was tolerable to its architects. The centralizing tendency of the nation-state, drawing powers and functions from the localities to the capital, was described earlier.[6] Now is the place to discuss the external relations of nationalism.

As in other respects the doctrine that was the maid-of-all-work for the nation-state—the theory of sovereignty—here, too was enlisted into service. Sovereignty was construed to mean that the government of the nation-state supreme within its own jurisdiction over local bodies and churches, acknowledged no political or legal superior beyond its territorial boundaries. "My dogs," as Queen

Elizabeth I of England once phrased it, "shall wear no collars but mine own." Authority, allegiance, and law were to be the exclusive monopoly of the nation-state, and as such, were not articles for import across national frontiers. Were they, however, articles for export? There lay the inconsistency. Whatever its professions, the nation-state acted on a double standard. Both in external and internal affairs it claimed to be a law unto itself. Limitations on its freedom of action diminished its sovereignty and consequently were inadmissible. But, though unwilling to submit to control from outside, it professed to see no wrong in subjecting others to do its own will. Imperialism violated the principle of sovereignty by denying to others the self-government on which the nationalist insisted. In effect, throughout the entire era of the nation-state, the political ordering of humanity never conformed consistently to the ideal of having a number of separate units of government, each self-contained. Imperialism meant dividing humanity into elite peoples who ruled, and whose nationality could find outlets for expression; and subject peoples whose national aspirations were suppressed. Hence imperialism negated the first premise from which the nation-state proceeded. It is no accident that the twins, which were born together and have lived in perennial incompatibility, in this century are dying together.

This combination of nationalism with imperialism and the ensuing dilemma produced an economic counterpart. From the sixteenth century to the eighteenth, or before laissez-faire policies become prevalent prosperity was sought by applying political concepts to economics. The politics of nationalism was matched by the economics of nationalism, that being the essence of the mercantile system.[7] Correspondingly, political imperialism was yoked to economic imperialism. Colonies, considered as the "possessions" of the imperial power, were organised to supply it with raw materials and precious metals, as they were also to import its manufactures and carry their commerce in its ships. This is not to deny that additional motives influenced the settlement or acquisition of colonies. The desire of dissident minorities to emigrate; the strategic quest for bases, ports of call, and defensible frontiers; the missionaries who preached the Christian gospel-many a magnet, besides trade, attracted nations to plan their flags on distant shores. But that the single most important factor in empire building was the economic can hardly be denied. Through imperialism the nation-state could grow more prosperous—or so it was hoped.

From the standpoint of security an empire was as much a liability as an asset. True, the treasure yielded by some colonies could be used to build more warships and pay more troops in order to defend the mother country and keep subjects more surely in subjection. But colonies situated across oceans were remote and exposed. They might prove hard to defend against an invader or to hold against a rebellion. Furthermore, when the imperial power was itself in danger of attack on its home terrain, less force could be spared for garrisons abroad. By spreading its resources thin, the imperial nation-state exposed many hostages to fortune. It was therefore vulnerable to amputation at the extremities or attack at the heart. The latter risk was the primary concern of nation-statesmen, since colonies were of no avail if the motherland was insecure. Hence in every case the organisation of the nation-state passed through a phase of expansion and consolidation wherein the purpose was to arrive, if possible, at a defensible frontier. Let us observe what happened and the consequences.

The United Kingdom, as Great Britain is officially called, was created by absorptions and additions. England, itself a fusion of smaller and previously separate kingdoms, provided the nucleus for a larger union. Amalgamation with Wales was achieved by conquest in 1284. Scotland and Ireland, both larger than Wales and less accessible, presented more formidable problems. But their independence posed a threat to England since a continental enemy like France could form an alliance with the Scots or Irish and threaten England from the flank or rear. An island had an obvious frontier in its coastline. The union of England and Scotland, facilitated by the triumph of Protestantism both north and south of the border, was formally effected in 1707. "John Bull's other island,"[8] whose proximity made it strategically vital, could be conquered,. but largely because of religious differences could not be absorbed. All that remained thereafter was for Britain to control the seas around her coasts and prevent any one power from dominating the European mainland. It this was done, its security was assured. The same problem confronted the continental nation-states, but with an important difference. They had a land as well as a sea frontier to defend. Besides navies, therefore, they had to maintain standing armies, which affected their internal politics, tending to reinforce the authoritarian structure of their government. Armies, more easily than navies, could reach the heart of an enemy state. Napoleon could cross the Pyrenees or the alps but not the channel, and Frenchmen and Germans marched in and out of each other's territories for centuries.

The military conditions imposed by geography go far toward explaining why it was Britain, and not any of her rivals, that emerged as the strongest power in the nineteenth century. But in that century new factors intervened which in the short run enhanced the might of Britain, yet in the long run contributed both to her decline and to that of the nation-state system. The intruding element was the technology of industrialism and the economic potentialities thus unleashed. Its immediate effect was to create a productive capacity exceeding the needs and resources of the nation-state. Britain had always engaged in foreign trade. But now in volume and extent this trade grew to unprecedented proportions.[9] The terrain that the nation occupied did not yield all the raw materials that manufacturers required. Nor did its population offer a market sufficient to consume their output. More than before, the prosperity of peoples became interdependent.[10] If somewhere in the world production was curtailed or purchasing power declined, if the price of a basic commodity fell or it was replaced by a substitute, other economies were intimately affected thousands of miles away.

ANARCHY AMONG NATIONS

The nation-state was not hopelessly caught in a tangle of contradictions. As if it were not already difficult enough to make the boundaries of state and nation coextensive, it became evident that the territorial unit chosen for military purposes was at variance with the area appropriate to economics. Protection was organised to run along national lines; prosperity, across them. The task of organizing a unit wherein the needs of nationality security, and prosperity would coincide harmoniously was well-nigh impossible, and the situation was rendered more chaotic by the competition between states for the same objective. An area which a state considered strategically necessary for its own protection might be inhabited by people whom a neighbour regarded as belonging to its own nationality. Valuable resources in the borderland between two states would be sought by both. Thus Alsace-Lorraine, the Low Countries, the Brenner Pass and the Trentino, Bohemia, the Polish Corridor, Suez, and Panama were scenes of international rivalry and conflict.

Under such circumstances, the nation-state became less and less capable of providing the minimal needs of protection and order. At its best, it maintained order within its own territory and minimised, without eliminating, the possibility of civil war; but it could not guarantee that international relations would be peacefully conducted. The doctrine of sovereignty, as it was applied, combined internal stability with external anarchy. In essentials, therefore, the history of the nation-state repeated (with a change of scale, because the unit was larger) the earlier experience of the city-state. International relations were like inter-*polis* relations, and the old drama was reenacted in modern dress. Like city-states before them, nation-states were small, medium-sized, or big. If small, their only chance of survival was to accept protection from the biggest power nearby, or if they lay between rival powers, to announce their neutrality and hope it would be respected. Medium-sised states could also serve as buffers to keep their larger neighbours from one another's throats. They might, however, be induced to enter into systems of alliances, since their support or opposition could have some effect on the balance of power. Their riskiest policy, of course, was to be afflicted with delusions of grandeur and dress in big-power costume without having the measurements to fill it.

The major states picked up the script which Athens. Corinth, Sparta, and Thebes had written. Each in turn strove for leadership. Each was destined to strut and fret its hour upon the stage-Spain,

Austria, France, Britain, and Germany. All had their periods of ascendancy. None could perpetuate its domination, because new challengers arose against every champion. The result was that throughout more than four centuries the nation-state system was incapable of securing a lasting peace. Major convulsions recurred with frightening regularity—the Thirty Years' War (1618-1648), the War of the League of Augsburg (1688-1697), the War of the Spanish Succession (1701-1713), Wars of the French Revolution (1793-1815), World War I (1914-1918), And World War II (1939-1945). These were interspersed with more limited conflicts, so that scarcely a decade went by without an outbreak of hostilities some where. The history of most countries contains testimony to prove that establishing a nation-state does not guarantee a continuous peace. The United States, for example, has engaged in four major wars (1776-1783, 1861-1865, 1917-1918,1941-1945) and six minor ones[11] (1812-1815, 1846-1848, 1898, 1950-1953,1965-1973, 1990-1991), so that, on the average, the peace has been broken in every third decade.

THE CONSOLIDATION OF LAND MASSES

The perennial anarchy of nation-states and the discordance between national politics and international economics were not the only reasons for the ending of an era. Another was the declining effectiveness of sea power. When this century opened, the peoples of the Atlantic seaboard were losing the advantages which had so long been theirs. Fresh opportunities for expansion were being discovered to the east and west. The new goal was to consolidate the continental land masses under the jurisdiction of a single state. Three attempts of this kind were made. The first was by Germany. The marriage of the Prussian army with the industries of the Ruhr and Rhineland created a formidable power in the north-center of Europe. From this base, with a strategy formulated in terms of land domination, the German *Reich* set out to unify the continent. Twice its leaders tried this in wars they instigated. Twice they were beaten, but at a dreadful cost. With its central position Germany enjoyed the advantage of interior lines and could be defeated only by encirclement. Thus, the Atlantic nations perforce were allied with Russia in World War I and again in World War II. Even the western front could not be maintained by Britain and France alone, who in both wars, and particularly in the second, needed American participation to defeat the common foe. Europe's loss of power after 1945 was the price paid by an entire continent for the necessity of curbing German ambitions.

The other two attempts had different results. From the Atlantic sea-board American democracy expanded westward to the Pacific. Czarist Russia had already fanned out eastward along northern Asia. Incorporating Siberia in its dominion and crossing the Bering Strait into Alaska. The phenomenon of states which spanned continents was noted by de Tocqueville, who in 1835 made this prophetic comment:

> There are, at the present time, two great nations in the world which seem to tend toward the same end, although they started from different points: I allude to the Russians and the Americans. Both of them have grown up unnoticed; and while the attention of mankind was directed elsewhere, they have suddenly assumed a most prominent place the nations; and the world learned their existence and their greatness at almost the same time. All other nations seem to have nearly reached their natural limits, and only to be charged with the maintenance of their power; but these are still in the act of growth; all others are stopped, or continue to advance with extreme difficulty; these are proceeding with ease and with celerity along a path to which the human eye can assign no term. . . . Their starting point is different, and their courses are not the same; yet of them seems to be marked out by the will of heaven to sway the destinies of half the globe.[12]

By the time the United States and Russia had attained a size which dwarfed the nation-states of Western Europe, the same technology which had already outmoded the economics of nationalism shattered its military defenses. It is nation-state floated into history on the wave of sea power, it sank under assault from the air. Blériot flew across the English Channel in 1909, in 1919 Alcock and Brown flew the Atlantic. Applied on only a limited scale in World War I, air power was decisive in the strategy of World War II. When the Nazis in 1914 defied the British control of the sea and captured Crete from the air, they rang down the curtain on an epoch. Four years later when the Japanese surrendered their islands after being the victims of two atomic bombs, they acknowledged realistically that the old politics must conform to the new physics. The foundations of the state have been relocated above and out of sight, in the stratosphere and in outer space.

COLLECTIVE INSECURITY

Abundant evidence confirms that the nation-state can no longer provide protection and prosperity within its own borders. In the first half of this century two wars occurred whose theatre of operations was the world. Together they demonstrated that the anarchy of the nation-state system breeds contagious insecurity and allows few to isolate themselves from its effects. The fears, suspicions, and distrust of nation for nation cause each to maintain whatever armaments it can afford, and their costliness is a drain on economies that otherwise could progress in the arts of peace. For other than military reasons, these same economies have become interdependent, rendering them vulnerable to worldwide movements over which no single nation has control. To this truth the depression of the early 1930s bore witness. As a plague sweeps across political frontiers, the same malady struck at one country after another, producing the same symptoms: falling prices, lowered purchasing power, rising unemployment, reduced revenues from taxation, unbalanced budgets, bankruptcies, and default on debts. Prosperity, as well as peace, had become indivisible.

This worldwide succession of event in a 30-year period-war, depression, and war again—offered the clearest proof that a global society was emerging for which the nation-state was an unsuitable unit of government. Not only in trade and commerce, but in cultural contacts and the movement of ideas communication between peoples had become easier and more rapid. As in the fifteenth and sixteenth centuries a national order could not predominate unless the localism of the medieval system was abandoned, so in the twentieth century a world order could not prevail if politics were conducted through national channels. Paradoxically the determination to build security within the borders of the nation-state contributed to everybody's insecurity. States behaved severally like individuals who place their reliance on self-protection and carry weapons on their person instead of resorting to public agencies such as police and courts. That system, whether imagined by Hobbes or practiced under frontier conditions, produces only disorder which is what has happened in a world of nation-states. The effort of each to build protection nationally has failed to protect us internationally. What is more, the particularism of nation-states has obstructed a development from the protection of each to an order embracing all. International politics had reached an impasse—and it illustrates the general problem of human association discussed in chapter 2. The relations between states were characterised by too much competition and too little cooperation. All suffered from the harmful effects of pursuing their aims in self-centred isolation. They were insufficiently aware that the objectives which all had sought separately could be better achieved if all cooperated collectively. Some method had to be devised of securing protection through order and of infusing the latter with a concept of justice. In short, the need to refashion the relations between states was similar in principle to that of harmonizing associations within the state. The jurisdiction of government had to become more nearly coextensive with the ambit of society.

THE SEARCH FOR REMEDIES

Because the problems are manifold the search for remedies has ranged the gamut from legal to military, from economic to political. Historically, the first attempt to mitigate the ferocity of the strong was the formulation of the body of international law.[13] Its rules were designed to regulate the competitive self-interest which governments practised in their mutual dealings. But independent means of enforcement were lacking. Only the threat of retaliation might serve to restrain an aggressor, and it seldom stopped the bigger bullies. Another method was to provide machinery for arbitration, so that disputes between governments could be resolved or compromised by a tribunal that both parties accepted Arbitration was notably extended in the later nineteenth century, especially in Anglo-American relations. But it depended on a prior willingness to submit to the machinery and to accept its outcome.

At the end of World War I, more ambitious experiments were launched. The International Labour Organisation—Composed of representatives of governments, employers and workers—was created to negotiate agreements for bringing industrial conditions to a common standard. The Permanent Court of International Justice provided a bench of jurists representing the principal legal systems of the world. They gave advisory opinions, when requested, or tried cases which governments asked them to adjudicate. Third in this trio was the League of Nations, whose central function was to preserve peace. This it sought by political means, establishing a forum for diplomacy and negotiation. When all else failed and war erupted, the League could evoke sanctions against the government that was declared the aggressor. But their application depended on the voluntary cooperation of the member states. Economic sanctions were attempted once, against Fascist Italy in 1935-1936 when Mussolini invaded Ethiopia. They failed because too many states refused to participate.

In all such experiments, a central problem emerged with stark clarity: the organisation of power in the international arena. Each of the institutions or procedures mentioned above was an exploratory device to govern an evolving international society. But the agencies employed to run the machinery were still, at this stage, the very nation-states which needed to be restrained. If these perceived enough of a common interest, they could agree to cooperate. But if their competing interests appeared paramount, how was a wider sphere of order to be maintained? No means were found to stop Japan's aggression against China, or Italy's against Ethiopia, or Germany's against Austria, Czechoslovakia, Poland, Norway, Denmark, and France. World War II was the price/paid for the shortcomings of the Versailles Treaty and the inadequacies of the League of Nations.

THE UNITED NATIONS

At the end of World War II humanity received its second chance within a generation to establish a stable world order. The problem confronting the victors in 1945 was even more urgent than in 1918 because prosperity and security were more seriously jeopardised. Not only were the economies of many countries shattered, but atomic bombs which could be delivered to distant targets constituted a greater menace to life than any previous destructive weapon. To organize a general economic recovery and police the world against future acts of aggression called for global solutions. So during the years 1944-1946, a number of new international bodies were established. All but one of these are specialised agencies in the sense that their work is limited to a particular function or service whose programmes are often technical in content.[14] The exception is the United Nations, which, as the successor to the League, took over the general responsibility of promoting cooperation between states and keeping them at peace.

A comparison of the League Covenant with the United Nations Charter shows that the latter was intended not merely to replace its predecessor but to remedy its defects. Though it embraces a wide range of international problems from declarations of human rights to control of atomic weapons, the United Nations organisation was influenced from the start by more realism and fewer illusions than its predecessor. The League did not measure up to the ordeals of the 1930s because it lacked bullets to enforce compliance with its ballots. Consequently, when the Charter was drafted, provisions for enforcement were included, and the Security Council became the cutting edge of the new organisation.

Its strength was quickly put to the test. Almost from birth, and before the bone structure had hardened, the United Nations was forced to adjust to major realignment. Several assumptions which were taken for granted in 1945 were quickly falsified. First, the expectation that the Kuomintang would rule China was not fulfilled. Their overthrow by Mao's forces brought one-quarter of the human race under communist control at one stroke, altering the balance of power in Asia with major consequences for relations between East and West. Next, the belief that Western states, after defeating Japan, could maintain their former empires over nonwhite peoples was unrealistic. The Dutch lost the East Indies, which become that state of Indonesia. The French, defeated at Dien Bien Phu, were forced out of Indochina, which was then subdivided into a trio of new states; in Africa they granted independence to their colonies and to Tunis, and eventually, after a long struggle, left Algeria to the Algerians—that is, to the Muslim majority. The Belgians, who did little to prepare the Congo for self-government, suddenly released their grip and abandoned the region to its own devices. As for Britain, a nation which in 1938 had accounted for one-fifth of the world's trade was too impoverished to shoulder its former commitments. The liquidation of empire proceeded inexorably. Beginning in 1948 with the independence of India, the ceremonies of withdrawal were reenacted throughout Asia and Africa. By 1990 the areas remaining under London's control were a scattering of insignificant possessions, mainly economic and military liabilities, and a few ports and islands strung out along the routes to vanished glories.[15]

Elsewhere, too, the sometime dominance of occidental peoples has evoked a reaction of angry outburst and violent challenge. Mossadegh led the way in Iran by taking over the properties of the Anglo-Iranian Oil Company. Nasser repeated this coup in Egypt by nationalizing the Suez canal, after which he set about fomenting movements throughout the Arab world to expel western influences. Indeed on every continent the opposition to Europen colonialism has become one of the most active political forces of our time. The words and deeds of 1776 have been much imitated and oft-repeated—sometimes with a sound that rings true, sometimes with a false note—in Accra, Cairo, Jakarta, Delhi, and other capitals.[16]

As the maritime empires disappeared from the map, the cumulative results of the transformation were visible in the expanding membership of the United Nations. What began in 1945 as an organisation of 51 states grew by 1992 to 178. When the government of China was finally seated in the early seventies, the United Nations became closer to the universality which is its ultimate rationale. But the institution, on which humanity's hopes for peace were centred, operated from the start under the severest handicap. The United Nations had been predicted on the belief that the coalition of states which won the war against fascism would continue to act in substantial harmony. Nor could one otherwise justify the veto power of the five principal states in the Security Council, since if they failed to cooperate the United Nations would be doomed to deadlock. For several decades the major activities of the United Nations—diplomatic, technical, and peacekeeping—were hampered by the formation of two potent and antagonistic blocs; one led by the United States, the other by the Soviet Union.

Indeed, the entire period from 1945 to 1990 not only exhibited a pattern which is unique, but it created a political context of infinite peril. The defeat of Germany, Italy and Japan, combined with the weakening of France and Great Britain, provided the occasion for de Tocqueville's prophecy to be fulfilled. For Several decades the influence of the two super-powers, the United States and the Soviet Union, was felt throughout the world, and their adversarial relationship—the Cold War, as it was called—set the stage on which the central drama of international relations was enacted. At the end of the 1980s, however, the Cold War at last gave way to a global warming. This *Denouement* makes it possible to analyze the last half century as a cycle in political evolution which in this one respect—the dangerous stakes of bipolar competition—is now complete. Rarely in world politics does a series of events unfold which clearly signify a turning point. Such, however, was true both of the years from 1945 to 1950, when the Cold War began, and of 1985 to 1990, when it ended.

THE COLD WAR

Much of the diplomacy conducted in the second half of the twentieth century was shaped within the framework of the competition between Washington and Moscow for global hegemony. That competition had different aspects. In the military sphere, it give rise to an arms race which impelled both governments to divert a significant proportion of their resources, budgets, and technical personnel to the production of weapons of a destructive capacity hitherto unimaginable. At the climax, each side possessed in its stockpile enough bombs to exterminate the principal centres of population of its rival many times over. Meanwhile, the domestic economy paid the price, and civilian consumers suffered. What is more, the two countries which Americans and Russians together had defeated in World War II, Germany and Japan, were able to initiate an economic recovery which was unimpeded by the demands of huge military outlays. By the 1980s the warnings of President Eisenhower in 1961 concerning the encroachments of the military-industrial complex were tragically fulfilled in the scandals and misplaced priorities of the Reagan Administration. Of the businessmen who came to Washington in that period to hold high offices in the executive branch, a large number abused their public positions for private financial gain or for the benefit of corporations to which they were linked.

No less striking were the diplomatic consequences of the Cold War. Bidding for hegemony, each side sought to build its coalition of allies and dependents. The latter's support or cooperation could take different forms—the supply of troops for joint undertakings, provision of bases, sharing of technology, supply of critical raw materials and voting for the same resolutions at international meetings. Although these arrangements were conducted between patron and client, and although the former was a superpower, the leverage which a recipient of aid could exert was not inconsiderable. The United States gave assistance to Tito, thus helping him to maintain his independence of Moscow. Naturally the Soviet Union reciprocated by supporting Castro, whose economy continued for decades to be a charge on its budget. Each side allowed itself to become involved in protracted civil wars in order to prop up or install a regime to its liking. Witness the cases of Vietnam and Afghanistan, each a tragedy for the superpower involved. Also, within the region considered as its sphere of influence neither government hesitated to launch invasions so as to ensure that the ruling group was sympathetic to its own philosophy—as Hungary and Czechoslovakia, the Dominican Republic and Grenada, may bear witness.[17] The competition to recruit members for their blocs impelled both Washington and Moscow to grant support to numerous unsavoury regimes, as long as they satisfied the basic condition of being, respectively, anticommunist or ant capitalist. Thus Moscow numbered Kim Il Sung anti Honecker among its clients, while Washington had Somoza and Marcos on its payroll.

This last point touches on yet another aspect of the cold War, the ideological. The conflict between the United States and the Soviet Union was perceived on both sides as a struggle concerning whose values and what kind of society would prevail. The Soviet system was dedicated to the doctrines of Karl Marx, with his theories of scientific materialism and the class war, plus his vision of an eventual classless society. The United States was founded on the individualistic doctrines of the Enlightenment, with a commitment to a pluralistic society and a government of limited powers obedient to the rule of law. Each sought to proselytize its creed and win new converts. Each at the same time showed intolerance toward any in its midst who sympathised with the values of its opponent. Think of McCarthyism in Washington in the early 1950s and Brezhnev's brutal persecution of dissenters. The propaganda war of that period—intensified emotionally by the conduct of espionage on both sides—was raised almost to a pitch of religious zeal, in some ways reminiscent of the mutual antipathies of Catholics and Protestants during the Reformation and Counter-Reformation.

The ending of the Cold War was a result of the advent to power of Mikhail Gorbachev and his frank recognition of the need for this country to change course. Since he had to reduce military expenditures in order to stimulate a declining economy, he displayed to the West a conciliatory face. The fruits of the new atmosphere of cooperation were first plucked in Eastern Europe, then in the Persian Gulf where Moscow gave its support to the American led coalition which was assembled to curb the ambitions of Saddam Hussein.

Who won the Cold War, it will be asked? In the truest sense, no one did. All were losers, because international politics for decades was poisoned by the animosities and misunderstandings which it generated. In a relative sense, however, the United States came out ahead of its rival. The evidence for that lies in the fact that the countries which previously were ruled by Communist Parties are nowadays discussing which features of the western political and economic system they can successfully introduce, whereas nobody in any part of the would is talking of converting to Marxism. If the United States did win the Cold War, however, it was at the heavy price of losing economic supremacy to Japan. The Japanese have learned that it is wiser to manufacture automobiles and television sets than aircraft carriers and tanks, and easier to buy Hawaii than to bomb it. Only in 1991 did the United States and the Soviet Union agree to a treaty under which both will at last begin reducing their long-range strategic missiles, i.e., those with the capacity for mass extermination. But the process will be long and slow, and expensive as well. Meanwhile, both economies will continue to suffer from being overextended by the insanity of the arms race. How often is the student of international relations constrained to exclaim with Shakespeare's Puck: "Lord, what fools these mortals be!"[18]

KEEPING THE PEACE

As long as the Cold War lasted, the United Nations had difficulty in discharging its major responsibility, which was to keep the peace. In June 1950, when North Korea attacked South Korea, it proved possible for the Security Council to authorize collective aid to the South only for the reason that the Soviet delegate had walked out[19] six months earlier and the Russian seat was empty at that moment.

In 1956, at the time of the Suez affair,[20] the United Nations emerged as the effective agent for ending hostilities in Egypt, inducing Britain, France, and Israel to withdraw their armies, and subsequently policing the Gaza Strip and Gulf of Akaba. The political reasons for this achievement invite reflection. In the first place the majority opinion throughout the world sided with Egypt. Although Britain, France and Israel had the military means to make their will prevail, a political fact—the concerted pressure of international opinion—compelled them to pull their armies back. The second, and conclusive, fact was the concurrence of the United states and the Soviet Union, both of whose governments at that time were unwilling to court the displeasure of the Arabs. But simultaneously with the events at Suez, the Soviet Union sent the Red Army into action in the streets of Budapest in order to reinstall the Communist government which had fallen from power through a popular uprising. Action by the United Nations against the Soviet Union, however, was not possible because of the widespread fear of initiating measures that could lead directly to a third world war between the superpowers.

Since then there have been other occasions when the United Nations has been charged with peacekeeping responsibilities—which means that various countries contributed contingents to serve under its flag and maintain order in areas where there was danger of war. This necessary, but unwelcome, service was performed in both the Congo and Cyprus, despite the objections of the Soviet Union and France which refused to pay a share of the expenses. Indeed, the United Nations undertook those particular functions on the basis of votes in the General Assembly, where, unlike the Security Council, the veto of the five principal members does not apply. However, it was shown in May 1967 that the opposition of the government of the country in which the United Nations places its forces can constitute a veto of its own. When Nasser demanded that the United Nations withdraw its peacekeeping units from the Gaza Strip and from Sharm-el-Sheik at the entrance to the Red Sea, the Secretary-General complied. The consequences were immediate. Egypt began closing the Gulf of Akaba to Israeli shipping. Then the six-day war erupted in which Israel crushed the combined forces of Egypt, Jordan, and Syria. Not until 1974, after the fourth bout of hostilities between Egypt and Syria on the one side and Israel on the other, was the flag of the United Nations brought back to the centre of this battlefield to police the cease-fire along the Suez Canal and the Golan Heights. And necessarily so. No other agency existed, national or international, in which the belligerents, as well as the United States and the Soviet Union, could acquiesce.

Subsequently, however, in that very same region the limitations on the United Nations as a peacekeeper were glaringly exposed. After the Palestine Liberation Organisation was driven from Jordan, it moved into Lebanon, taking control of much of its territory and upsetting the ever-delicate balance between the Christian and Muslim communities. Soon, Lebanon disintegrated into civil war. Syria then marched in and occupied the north, while the Israelis backed a Christian militia in the south as a buffer between their northern frontier and the PLO. The United Nations dispatched a peacekeeping force to keep the hostile groups apart, but to no avail. Bent on destroying the PLO, the Israelis drove to Beirut in 1982, and, when they later withdrew south, the UN contingents were caught in the cross-fires of warring Lebanese militias. Since the United Nations does not have overwhelming force at its disposal, it can only function where the belligerents are ready for a truce and can be induced to observe it.

New life, however, was breathed into the world body with the ending of the Cold War. As the adversarial relationship between Washington and Moscow was replaced by willingness to cooperate, the United Nations started to come into its own. Forty years after its founding, the principal member governments made a practice of utilizing its services as the indispensable agency for moderating disputes and enforcing a rule of law. In southern Africa, for example, the United Nations helped to negotiate the independence of Namibia from South Africa as well as the conclusion of the civil war in Angola and the withdrawal of foreign forces. Its mediation was similarly instrumental in settling the hostilities in Afghanistan and Cambodia. Most spectacular of all was the role it played after Iraq occupied Kuwait in August, 1990. Militarily, it was the United States and its allies in the coalition assembled by President Bush who compelled the Iraqi dictator, Saddam Hussein, to withdraw his forces. At the diplomatic level, however, a series of resolutions in the Security Council, not vetoed by any of the five permanent members, authorised the sanctions—economic and military—against the aggressor government and enunciated the principles which the world community sought to uphold in the Persian Gulf. It is a revitalised United Nations which now prepares for the advent of a new millennium.

In terms of the loss of life and general devastations, it should be noted that the most murderous conflicts since 1960 originated as civil wars in which other governments involved themselves. Such were the attempt of Biafra to secede from Nigeria, which failed; the split between East and West Pakistan, where the former became the independent state of Bangladesh; and Vietnam, where, contrary to the Geneva Agreement of 1954, the United States backed a separate regime in Saigon to oppose the one in Hanoi. In none of these cases was the United Nations effective in mitigating or ending the hostilities. What did have a decisive effect was the amount of aid or direct military intervention from outside. Thus, Great Britain helped Nigeria; India sided with Bangladesh; While the United States struggled in vain to prop up a rickety regime for South Vietnam. Relations between the United States and the United Nations were at their lowest point during the Johnson and Nixon administrations, when American forces were fighting in or over Vietnam, Laos, and Cambodia, while the Secretary-General of the United Nations, U Thant, was Burmese and Buddhist. In that same area, after America's involvement ended, Cambodia was the stage for one of the most horrifying tragedies of this century. Civil war was compounded by the rival ambitions of China and a Soviet-supported Vietnam to control this hapless peasant society—one third of whose people are believed to have perished.

INTERNATIONAL RELATIONS IN A DOUBLE-STANDARD WORLD

Although the rivalry of major powers is common enough, the raw materials for conflict are everywhere at hand in the inequality of conditions that divide vast sections of the human race. Throughout Asia, Africa, and South and Central America, most human beings are illiterate, under-nourished, squalidly house, and meanly clad. Poverty, disease, and ignorance dog their brief lives.[21] Probably the great majority of people have always fared this way—or at least have so fared throughout the few millennia over which historical records extend. It is manifestly impossible for a double-standard world to be a contented one, and inequality, as Aristotle noted, has ever been a fertile source of revolution. But, though social upheavals have not been wanting in the past, their effects were formerly less widespread and less interconnected than those that characterize our epoch. Uintil a few centuries ago, large segments of humanity and entire civilisations endured in isolation from one another. A Change of dynasty in China stirred not a ripple in Europe. The death of a Russian autocrat caused little concern beyond the borders of Muscovy. Discussions or decisions on the banks of the Potomac, the Thames, or the Seine did not make the whole welkin ring. The supply and control of oil, iron ore, and uranium were not matters of global life or death.

All that has changed. For our woe or weal, we have made of all the world a single stage where the drama of human fate is enacted in scenes that shift rapidly from place to place but form part of one plot. What distinguishes our age from those that have gone before, and complicates the solution of its problems, are the extension of the community of interests to an area as wide as the world, the greater volume of information and speed in communicating it, and the deeper awareness by millions of their common lot. The huddled masses of humanity—"the wretched of the earth," as Fanon described them—not only yearn to breathe free; they also crave a share in things they have never enjoyed. The demand for economic development, to be achieved rapidly, has become the item of first priority for governments of countries with a backward technology and a traditional social system. Such circumstances make a spawning ground for political movements of many kinds. People who resent their underprivileged status, but who are politically unsophisticated, will readily listen to promises and follow a prophet. If lucky, they discover honest counsellors whose government has their interests at heart, a Nehru or a Nyerere. But they are just as likely to find that their prophet is a fraud and the promises were bogus. Or, they many encounter obstruction by those who reject the claims of the masses to more equal treatment. Out of this milieu come regimes which may be fascist, communist, nationalist, racist, militarist, theocratic, or democratic. Once the top is off the bottle and the genie is out, there is no telling what shape it will assume.

When the Charter of the United Nations was written, many recognised that colonial aspirations for independence and the general desire of people in underdeveloped areas for higher living standards are a constant source of friction and hence a possible cause of war. For this reason the structure included among its principal organs both a Trusteeship Council and an Economic and Social Council. The former was intended to safeguard the interests of weaker peoples, whose government the United Nations entrusts to another state. The goal of the Economic and Social Council is to lessen the gap between the technologically advanced communities and the backward. Despite inadequate budgets, significant aid has been rendered to underdeveloped countries by the United Nation through its Technical Assistance Administration and specialised agencies. Besides the granting of loans, this help consists in gathering and publishing information, disseminating scientific knowledge, and recruiting teams of experts and individual technicians who go to work in countries which request assistance. Their programmes for the most part are practical and specialised: a loan to build a steel mill or a dock, eradication of malaria, development of fisheries or reforestation, control of narcotics, reduction of illiteracy, the installation of a tax system, and so on.

PROBLEMS OF INTERNATIONAL COOPERATION

However constructive, such activities do not lack their quota of difficulties. The budgets of international agencies are grossly inadequate. Their poorer members, which need the help, have nothing to give. The wealthy, which must contribute most of the total, may be self-centred or may feel that they are already paying enough.[22] They may then oppose a budgetary increase, since they are the donors, not the recipients, of aid. Competent personnel are hard to recruit, because many persons see better opportunities in their own national civil service or because governments are sometimes disinclined to offer their best staff to an international agency. Because of political obstruction, some of it unrelated to the issue at hand, it may be impossible for the delegates at a conference to pick the best programme from the alternatives available. The Arab governments, supported by the Communist regimes, have used such occasions to reprimand Israel, while Black African states make white-dominated South Africa their target. Will the FAO always adopt policies which run counter to the profits of agribusiness and giant food-processing corporations? Can WHO sponsor programmes for contraception or abortion in areas of poverty and over-population when these are denounced by the celibate male clerics of the Catholic Church? Similarly in the ILO, which treads the thorny path of employer-employee relations, or at UNESCO, which seeks to combat ignorance and enrich humanity with the treasures of mind and spirit the conflict between competing interests or opposed philosophies is a hindrance to positive action. What accentuates these problems is the touchiness of national governments whenever an issue is raised that they deem vital. Where a great power is involved, other states are reluctant to outvote, and cannot coerce it. But small states too produce governments and leaders who can be particularly stubborn and self-willed in what seems to them their special interest. In particular, the rulers of countries that emerged recently from a dependent or colonial status are torn two ways. Without aid from outside—loans, investment, goods, and technicians—they cannot develop their economies and raise their living standards to the level they desire. But aid will normally be accompanied by some list of conditions, some attachment of strings, which then is interpreted in the guise of "foreign control"—especially when the aid is received from a single government instead of from an international source. Those who were recently subject to another power will chafe at new restraints, even when their source is an international agency. Furthermore, those who in opposition consistently proclaim fine-sounding principles can be seen making concessions to expediency when in office.

The crux of the problem can be simply stated: All over the world there are people who are dependent in their economics and technology but have strong feelings about their political independence. That paradox is explicable by the time lag in the spread of the nation-state. This unit of government, as we saw, originated in Western Europe in the fifteenth and sixteenth centuries. Its full force was not felt in Eastern Europe until the nineteenth. Among colonial peoples the first effective blow for national independence was struck in North America in 1776, with Latin America following suit five decades later. In the closing decades of the nineteenth century the force of nationalism began to explode in Asia, and the results have been manifest in recent history. Last came Africa, where much writing is already visible on the wall—and more will be written.

Contrary to my theme, however, some will maintain that today's world expresses the final triumph of the nation-state which has at last covered the globe. Now that the old colonial empires have virtually disappeared and the membership of the United Nations has trebled, is this not evidence of the vitality of nation-states? And is it not true that national sentiment continues to be a powerful force in many countries?

The facts are not in dispute, but I interpret them differently. The strength of national feelings is a familiar example of the normal time lag between a change in reality and the perception of it. In the history of politics and the evolution of society, sentiments which have been attached to an institution will remain strong for several generations after its potency has been eroding away. Today's nationalism often exists in inverse relation to the realities that could support and justify it. In addition, I would contend that the contemporary proliferation of new states, supposedly sovereign and independent, signifies not so much the success of the system as its *reductio ad absurdum*. Just as the splitting and subdivision of the *Polis* produced eventual chaos around the Mediterranean in the fifth and fourth centuries B.C., so has the liquidation of empires and the grant of self-government to former colonies multiplied the areas of disorder in the second half of the twentieth century.

To construct an international order out of today's disparate elements is truly a formidable task. The mansion of peace and prosperity must be built with bricks of different materials and varying shapes and sizes. The edifice includes once-mighty states like Britain and France; states which now stand in the forefront, like the USA; those with huge populations, like China and India, which nurtured ancient civilisations and will again be mighty when their potentialities are unleashed; states which give few thanks to the past, but consider themselves, as does Brazil, "lands of the future", those that made their bid for imperial hegemony and failed, but have fully recovered in economic strength and political influence, such as Germany and Japan; medium-states, some developing peaceably, others aggressively in wish or deed; others again of which little need be said except that they exist; and then an odd assortment of small fry-buffer states such as Belgium, Austria, or Uruguay; a few neutrals of the Swiss or Swedish model; the client-states like Bulgaria, Liberia, Cuba, or the Philippines; the Phoenix-style creations of Poland or Israel; and the anomalies of Iceland, Luxembourg, Botswana, two Koreas, and Tuvalu. Among recent additions to the list are many which are states by fictions, governments by courtesy, and nations only in the imagination. Nevertheless, all are clothed in the panoply of juridical attributes which other states accord to each new member of the club. Yet, looking at them, one cannot fail to see—as the boy said of the emperor in the fairy tale—that they are naked. It statesmanship be an art, as some aver, what artist ever worked in so intractable a medium?

Whatever one's political viewpoint, nobody can deny that, as we enter the final decade of the second millennium A.D., the world is characterised by much tension, conflict, and outright hostility between states and that most human beings on every continent exist in an atmosphere of insecurity. Many factors contribute to this, but in a political analysis, which concerns itself with the activities of states, the root-cause can be simply diagnosed. We are beset with a fundamental contradiction between the old political divisions of humanity into a multiplicity of nation-states and the newer realities of an emerging world society. The latter are particularly evident in the economic sphere and in matters technological and military. In today's world, there is but one economy and it is global. Within this, all countries are interdependent, and within it there operate at will the huge multinational corporations which transcend national boundaries. Assets counted in the billions can nowadays be transferred from market to market, or continent to continent, in the time it takes to place a telephone call. Plants which employ thousands, on which a whole locality may depend for its livelihood, are constructed, closed, or reorganised, as a result of decisions in a corporate office on another continent.

Add to this the complications which the newest technologies inject. Sometimes a boon to humanity, they can also be a curse. Think of the aftereffects and all the international ramifications of the disasters at Union Carbide's factory in Bhopal, India, and the nuclear power plant at Chernobyl in the Ukraine. The pollution caused by acid rain is a continuous source of friction between the United States and Canada, between Norway, Germany, and Great Britain. Everybody, it has been said, is upstream or downstream from somebody else. The sources of many of today's difficulties are located within national jurisdictions, but the fall-out is international.

Added to that is the military dimension, itself a product of the newest technology. A strategic missile launched nowadays from either the United States or Russia would reach its target, with a trajectory over Canada, in 20minutes or less. In 1945, only three atomic bombs existed, all in the hands of the United States. By the 1980s, there were estimated to be over 50,000 nuclear warheads in the stockpiles of five governments: namely, the United States and the Soviet Union, which together possessed the vast majority, plus China, France, and Great Britain.[23] Yet new weapons are added every year, and smaller governments including some which are thoroughly disreputable, are encouraged to buy conventional weapons of increased sophistication and destructiveness. Add up the military expenditures of all governments on our planet, and you find that the world spends two millions of dollars for this purpose ever single minute. More in consumed annually by the military than by health and education combined. Indeed, the world spends for war in one day as much as the peace-keeping agency, the United Nations spends in an entire year for peace. These figures amount to a collective insanity-and the agency primarily responsible is the nation-state which divides human beings from one another and therefore engenders distrust and rivalry.

Though it has acted constructively in several disputes, all too frequently the United Nations is powerless to do more than debate, declare and deplore. On most major issues it has been so rent by internal hostilities that it lacks the capacity to decide and enforce.

Speakers, in the Security Council and the General Assembly often talk to their home audiences with scant prospect of influencing their principal antagonists. Nevertheless even in its restricted role, this institution performs an indispensable function. It is the only association that houses the divided fragments of humanity. It is the closest we have yet come to a common deliberative forum for the conscience of mankind. Its freedom of debate impels all governments to reply in public to the worst criticisms that foes can hurl, whether merited or false. Its survival for half a century marks a step toward the ultimate goal of "the Parliament of Man, the Federation of the World."[24]

REGION-STATES IN THE MAKING?

But the realisation that politically the world is not yet one in heart and spirit has persuaded some that prosperity and security may perhaps be organised through institutions intermediate between the nation-state, which is outmoded, and a global state, which humanity is still too divided to operate. There are signs that a new unit of government is already evolving. The peoples who live around the coasts of the Atlantic have begun experimenting with a variety of novel unions. On the mainland of Western Europe there are the European Community and the Council of Europe. Linking the two sides of the ocean are the Organisation for Economic Cooperation and Development and the diplomatic and military agreements of the North Atlantic Treaty Organisation. These schemes enlarge the area for military, political, technical, and economic cooperation among peoples who mainly[25] share the same civilisation . Indeed, when one reflects on the divisions which have marked the history of Europe or the differences of attitude between the New World and the Old, what was accomplished in one generation was truly remarkable.

Among the positive gains are the postwar recovery of the Western European economies; Their steps toward integration in such essential matters as coal and steel, atomic energy, for peaceful uses, and tariff policies; the coordination of peacetime planning for military defense; the regular consultations and informal discussions between their heads of government, foreign secretaries, and leaders of opposition parties; and finally the growing realisation that their interests are intertwined. Most importantly, the United States and Canada Jointly helped to underwrite and stimulate the union, declaring a common interest with Western Europe in the vital concerns of safety and prosperity. If these relationship continue, an ocean will become, not a barrier that separates, but a highway that unites. As was the Mediterranean to the *pax Rommana,* so may the Atlantic prove to be the "inland sea" of the Western civilisation Nothing in this, however, is certain Whereas the decade of the 1950s witnessed an acceleration in the regional integration of nation-states, during the sixties that movement slowed down. In some spheres it was even halted by a resurgent nationalism, which was most evident in France and was stimulated by de Gaulle—although this phenomenon was by no means confined to him or restricted to his country. After the presidency of France changed hands, however, the European Community was able to add three new members, including Great Britain, and, later on, still another trio, bringing its total to twelve. Subsequently, the Turks applied for membership; and, after the communist systems collapsed in eastern Europe, several of the governments of that region as well as some of the neutrals (e.g., the Swedes and Austrians) Displayed a similar interest. The twelve existing members then had to decide which to do first: broaden their membership, but slow up the process of integrating their separate states into an effective union, or speed up their union while delaying the admission of new members. That is their big question for the decade of the nineties.

Meanwhile, the demonstration that the Community is succeeding has prompted imitations elsewhere—with limited and varying results. An equivalent in eastern Europe, the Council for Mutual Economic Assistance (Comecon, for short) was established in 1959 on Moscow's initiative, as was the military alliance known as the Warsaw Pact. Both organisations, however, were simply an extension of Moscow's sphere of control over its western neighbours. Both were dissolved in 1990 when the communist systems collapsed. In Latin America, both Central and South, regional experiments have been launched, but have not amounted to much more than the creation of areas for freer regional trade.

The same is true of the Efforts along the same lines conducted in parts of Asia and Africa. Unless there is sufficient stability in the component units, a structure assembled from faulty materials will not hold up. But it is reasonable to predict that when western Europe creates a new union-political, economic, and military—this will be the wave of the future. Other regions which are sufficiently developed are then likely to follow suit.

If we extrapolate the developments of the last three decades and do not fly too far ahead of the facts, we can discern the possibility of a new and wider unit of government. To distinguish this from the nation-state or a world-state, could we not call it the "region-state"? Through the nascent region-state, some portions of humanity may perhaps construct their political defenses against economic blizzard and nuclear annihilation. How urgent is the need can be gauged by projecting into the future two contemporary facts. One is the worldwide rise in population, increasing now so rapidly that its implications have been termed "explosive" by demographic experts. The reduction of the death rate, improvement of health, and material gains from industrialism will do For Asia, Africa, and Latin America what they did for Western Europe and North America. There will be millions more to feed in each coming decade—to feed, let alone to be prosperous. If the "Malthusian checks" of poverty and war are no longer acceptable, wider political unions and more enlightened policies will be required to augment the supply of food and industrial goods. The second inescapable fact is the technology which enables us to place satellites in orbit around the earth or propel them beyond the gravity of our planet. Already human beings have walked on the moon and satellites have reached the planets of the solar system. Now that we have voyaged into outer space, air power is being superseded by a yet more formidable weapon. Where will our endangered species locate our military defense tomorrow? Humanity arrived on the moon long before peace was constructed on earth. Is it not self-evident that the nation-state, a unit which evolved under the special conditions of the sixteenth and seventeenth centuries, is inadequate to govern us under the conditions of the twentieth? The new population and the new pollutions, the new technology and the new weapons, point ultimately to a new unit of government.

—

CONTOURS AND CONTENTS OF REGION-STATES

Yet a word of caution is necessary, lest hopes be raised too high and then be cruelly dashed. A region-state will present problems of organisation fully as complex as its predecessors. If it was difficult to delimit the boundaries of the nation, will it be easier to define those of the region? An example is the North Atlantic Treaty Organisation, which already reaches as far east as Greece and Turkey. Some states, moreover, have interests in more than one region. Thus the United States belongs to the North Atlantic Treaty Organisation as well as to the Organisation of American States and we have a major stake in the affairs of the Pacific with contractual commitments to Australia, the Philippines, and Japan. Nor should one assume that wars between region-states are impossible. The region-state can justify itself only if it provides a broader framework for enhancing the economic well-being of all its members, and if each presents such a picture of strength to a possible antagonist that nobody will run the risk of initiating a third general war from which none can emerge unscathed. Some of the same factors that impede the task of international organisation can also be obstacles to the formation of region-states. To create the latter, a union may be required between a superpower and a group of medium-sized and smaller countries. But nationalism or differences of living standards may provoke a rift in that relationship, and the superpower may even aggravate the difficulties of leadership by demonstrating that might is not always correlated with wisdom.

Since 1947, the United States has been the nucleus of a large and loosely structured coalition which includes virtually all of the world's most advanced communities and many that are backward. Out of their rich resources, financial strength, and great productive capacity, the American people rendered economic and military assistance to numerous governments in the hope that such aid would increase their means of resistance to armed aggression from without and political upheaval from within. The results of this programme have been as varied as the characters of the recipients. Where the government is honest and the people in general are hardworking and self-disciplined, the American contribution was successful. In some instances, however, corrupt cliques and incompetent governments misused or squandered much of the aid that was granted. Thereafter, the donors feel disposed to attach conditions that the recipients must fulfil. But when that happens, the nationalistic pride of the latter is outraged and they will voice angry protests that their "Sovereignty" is being invaded. The American public sees a portion of its tax dollar appropriated to finance foreign aid programmes which, while they help other countries, are thought the to promote simultaneously the interests of the United States. That such efforts sometimes provoke resentment rather than thanks may surprise those who provide the money. But it is not normal in the relations between groups, anymore than in the relations of individuals, for the stronger, wealthier, and luckier to meet with gratitude and affection, or for the dependent to relish their position. Moreover, in numerous instances those assisted by the United States happen to be privileged oligarchies, which have no intention of sharing power and its perquisites with their own have-nots. Consequently, the weapons which the United States has placed at the disposal of such oligarchies have been employed in internal contests for power—with the obvious result of fostering anti-Americanism among the victims.

The hand of a great power unusually rests heavily on the smaller states close by, which it considers as lying within its sphere of influence. In this respect, the record of successive American governments in the Caribbean and Central America has repeated the unsavoury pattern of other dominant states throughout the history of Europe and Asia. For almost a century, the United States has infiltrated, intervened, and invaded installing governments to its liking wherever possible. The history of our relations with Cuba, the Dominican Republic, Grenada, Haiti, Mexico, El Salvador, Panama, and Nicaragua has been that of an imperial power toward its dependencies. In the 1980s the Reagan administration was actively assisting a centrist regime in El Salvador against its opposition of left-wing guerrillas. In Nicaragua, it was helping right-wingers, who include supporters of the ex-dictator, Somoza, in their military effort to overthrow the Marxist Sandinista regime. What meanings attach to the fictions of "independence" or "Sovereignty" under these conditions?

The same can be said of the international behaviour of communist regimes wherever they have been in control of governments. Despite the Marxist indictment of imperialism, which was interpreted as the last stage of capitalist exploitation, the Communists were determined to continue the empire which the Czars had built. Moreover, their hold over eastern Europe—a Combination of military, political and economic supremacy—was as imperialistic as any treatment of their colonies by western powers. That is why, when the grip of the Communist Party was broken between 1989 and 1991, so many of the former client-states rapidly proclaimed their independence of Moscow. As for the other Communist giant, its conduct too exhibits a similar pattern. China's treatment of Tibet is nothing but naked imperialism on the part of a regime which has always denounced the West and the Japanese for their imperial incursions. "The pot calling the kettle black" is a perennial phenomenon in the relations between states.

Like any established system, nationalism, dies hard. Old sentiments and old ideas continue to have their force in the present, sometimes most fiercely among those to whom they have come late, for no nationalism is as prickly and sensitive as a new one. Although the old empires are liquidated, the fragmentation is occurring faster than the reverse process of merging. Region-states may be in the making. They could help in organising the larger areas in which we may find our safety and prosperity. But in any case, region states alone will not be enough. They, too, have to learn to live together within one world, for which a truly global organisation is required. Such problems as the population explosion (with all its implications of a death explosion as well), the gulf between haves and have-nots, and the control of nuclear weapons are of universal concern. Hence, the region-states, too, if indeed they do succeed in becoming organised, will need ultimately to realize that to live means also to let live. Otherwise they are certain to start in motion a train of rivalry that could lead to the destruction of the human species.

The conclusion is self-evident. Political inventiveness must find a way to substitute cooperation for competition and simultaneously consolidate both the world and its regions.

—Leslie Lipson

References

1. The concept of expansion from a city to the world (*ab urbe ad orbem)* was a rhetorical flourish, never a political reality.
2. E.g., the Kurds, who are partitioned among Iraq, Iran, and Turkey.
3. John Churchill, first, Duke of Marlborough, victor of the battles of Blenheim (1704) and Ramilles (1706), was an ancestor of Winston Churchill.
4. This principals was first officially recommended for Canada in Lord Durham's Report (1839) and applied in that country in 1846-1847.
5. Except in the ecclesiastical sphere, where the international power of the church was more than theoretical.
6. "Sovereignty and Absolutism in the Nation-State."
7. "Medievalism and Mercantilism."
8. The title of a play set in Ireland by G.B. Shaw.
9. A century and a half ago, half of the trade of the entire world passed through the port of Liverpool. In the second half of the twentieth century, Liverpool's chief claim to international attention lay in its having exported the Beatles.
10. The British adoption of free trade in the 1840s was a frank recognition of this fact.
11. This distinction means that victory in a major war requires the mobilisation of a people's entire resources in order to survive, while a minor war requires only a limited effort and does not involve a danger to survival.
12. Alexis de Tocqueville, *Democracy in America,* part I, trans. Henry Reeve (New York: J. & H.G. Langley, 1841), pp. 470-71.
13. Grotius. The Latinised name of the Dutchman de Groot, published the foundation work in this field in 1625.
14. Examples are the International Monetary Fund; the International Bank for Reconstruction and Development; the Food and Agriculture Organisation; the World Health Organisation (WHO); and the United Nations Educational, Scientific, and Cultural Organisation (UNESCO).
15. Hong Kong, the most populous of these, will revert to China in 1997. Spain wants Gibraltar back, but the Gibraltarians prefer their

link with Britain. The Falklanders, all 1800 of them, remain under the Union Jack as a result of the British victory over the Argentines in 1982, an anachronistic conflict reminiscent of the nineteenth century.

16. The second edition of this book, published in 1960, contained this prediction (p.394)"Indeed, if one projects into the future the trends of the last 12 years, it seems certain that the French cannot maintain their hold on Algeria, that a handful of British planters cannot monopolize the Kenya highlands, and that the Afrikaner nationalists cannot perpetuate the privileges of Europeans in Sooth Africa." Two of those predictions have come true. The third will also, but it is taking longer.

17. The Soviet Union crushed an anti-Communist revolt in Budapest in 1956 and overthrew a reformist regime in Prague in 1968. President Johnson sent U.S. Forces into the Dominican Republic in 1965 to install a regime to his liking; President Reagan invaded Grenada in 1983 to oust a junta which tilted toward Moscow and Havana.

18 A *Midsummer Night's Dream,* Act II, sc. II, line 115.

19. Over the issue of the Council's refusal to place a representative of Beijing in China's seat.

20. In october1956, Israel sent its army to occupy the Gaza Strip from which Egypt was mounting commando raids against Israeli settlements. The British and French sent in their forces to retake the Suez Canal, which Nasser had nationalised earlier.

21. The World Bank's annual "World Development Report" stated in July 1990 that 1.1 billion people-a fifth of the world's population—still live with annual incomes of less than $ 370 a year. *New York Times,* July 16, 1990.

22. In fact, they do not give nearly enough. The Organisation for Economic Cooperation and Development, whose members consists of the advanced industrial economies, has recommended that each country give at least 0.7 per cent of its GNP to help the less developed. In the 1980's,. only Sweden, Norway, and the Netherlands exceeded that. The United States continues to be the single biggest donor, in absolute figures. But US aid has steadily dropped as a percentage of the GNP. In the early 1960s it stood at 0.75 per cent, but it fell to under 0.25 per cent in the 1980s.

Moreover, in the years of the Reagan Presidency, the bulk of the aid given was military, not economic.

23. India, which has conducted an atomic explosion, and several other governments reportedly have the capacity to assemble a nuclear bomb at short notice.

24. Tennyson's words from the Poem "Locksley Hall."

25. I add this qualification because Turkey is a member of NATO, and Japan of OECD.